Astrological Relationship Handbook

Other Books by Kevin B. Burk

Astrology: Understanding the Birth Chart
(Llewllyn, 2001)

The Complete Node Book
(Llewellyn, 2003)

The Relationship Handbook:
How to Understand and Improve Every Relationship in Your Life
(Serendipity Press, 2004)

The Relationship Workbook:
How to Understand and Improve Every Relationship in Your Life
(Serendipity Press, 2004)

Astrology Math Made Easy
(Serendipity Press, 2005)

The Relationship Workbook:
How to Design and Create Your Ideal Romantic Relationship
(Serendipity Press, 2005)

The Relationship Workbook:
The Secrets of Successful Team Building
(Serendipity Press, 2005)

Astrological *Relationship* Handbook

How to Use Astrology to Understand *Every* Relationship in Your Life

Kevin B. Burk

Serendipity Press

SAN DIEGO, CALIFORNIA

ISBN 0-9759682-8-9

© 2006 Kevin B. Burk. All rights reserved. No part of this publication may be reproduced, transmitted, transcribed, stored in a retrieval system, or translated into any language, in any form, by any means, without written permission of the author.

Printed in the United States of America.

Published by
Serendipity Press
6161 El Cajon Blvd. #306
San Diego, CA 92115

Portions of this work appear in slightly different versions in *The Relationship Handbook: How to Understand and Improve Every Relationship in Your Life,* © 2005 Kevin B. Burk, and in *Astrology: Understanding the Birth Chart,* © 2001 Kevin Burk.

All horoscope charts in this book were generated using Solar Fire™, © Astrolabe, Inc.

Book design and cover design by Kevin B. Burk.

Contents

1
Introduction to Relationship Astrology
1

How to Use This Handbook 2
The Laws of Relationship Astrology 3
The Secret to Completely Accurate Interpretations 5
The Right Tool for the Right Job 5

2
Introduction to Human Relationships
7

Being Human 7
The Ego 8
What are Relationships? 10
Relationship Needs 12
    Need Bank Accounts 13
    Relationship Needs Bank Accounts 14
Relationship Checklists 15
    Wants vs. Needs 16
Relationship Checklist Languages 16
Relationship Blueprints 18

3
Using Classical Astrology to Create a Context to Find the Relationship in the Natal Chart
21

Elements and Modalities 21
    Elements 21

        Fire 22
        Earth 22
        Air 23
        Water 24
    The Modalities 25
        Cardinal 25
        Fixed 26
        Mutable 27
TEMPERAMENT: QUADRANTS AND HEMISPHERES 28
    The Southern Hemisphere 29
    The Northern Hemisphere 29
    The Eastern Hemisphere 29
    The Western Hemisphere 29
    The Quadrants 29
INTRODUCING CLASSICAL ASTROLOGY 30
    Introduction to Essential Dignities 30
        Rulership 32
        Exaltation 32
        Triplicity 33
        Term 33
        Face 34
        Detriment 34
        Fall 35
        Peregrine 35
    A Word About Classical Interpretations 36
    How the Outer Planets Fit In 36
    Dispositor Trees 37
CREATING A CONTEXT TO FIND THE RELATIONSHIP: ELIZABETH TAYLOR 42
    Part 1: Elements and Modalities 44
    Part 2: Temperament 44
    Part 3: Essential Dignities 45
    Part 4: Dispositor Tree Diagram 45

❧ 4 ❧

SAFETY NEEDS (THE MOON)

47

EXPLORING OUR SAFETY NEEDS 47
    Survival Needs 47

  Need to Know What to Expect 48
 Emotional Connections 49
 Boundaries and Personal Space 49

How Do We Know We're Feeling Unsafe? 50
Safety Checklists: The Moon 50
  Fire Safety Checklists 51
   The Moon in Aries 52
   Moon in Leo 53
   Moon in Sagittarius 55
 Earth Safety Checklists 57
  Moon in Taurus 58
  Moon in Virgo 60
  Moon in Capricorn 62
 Air Safety Checklists 64
  Moon in Gemini 65
  Moon in Libra 67
  Moon in Aquarius 69
 Water Safety Checklists 72
  Moon in Cancer 73
  Moon in Scorpio 75
  Moon in Pisces 77

✲5✲
Validation Needs (Venus)
80

Exploring our Validation Needs 80
 Group Acceptance Needs 81
  Acceptance by the Group 81
  Equality within the Group 82
  Prominence in the Group 82
 Self Acceptance Needs 83
  Asserting Individuality 83
  Equality as an Individual 84
  Self-Esteem 84
Praise, Gratitude and Love 85
Validation Checklists 85
 Fire Validation Checklists 86
  Venus in Aries 87

Venus in Leo	89
Venus in Sagittarius	90
Earth Validation Checklists	92
Venus in Taurus	93
Venus in Virgo	95
Venus in Capricorn	97
Air Validation Checklists	99
Venus in Gemini	100
Venus in Libra	101
Venus in Aquarius	103
Water Validation Checklists	104
Venus in Cancer	105
Venus in Scorpio	107
Venus in Pisces	108

❖6❖
CAN WE MEET OUR NEEDS?
111

FEELING SAFE AND FEELING VALIDATED (PICK ONE)	111
Identical Moon and Venus	112
Compatible Moon and Venus Signs	112
Balancing Acts	114
Conflicts of Interest	114
No Common Ground	115
SATURN ASPECTS: CHECKLISTS FROM HELL	116
Moon-Saturn Aspects	117
Moon conjunct Saturn	118
Moon square Saturn	118
Moon opposite Saturn	119
Moon quincunx Saturn	119
Venus-Saturn Aspects	120
Venus conjunct Saturn	120
Venus square Saturn	121
Venus opposite Saturn	121
Venus quincunx Saturn	122
URANUS ASPECTS: EXPECTING REJECTION, FEARING ABANDONMENT, AND ASSUMING UNRELIABILITY	122
Moon-Uranus Aspects	123

    Moon conjunct Uranus 124
    Moon sextile Uranus 124
    Moon square Uranus 125
    Moon trine Uranus... 125
    Moon opposite Uranus 126
    Moon quincunx Uranus 126
  Venus-Uranus Aspects.. 126
    Venus conjunct Uranus 127
    Venus sextile Uranus... 127
    Venus square Uranus 128
    Venus trine Uranus... 128
    Venus opposite Uranus 128
    Venus quincunx Uranus 129

NEPTUNE ASPECTS: BAD BOUNDARIES AND HOPELESS ROMANTICS 129

  Moon-Neptune Aspects... 130
    Moon conjunct Neptune... 130
    Moon sextile Neptune... 131
    Moon square Neptune... 131
    Moon trine Neptune... 132
    Moon opposite Neptune 132
    Moon quincunx Neptune.. 133
  Venus-Neptune Aspects... 133
    Venus conjunct Neptune... 134
    Venus sextile Neptune... 134
    Venus square Neptune... 134
    Venus trine Neptune... 135
    Venus opposite Neptune 135
    Venus quincunx Neptune.. 136

PLUTO ASPECTS: POWER, CONTROL, MANIPULATION AND ABUSE 136

  Pluto and Abuse 137
  Moon-Pluto Aspects.. 138
    Moon conjunct Pluto 139
    Moon sextile Pluto 139
    Moon square Pluto 139
    Moon trine Pluto 140
    Moon opposite Pluto.. 140
    Moon quincunx Pluto 140
  Venus-Pluto Aspects.. 141
    Venus conjunct Pluto 141
    Venus sextile Pluto 142
    Venus square Pluto 142

    Venus trine Pluto..142
    Venus opposite Pluto..142
    Venus quincunx Pluto 143
CHIRON ASPECTS 143

❖7❖
RELATIONSHIP WANTS: THE DESCENDANT AND THE VERTEX
145

UNDERSTANDING THE ANGLES..145
THE ARIES-LIBRA AXIS 147
    Aries Ascendant/Libra Descendant 147
    Libra Ascendant/Aries Descendant 147
THE TAURUS-SCORPIO AXIS 148
    Taurus Ascendant/Scorpio Descendant..148
    Scorpio Ascendant/Taurus Descendant 149
THE GEMINI-SAGITTARIUS AXIS..149
    Gemini Ascendant/Sagittarius Descendant..149
    Sagittarius Ascendant/Gemini Descendant..150
THE CANCER-CAPRCORN AXIS 150
    Cancer Ascendant/Capricorn Descendant 150
    Capricorn Ascendant/Cancer Descendant 151
THE LEO-AQUARIUS AXIS 151
    Leo Ascendant/Aquarius Descendant..152
    Aquarius Ascendant/Leo Descendant..152
THE VIRGO-PISCES AXIS 153
    Virgo Ascendant/Pisces Descendant 153
    Pisces Ascendant/Virgo Descendant 153
THE VERTEX 154
    Vertex in Aries 155
    Vertex in Taurus 155
    Vertex in Gemini 155
    Vertex in Cancer..155
    Vertex in Leo 156
    Vertex in Virgo 156

Vertex in Libra 156
Vertex in Scorpio 157
Vertex in Sagittarius 157
Vertex in Capricorn 157
Vertex in Aquarius 158
Vertex in Pisces 158
WHAT ELSE DO WE WANT? WHAT ELSE DO WE LACK? 158
Planets in the 7th and 8th Houses 158

☙ 8 ❧
PUTTING IT TOGETHER PART 1: RELATIONSHIP NEEDS AND WANTS
160

ELIZABEH TAYLOR (CONTINUED) 160
Part 5: Relationship Needs 160
    Safety Needs 160
    Validation Needs 161
Part 6: Can Needs Be Met? 161
    Feeling Safe and Feeling Validated (Moon and Venus Connection) 161
    General Safety Issues 161
    Uranus Aspects: Issues with Rejection, Abandonment and Unreliability 162
    Pluto Aspects: Power Control, Manipulation and Abuse 162
Part 7: Relationship Wants 163
    Conscious Desires: Descendant in Gemini 163
    Unconscious Desires: Vertex in Cancer 163
RICHARD BURTON 163
Part 1: Elements and Modalities 165
Part 2: Temperament 165
Part 3: Essential Dignities 166
Part 4: Dispositor Tree Diagram 166
Part 5: Relationship Needs 167
    Safety Needs 167
    Validation Needs 167
Part 6: Can Needs Be Met? 168
    Feeling Safe and Feeling Validated (Moon and Venus Connection) 168
    General Safety Concerns 168
    General Validation Concerns 168

Part 7: Relationship Wants 168
    Conscious Desires: Descendant in Capricorn 168
    Unconscious Desires: Vertex in Sagittarius 168

❖9❖
Relationship Houses
170

Friends, Lovers or Spouses? 171
Evaluating the Parents in the Natal Chart: Uncovering the Marriage Blueprint 173
Relationships to Authority 174
Other Relationship Houses 176

❖10❖
Putting It Together Part 2: Finding the Relationship in the Natal Chart
177

Elizabeth Taylor (Continued) 177
    Part 8: Parents & Marriage Blueprint 177
    Part 9: Friends, Lovers or Spouses? 178
Richard Burton (Continued) 179
    Part 8: Parents & Marriage Blueprint 179
    Part 9: Friends, Lovers or Spouses? 179
Jennifer Aniston 179
    Part 1: Elements and Modalities 181
    Part 2: Temperament 181
    Part 3: Essential Dignities 182
    Part 4: Dispositor Tree Diagram 182
    Part 5: Relationship Needs 183
        Safety Needs 183
        Validation Needs 183
    Part 6: Can Needs Be Met? 183
        Feeling Safe and Feeling Validated (Moon and Venus Connection) 183
        Uranus Aspects: Issues with Rejection, Abandonment and Unreliability 183

Pluto Aspects: Power, Control, Manipulation and Abuse	184
Part 7: Relationship Wants	184
Conscious Desires: Descendant in Aries	184
Unconscious Desires: Vertex in Gemini	184
Part 8: Parents & Marriage Blueprint	184
Part 9: Friends, Lovers or Spouses?	185
BRAD PITT	**185**
Part 1: Elements and Modalities	187
Part 2: Temperament	187
Part 3: Essential Dignities	188
Part 4: Dispositor Tree Diagram	188
Part 5: Relationship Needs	189
Safety Needs	189
Validation Needs	189
Part 6: Can Needs Be Met?	189
Feeling Safe and Feeling Validated (Moon and Venus Connection)	189
Part 7: Relationship Wants	190
Conscious Desires: Descendant in Gemini	190
Unconscious Desires: Vertex in Cancer	190
Part 8: Parents & Marriage Blueprint	190
Part 9: Friends, Lovers or Spouses?	190

❖11❖
EVALUATING COMPATIBILITY
191

THE MYTH OF COMPATIBILITY	192
COMPATIBILITY PART 1: ELEMENTAL COMPATIBILITY	193
COMPATIBILITY PART 2: SAFETY AND VALIDATION NEEDS	196
COMPATIBILITY PART 3: COMMUNICATION STYLES	197
INTRODUCING THE SYNASTRY GRID	198
Inter-Personal Connections (Personal to Personal)	200
Karmic Connections (Outer to Personal)	200
Generational Connections (Outer to Outer)	200
Reinforced Aspects	201
Double Aspects	201
Aspects in Synastry	201
Conjunctions	202

   Oppositions 202
   Trines 202
   Squares 202
   Sextiles 202
   Quincunxes 202
   Semi-Squares and Sesquiquadrates 203
  Planets in Houses in Synastry... 203
COMPATIBILITY PART 4: INTER-PERSONAL CONNECTIONS 203
COMPATIBILITY PART 5: KARMIC ASPECTS 204
COMPATIBILITY PART 6: SYNTHESIZING SYNASTRY 205

12
COMPOSITE CHARTS
207

13
PUTTING IT TOGETHER PART 3: COMPARING CHARTS
209

ELIZABETH TAYLOR AND RICHARD BURTON 209
 Part 1: Elemental Compatibility.. 209
 Part 2: Safety and Validation Needs 211
 Part 3: Communication Styles 211
 Part 4: Inter-Personal Connections... 212
 Part 5: Karmic Aspects 212
  Richard Burton's Planets Aspecting Elizabeth Taylor's Planets 212
  Elizabeth Taylor's Planets Aspecting Richard Burton's Planets 213
 Part 6: Synthesizing Synastry 213
JENNIFER ANISTON AND BRAD PITT.. 214
 Part 1: Elemental Compatibility.. 214
 Part 2: Safety and Validation Needs 216
 Part 3: Communication Styles 217
 Part 4: Inter-Personal Connections... 217
 Part 5: Karmic Aspects 218
  Jennifer Aniston's Planets Aspecting Brad Pitt's Planets 218
  Brad Pitt's Planets Aspecting Jennifer Aniston's Planets 219

Part 6: Synthesizing Synastry 219
COUPLE NUMBER 3: PAUL NEWMAN AND JOANNE WOODWARD 220
PAUL NEWMAN 220
Part 1: Elements and Modalities 222
Part 2: Temperament 222
Part 3: Essential Dignities 223
Part 4: Dispositor Tree Diagram 223
Part 5: Relationship Needs 224
    Safety Needs 224
    Validation Needs 224
Part 6: Can Needs Be Met? 225
    Feeling Safe and Feeling Validated (Moon and Venus Connection) 225
    Pluto Aspects: Power Control, Manipulation and Abuse 225
Part 7: Relationship Wants 225
    Conscious Desires: Descendant in Cancer 225
    Unconscious Desires: Vertex in Leo 226
Part 8: Parents & Marriage Blueprint 226
Part 9: Friends, Lovers or Spouses? 227
JOANNE WOODWARD 227
Part 1: Elements and Modalities 229
Part 2: Temperament 229
Part 3: Essential Dignities 230
Part 4: Dispositor Tree Diagram 231
Part 5: Relationship Needs 232
    Safety Needs 232
    Validation Needs 232
Part 6: Can Needs Be Met? 232
    Feeling Safe and Feeling Validated (Moon and Venus Connection) 232
    Saturn Aspects: Checklists from Hell 233
    Uranus Aspects: Rejection, Abandonment and Unreliability 233
    Pluto Aspects: Power Control, Manipulation and Abuse 233
Part 7: Relationship Wants 234
    Conscious Desires: Descendant in Cancer 234
    Unconscious Desires: Vertex in Leo 234
Part 8: Parents & Marriage Blueprint 234
Part 9: Friends, Lovers or Spouses? 235
PAUL NEWMAN AND JOANNE WOODWARD 235
Part 1: Elemental Compatibility 235
Part 2: Safety and Validation Needs 237
Part 3: Communication Styles 237

Part 4: Inter-Personal Connections..238
Part 5: Karmic Aspects 238
    Paul Newman's Planets Aspecting Joanne Woodward's Planets..................................238
    Joanne Woodward's Planets Aspecting Paul Newman's Planets..................................239
Part 6: Synthesized Synastry 240

❖14❖
Relationship Counseling
242

The Six Steps to Improve Every Relationship in Your Life 245
    Step 1: Identify What Needs Aren't Being Met in the Relationship 245
    Step 2: Identify How We Would Like Those Needs to Be Met 246
    Step 3: Reality Check—Are Our Expectations Reasonable? 246
    Step 4: Determine What Needs We Aren't Meeting 247
    Step 5: Meet Our Partner's Needs First 247
    Step 6: Ask to Have Our Needs Met 248

❖Appendix A❖
Relationship Astrology Worksheets
A-1

Natal Chart Relationship Interpretation Worksheet A-2
Relationship Compatibility and Synastry Worksheet A-8

List of Figures

Figure 1: Maslow's Hierarchy of Needs (With Annotations) 12
Figure 2: Maintaining the Minimum Balance in our Need Accounts 13
Figure 3: Relationship Need Accounts 14
Figure 4. Quadrants and Hemispheres 28
Figure 5: Ptolemy's Table of Essential Dignities and Debilities as shown in *Essential Dignities* by J. Lee Lehman, Ph.D. 31
Figure 6: Liza Minnelli's Natal Chart and Dispositor Tree 39
Figure 7: Meryl Streep's Natal Chart and Dispositor Tree 40
Figure 8: Sylvester Stallone's Natal Chart and Dispositor Tree 41
Figure 9: Elizabeth Taylor's Natal Chart 43
Figure 10: Richard Burton's Natal Chart 164
Figure 11: Jennifer Aniston's Natal Chart 180
Figure 12: Brad Pitt's Natal Chart 186
Figure 13: Synastry Grid 199
Figure 14: Elizabeth Taylor and Richard Burton Synastry Grid 210
Figure 15: Jennifer Aniston and Brad Pitt Synastry Grid 215
Figure 16: Paul Newman's Natal Chart 221
Figure 17: Joanne Woodward's Natal Chart 228
Figure 18: Paul Newman and Joanne Woodward Synastry Grid 236

List of Tables

Table 1: Compatible Moon and Venus Signs 113
Table 2: Opposing Moon and Venus Signs 114
Table 3: Conflicting Moon and Venus Signs 115
Table 4: Moon and Venus Signs with No Common Ground 116
Table 5: Classification of the Signs 194
Table 6: Compatibility Relationships Between Signs 196

Acknowledgments

Writing the acknowledgments for a book, for me, seems to have a great deal in common with writing one's acceptance speech for the Academy Awards®. There's never enough time (or, as it were, space) to thank everyone who truly deserves it, and even if one made a good faith effort to list every single person who made some significant contribution to one's success, someone will inevitably be left out.

For me, that list would include every one of my astrology teachers, every one of my astrology students (who are some of my most important and powerful teachers), every one of my counseling clients, and indeed everyone who has ever visited my website (or at least everyone who has ever written me with an astrology question).

Obviously, we'll have to settle for the short(er) list.

First, I am eternally grateful to the truly amazing individuals with whom I have studied astrology. These master astrologers include Terry Lamb, Michael Lutin, Dr. J. Lee Lehman, Ph.D, and Jim Shawvan. I could not ask for finer teachers of the art of astrology.

I also had the great fortune to learn the art of spiritual counseling from other master teachers and powerful individuals. My love and thanks go out to Argena Marie Berne, Rev. Alicia Light and Rev. Dorothy Lee Donahue.

I want to thank the San Diego Astrological Society, the Oregon Association of Astrologers, Astrology et al bookstore in Seattle, Washington and Body, Mind & Soul Bookstore in Houston, Texas for their support and encouragement, and for sponsoring the Relationship Astrology Workshops that helped to shape and create this handbook. I also want to thank Jessica McKeegan Jensen, Douglas Askew and Cinda Johnson for their support and assistance in hosting and promoting the Relationship Workshops. Finally, I want to thank Julie Braden and Terri Trainor for hosting the Relationship Astrology classes in San Diego. Julie hosted the very first Relationship Astrology class and helped birth this handbook; and Terri hosted the Relationship Astrology Correspondence Course, based on the completed handbook.

❖ 1 ❖
Introduction to Relationship Astrology

When most people begin to study astrology, the first thing they want to know is what their birth chart has to say about them. The second thing they want to know is what their birth chart has to say about their relationships.

This is hardly surprising. Relationships are the most important aspects of our lives. From the moment we arrive on Earth to the moment we depart, we experience relationships of all kinds with other individuals. Sometimes these relationships are supportive, and sometimes they present challenges. Some people seem to have a knack for maintaining strong and healthy relationships. The rest of us, however, often wish we had some help.

Astrology can be a very powerful tool to help us to understand and improve our relationships. However, human relationships are complex and intricate, and while astrology is a powerful tool to help us to unravel and understand them, using this tool takes a certain amount of skill.

Mastering the language of astrology involves more than simply learning how to interpret the various symbols: the planets, signs, houses and aspects. The real art of astrological interpretation involves knowing how to sift through the overwhelming amount of information in a chart and identify the structure, locate the patterns and themes, and separate the truly important and useful information from the vast sea of background noise. When using astrology to help understand interpersonal relationships, we have more than twice as much information to sift through because we first have to understand the two individual natal charts, and then explore how those charts interact with each other.

To most astrologers, relationship astrology is about comparing two birth charts, and exploring how the planets in each chart interact with each other. While this is certainly a part of relationship astrology, it's a technique that comes at the very end of the process, not at the beginning. Without a solid foundation and a thorough understanding of the individual charts (not to mention of the individuals themselves), we have no context to make use of the information we uncover when comparing two charts.

In this handbook, you will learn everything you need in order to use astrology to understand and improve your relationships. You will learn how to use classical astrology to create a context for understanding each individual chart. You will learn how to create your own, synthesized interpretation of the key relationship issues and patterns in a natal chart. And finally, you will learn how to build on this foundation and discover how to compare two natal charts and identify the key challenges and opportunities in any relationship.

How to Use This Handbook

This book is part of *The Relationship Handbook* series. In fact, the *Astrological Relationship Handbook* is designed to be a companion to *The Relationship Handbook: How to Understand and Improve Every Relationship in Your Life.* This handbook covers the astrology behind *The Relationship Handbook* in great detail. It is a guide to how to use astrology in relationship counseling—or to be more precise, a guide to how *I* use astrology in my relationship counseling practice.

Although this book may read like it's written for professional astrologers who see clients on a regular basis, it is, in fact, written for *all* astrologers. I've yet to meet an astrologer who could resist sharing his or her knowledge with a few close friends or acquaintances. The advice on how to relate to clients ethically, spiritually, compassionately, and responsibly applies whether you are being paid for your time or not. Even if you are new to astrology, please take this to heart.

What you will learn from this handbook are the astrological techniques that I use to identify key relationship patterns in the birth chart. This is the "behind the scenes" information that I use when I prepare for an astrology consultation or a relationship coaching session.

I never share this information with my clients.

As a counselor, my goal is to help my clients to understand themselves better, to become aware of the patterns and choices they've made in their lives so far, and to support them in making more elegant choices for themselves. I want to empower my clients. Therefore, I'm very careful about how much astrology I bring into the picture.

Anytime I talk about a planet, sign, or aspect with a client, I always make sure that they understand how the symbol works. I help them to appreciate the archetypal nature of the astrological symbols. Most importantly, I do my best to help my clients understand that every symbol in the chart has an infinite range of expression. There are no "good" or "bad" planets. The most we can say is that there are skillful and not-so-skillful ways of expressing the energies in the chart. We have absolute free will. My objective is to support my clients in making more elegant and skillful choices, if that is what they choose to do.

When most people think about astrology, they think about how our destinies are written in the stars. This goes for the vast majority of astrologers, both amateur and professional. We look at an aspect or a pattern in our charts, and we see it as limiting. If we have the Sun opposite Saturn, we may believe that we will always have issues with authority figures, and there's nothing we can do about it. Even worse, if we have Venus square Saturn, we may believe that we will always be unlucky in love, because that's the only interpretation we've ever read of this aspect.

If we have a client who has come to us for relationship advice, and we tell them that they have Venus square Saturn in their chart, we are doing them a tremendous disservice. If we tell them that Venus square Saturn means that they'll be unlucky in love, they now believe that they are *destined* to be unlucky in love, and that there's nothing they can do to change this. It's essential that our clients understand that we have absolute free will, and that we can learn to work with the symbols in the birth chart in skillful, supportive and positive ways.

This handbook covers the astrological interpretations, including examples of more skillful and supportive ways to express each element in the chart. Even so, it is designed to help you, the astrologer, to expand and deepen your understanding of the astrological symbols. It does not cover how to make use of that information in a practical manner. That information is contained in *The Relationship Handbook: How to Understand and Improve Every Relationship in Your Life*.

The Laws of Relationship Astrology

When most astrologers think of relationship astrology, they immediately think of synastry: analyzing and interpreting the aspects between two natal charts. Almost every book on relationship astrology focuses entirely on synastry.

Almost every book on relationship astrology is completely worthless.

Synastry is certainly a useful tool, but it has very specific and limited applications. *It is not possible to look at the aspects between two charts and predict how successful a relationship will be.* The reason for this is the **First Law of Relationship Astrology:**

Relationships Occur Between Two Individuals and Not Between Two Charts.

Just as it's not possible to predict how an individual will behave based on his or her natal chart, it's also not possible to predict how two individuals will relate to each other based on how their charts connect. We must understand the individual first.

From this, we derive the **Second Law of Relationship Astrology:**

Every Relationship Pattern Can Be Found in the Natal Chart.

The first two thirds of this handbook is devoted to teaching you how to identify relationship patterns in the natal chart. You will be amazed at how much information is available in the natal chart, once you know where to look.

In the last third of this handbook, you will learn how to use synastry to explore and interpret the dynamics of a relationship between two individuals. When comparing two charts, however, we must always remember the **Third Law of Relationship Astrology:**

Everything Must Be Interpreted in the Context of the Natal Chart.

Here's an example that will both illustrate the Third Law of Relationship Astrology and demonstrate why most books on relationship astrology are completely worthless. Every book on relationship astrology I've ever encountered basically says that you should look for "soft" aspects between two charts: Trines and sextiles indicate the most successful relationships. While this may be the case for an individual with nothing but easy aspects in her chart, it does not hold true for someone with a more active natal chart.

An individual with squares and oppositions in her natal chart will need to be challenged and stimulated by her partners in relationships. She's far more likely to enjoy relationships with lots of squares in the synastry. She will probably find the trines and sextiles tedious and boring.

Everything must be interpreted in the context of the natal chart.

In order to understand the dynamics of a relationship, we must first understand the two individuals involved in the relationship. In order to understand human relationships, we must first understand the individual humans. (And since most of us need a refresher course on what it really means to be human, we'll be covering that in the next chapter). Since we're exploring human relationships, we must also remember the **Universal Law of Relationships:**

Our Partners in Relationships are our Mirrors: They Reflect Our Own Issues Back to Us.

We'll explore the basis for this law in the next chapter. For now, let's simply acknowledge that because of the Universal Law of Relationships we know that nothing in any relationship is *ever* about the other person. It's all our own stuff.

The Secret to Completely Accurate Interpretations

When we look at a client's chart, we are making educated guesses about who that individual is and how he or she is experiencing and expressing the symbols in the chart. Astrology operates on the symbolic level. Through the symbols and archetypes, we can grasp the spirit, although we can't always predict the manifestation.

We can look at a chart, and see that a client has Moon square Uranus. Immediately (or at least immediately after reading Chapter 6), we can hypothesize that our client has core issues with rejection and abandonment. What we cannot know, however, is how these issues are manifesting in our client's life at this time. We don't know if these issues are overwhelming them, or if they've spent the past 20 years in therapy addressing and mastering them.

There is, however, one technique that will always reveal the truth. This technique rarely fails, and it provides the greatest amount of accurate, detailed information about how the client is experiencing and expressing his or her chart:

Ask.

Ask the client how they're experiencing or expressing a certain energy. Ask them how a particular pattern has shown up in their life. *Ask the client!*

I'm not a mind reader. I don't know how my clients are expressing and experiencing their charts. I have hypotheses, of course. I make notes to myself, and form theories based on the astrology, and sometimes these theories prove to be exceptionally accurate. The way that I find out, however, is by *asking*. Sometimes, I'm completely off base. But what matters is that while I was off base in the particular manifestation of a symbol, my understanding of that symbol was still accurate. And now that I know how that symbol is manifesting in my client's life, I can help them to understand that symbol better, so they can express it and experience it in more elegant and supportive ways.

Personally, I ask open-ended questions. I know what answer I expect because of what I've seen in their natal chart (and by the time you finish this handbook, you will, too!), but I don't share that answer in advance. For example, I'll ask, "Tell me about your parents' relationship," and not "How old were you when your father abandoned your alcoholic mother and ran off with his mistress?"

The Right Tool for the Right Job

Astrology is a tool. As tools go, however, it's definitely of the "Swiss Army Knife" variety. Astrology can be used in a great many ways both as a predictive tool and as a tool for personal and spiritual growth. Useful as astrology is, it's important to remember that at the end of the day, it is only a tool, and sometimes, it is simply not the best tool for the job.

In terms of understanding relationships, I find astrology to be exceptionally useful. However, in terms of relationship counseling, astrology will only take you so far. There are some very important elements that can only be understood by asking the client.

Astrology will immediately, clearly, and accurately identify an individual's core relationship needs (safety and validation) and illustrate the language that individual speaks to have those needs met. Astrology will also point out any patterns that may make it difficult for that individual to meet his or her needs. As you will discover in Chapter 2, our Safety and Validation Needs are the single most important parts of human relationships. When we understand the kinds of things that make us feel safe and validated, and learn how to meet these needs (and overcome any beliefs and patterns that may make meeting these needs challenging), we have mastered 75% of everything we need to know in order to improve every single relationship in our lives. This information alone is enough to transform every relationship.

Astrology is a powerful tool for identifying our core needs and motivations. What astrology does not do, however, is predict behavior. Often times, the key to improving our relationships will be found in our Relationship Blueprints (which you will learn more about in Chapter 2), and while astrology can shed some light on our Relationship Blueprints, it's ultimately not the right tool for the job. *Asking* is the right tool for the job when it comes to understanding our Relationship Blueprints. To learn more about Relationship Blueprints and the kinds of questions to ask, see *The Relationship Handbook: How to Understand and Improve Every Relationship in Your Life.*

❖2❖
Introduction to Human Relationships

Before we dive into the astrology, we need to ground ourselves in the humanity. This chapter contains key excerpts from *The Relationship Handbook: How to Understand and Improve Every Relationship in Your Life.* Here, you will learn about what it really means to be human, how to master the ego, and the true nature of relationships.

Being Human

Sometimes we need to be reminded of the truth of who we are. Certainly, most of us have forgotten our true natures.

Each one of us is a multi-dimensional, eternal aspect of the Universe. We are whole and complete, and connected to all of creation. We are, in fact, aspects of All That Is[1]. We are all-powerful because we are part of All That Is. We are each part of whatever name or concept we give to the Ultimate Creative Force in the Universe. We're also currently having a human experience, and we're having this human experience on the planet Earth. If you've ever had to change planes in Atlanta, it's kind of like that. In the grand scheme of our eternal existence, the human experience has a lot in common with a really long layover in Atlanta.

I don't mean to belittle our time here. In fact, we chose to have our human experiences because we wanted to explore the third dimension and to gain a greater understanding of certain aspects of ourselves. It's simply not the most pleasant part of our journey. It does,

---

[1] Throughout this handbook, you will notice a variety of names and concepts that refer to the Ultimate Creative Force in the Universe. You may know this force as God, Goddess, Christ, Allah, Great Spirit, a Higher Power or Brahma, just to mention a few of the more popular names. When I refer to "All That Is," "the Creator," or "the Source," please know that I am referring to whatever name or concept you personally associate with the energy of Divine Love.

however, share certain things in common with the layover in Atlanta: we often feel trapped, crowded, isolated, tired, stressed, and disoriented. Plus, we worry about losing our luggage.

No one is at his or her best when they're stranded in an airport waiting for a connecting flight. In much the same way, it's often difficult for us to connect with our true, divine nature when we're having our human experiences.

This is one of the drawbacks of the third dimension: In order to truly experience it, we have to pretend that we're a part of it. Shortly after we're born, we begin to forget that we are eternal, multi-dimensional beings, connected to all of creation. And the less we remember that truth, the more our human experience starts to look like Atlanta International Airport.

Bernard Gunther describes it perfectly in his book, *Energy Ecstasy:*

"The game we play is Let's Pretend and Pretend We're Not Pretending."[2]

Most of us have gotten so good at pretending we're not pretending, that we've completely forgotten that we're pretending in the first place. One of the goals of the game we play is to remember our true selves. We came here to learn how to master the third dimension. Our purpose is to wake up to our true spiritual natures, and to help everyone else on the planet to wake up as well.

Fortunately, we're not alone—we are having a human experience with many other souls that are also having human experiences. And our relationships to others are one of the most important tools to help us to remember our true power and potential.

In order to do this, however, we have to learn how to master the ego.

The Ego

When we begin our human experiences, we're given a very useful tool to help us to interact with the third dimension: the ego[3]. The ego is entirely a third-dimensional construct. In a sense, we put on an "ego suit" so that we can experience and explore the third dimension from a unique and specific point of view. The ego helps us to pretend that we are individuals; more specifically, the ego helps us to pretend that we're not, in fact, connected to each other as part of All That Is.

As tools go, the ego is very useful. The more we use it, the more uses we find for it. In fact, we can become pretty darned dependent on the ego without realizing it. To illustrate, it may help to think of our egos the way many of us think of our computers.

---

[2] Gunther, page 1.

[3] Many individuals who have had some experience with traditional psychology have a very specific understanding of the ego, usually based on Freud's theory of the *id*, the *ego* and the *superego*. The ego featured in this handbook is not quite the same thing. If you are used to the Freudian definition of the ego, it might help to substitute another name for the ego described in this handbook. I recommend calling it the "inner parent."

More and more people today can't imagine living their lives without their computers (or PDAs, or cellular phones, or any of the hundreds of other technological tools that are supposed to make our lives easier). The more we use our computers, the more ways we find that they can help us. Computers started out as tools to help us be more productive at work, but they've become sources of entertainment for us as well. We can store and organize our lives on our computers! We can even use our computers to stay in touch with people. We can communicate with people across the entire planet without ever having to experience any actual human contact, in fact.

But soon, in subtle ways, the computer begins to take over our lives. We spend hours on the phone with technical support to make sure that our computers run the way we want them to. We feel isolated and cut off if our Internet access is disrupted and we can't check our e-mail. And let's not forget the crushing panic that comes when something serious goes wrong: If the hard drive goes bad, we could lose our entire *lives*.

Even if this doesn't describe you, you probably know someone that it *does* describe. We've become so dependent on our computers that they've stopped being just tools.

But consider this: What if it went even further than that? What if our computers were advanced enough that they could think? What if they were afraid of being damaged—or even of being shut down? What if they realized how dependent we had become on them? What if, in fact, our computers recognized that even though we still had the ultimate power over them, that we had *forgotten this*?

Oh, our computers would still have our best interest in mind, of course. Only what our *computers* believe is in our best interest may not really be what is in *our* best interest. And as long as we remained dependent on our computers, as long as we believed that we couldn't survive without them, they could control and manipulate us. Instead of serving our needs, computers would be fundamentally concerned with staying alive.

The HAL9000 computer in *2001: A Space Odyssey* is an excellent example of what can happen when we let a tool take control of our lives.

It's also a very good description of our relationships with our egos.

Our egos are tools that are designed to help us to pretend to be separate individuals so we can experience the third dimension. Ultimately, our egos are designed to help us to remember where we left our car keys, and not much else.

The problem is that our egos don't know this.

Our ego believes that its job is to protect us from what it perceives to be a very cruel and dangerous universe. Since the ego was created to help us maintain the illusion of separation from the Source, separation is all that the ego knows. The ego feels lost, isolated and alone. In an attempt to protect us from the pain of the world, the ego increases our sense of separation. Of course, the greater the separation, the more the pain. The more the ego tries to protect us from the pain of separation, the more pain it causes.

The ego's single greatest fear is death. Everything the ego does, it does to try to prevent itself from being destroyed. The ego can be destroyed—it's a product of the third dimension, and therefore it's fragile and finite. *We*, on the other hand, are eternal, multi-dimensional beings who can never die or be destroyed because we are a part of All That Is. We get into trouble when we start to identify with our egos and forget our true natures. When we start to believe that we are our egos, we see the world from our ego's point of view and experience fear and pain.

All fear comes from the ego. All fear, in fact, is directly related to the ego's fear of being destroyed. Fear can only exist when we believe that we are separated from the Source. The more we believe the ego, the more we believe we are separate from the Source, and the more we experience fear.

Only two states of being exist: fear and love. We experience fear when we listen to the ego and buy into the idea that we're separated from the universe. We experience love when we remember the truth that we are whole and complete. It's not possible to experience both states of being at the same time, although most of us are masters at switching between them almost instantly.

One of the most important lessons while we're having our human experience is to learn how to manage the ego. We have to keep it in its proper place. When we remember that we're playing a game—a role-playing game in a very literal sense—we can remember that our egos are not our true selves. Then, we can reconnect with our higher selves, with our souls, and let ourselves be guided from a love-based perspective instead of from the ego's fear-based perspective.

In order to experience true spiritual connections in our relationships, we have to put our egos aside. When we keep our egos in check, our relationships can remind us what it feels like to be connected to another individual. Then, we can begin to remember that we're not only connected with that particular individual, but also with every other person on Earth, and with the rest of creation as well.

What are Relationships?

Relationships are first and foremost ways that we can learn our spiritual lessons in the most effective and efficient manner. This applies to *all* types of relationships, not only to romantic and/or sexual relationships. We must always remember the **Universal Law of Relationships:**

Our partners in relationships are our mirrors: They reflect our own issues back to us.

Nothing in any relationship is *ever* about the other person. It's *all* our own stuff. *Always.*

It's *never* about the other person.

Everything we've ever admired in another person—everything we've ever hated about another person—it's *all our own stuff.* When people upset us, when our partners "push our buttons," the lesson is to make us *aware* that we have a button in the first place. Once we've acknowledged this, we can accept responsibility for the button, and *own* it. Then, we can *choose* to release the button. Once we've released a button it can no longer be pushed by anyone.

This applies to *every single relationship in our lives.* It applies to our romantic relationships, to our professional relationships, to our family relationships, to the relationships we have with the people we meet on the street. *Every single relationship.* This, in fact, is the entire reason we *have* relationships—they help us to recognize and acknowledge the parts of ourselves that we have yet to accept or integrate. What we do instead is give these parts of ourselves away. We project our own issues onto others and experience these lessons as if they were coming from outside us. And don't forget: our partners are doing the same thing to us. So, while we're learning about ourselves from them, they're learning about themselves from us.

Because our relationships are designed to help us to learn our spiritual lessons, relationships will last as long as both individuals are learning their lessons from each other at the same rate. If one person learns their lessons, and the other person does not, the relationship will end. Each person will create a new relationship, where they can continue to grow at their own pace. If we've learned our lessons, we'll attract a partner who will give us the chance to move on to the next set of lessons. If we didn't learn our lessons, we'll attract a partner who will give us another chance to learn our current lessons.

Of course, relationships end for many different reasons. We've all had friendships that were close and intimate for years and then seemed to fade away. In the work environment, we can be transferred or promoted, or change jobs, any of which would sever our workplace relationships and create new relationships in our new workplace. And we've had romantic relationships that ended because our life circumstances changed. However, the principles are the same. If we learned our lessons in our old relationships, we'll move on to our next set of lessons in our new relationships. And if we didn't learn our lessons in our old relationships, our new relationships will look just like our old relationships did, giving us another chance to learn our lessons.

Relationship Needs

Abraham Maslow first presented the theory that the key to human behavior is our needs. Everything we do in life has to do with finding ways to meet our unsatisfied needs, and we have to satisfy the lower needs before we can begin to address the higher needs. Maslow's Hierarchy of Needs is usually represented as a pyramid (as shown in Figure 1), because Maslow believed that the lower needs take precedence over the higher needs. He theorized that until we meet our lower needs, we won't be concerned with meeting our higher needs. He also believed that even when we've started to meet our higher needs, if any of our lower needs are interrupted, our focus will immediately shift to the lower needs. In other words, when we're laid up with the flu, we're more concerned with regaining our health (physiological needs) than we are with expressing our individual creativity (self-actualization needs).

Maslow's theories give us a starting point for understanding human relationships. We will build on Maslow's ideas to create a context for understanding and improving our relationships.

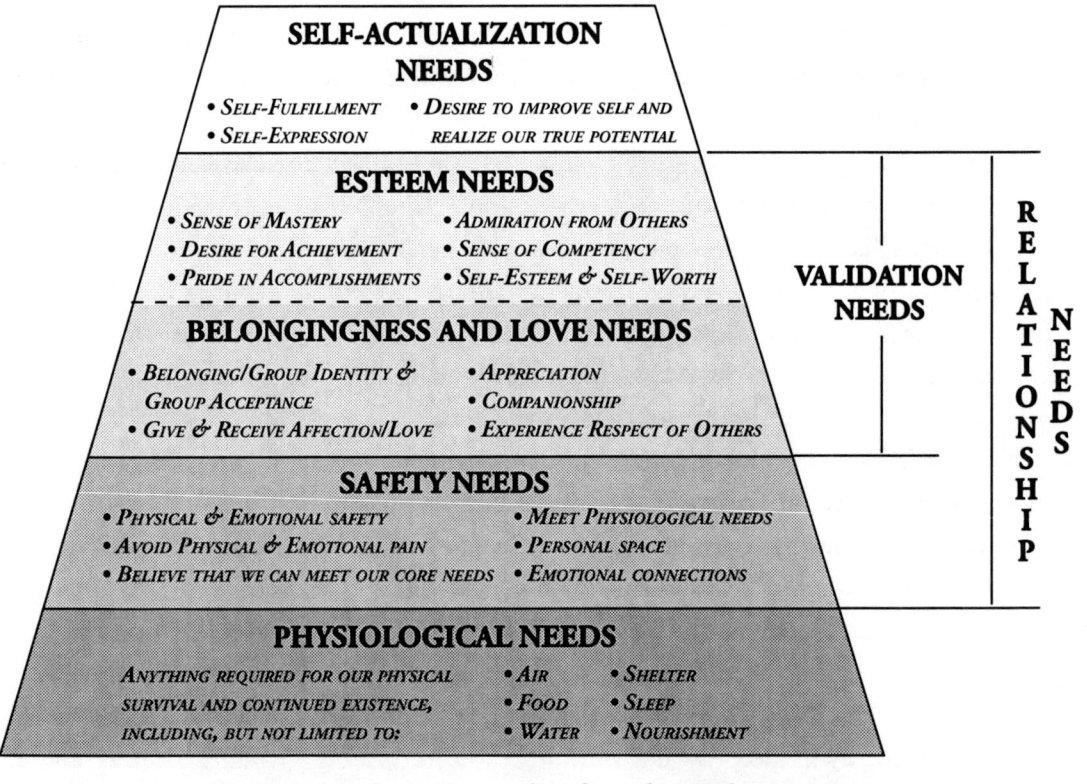

SELF-ACTUALIZATION NEEDS
- Self-Fulfillment
- Self-Expression
- Desire to improve self and realize our true potential

ESTEEM NEEDS
- Sense of Mastery
- Desire for Achievement
- Pride in Accomplishments
- Admiration from Others
- Sense of Competency
- Self-Esteem & Self-Worth

BELONGINGNESS AND LOVE NEEDS
- Belonging/Group Identity & Group Acceptance
- Give & Receive Affection/Love
- Appreciation
- Companionship
- Experience Respect of Others

SAFETY NEEDS
- Physical & Emotional safety
- Avoid Physical & Emotional pain
- Believe that we can meet our core needs
- Meet Physiological needs
- Personal space
- Emotional connections

PHYSIOLOGICAL NEEDS
Anything required for our physical survival and continued existence, including, but not limited to:
- Air
- Food
- Water
- Shelter
- Sleep
- Nourishment

Validation Needs: Esteem + Belongingness
Relationship Needs: Esteem + Belongingness + Safety

Figure 1: Maslow's Hierarchy of Needs (With Annotations)

In any relationship, we're concerned with meeting two categories of needs: *safety* and *validation*. Validation Needs encompass two levels of Maslow's hierarchy: the Belongingness and Love Needs and the Esteem Needs. As long as we feel safe and validated, we will be happy in the relationship. If our Safety Needs or our Validation Needs are not being met, we will experience problems in the relationship. *All* relationship problems stem from either Safety Needs or Validation Needs not being met.

But what about communication (I hear you cry)? Isn't communication the foundation of good relationships? Of course it is. Communication is essential in any relationship. Communication lets us inform our partners that our Safety or Validation Needs are not being met. Communication is a means to an end. Relationships are all about meeting our needs.

Need Bank Accounts

We have a separate bank account for each of our needs. We are responsible for maintaining a minimum balance in each account on our own. As each account reaches or exceeds the minimum level, our attention shifts to filling the next higher account, as shown in Figure 2. Notice that even though the Safety Needs in Figure 2 haven't reached the minimum balance, we still have some credit in the "higher" need accounts, Validation and Self-Actualization. Even so, our primary objective is to meet our Safety Needs and bring that account to its minimum balance. We may make incidental deposits in the other accounts, but for the most part, we won't be conscious of the balance or activity in those accounts.

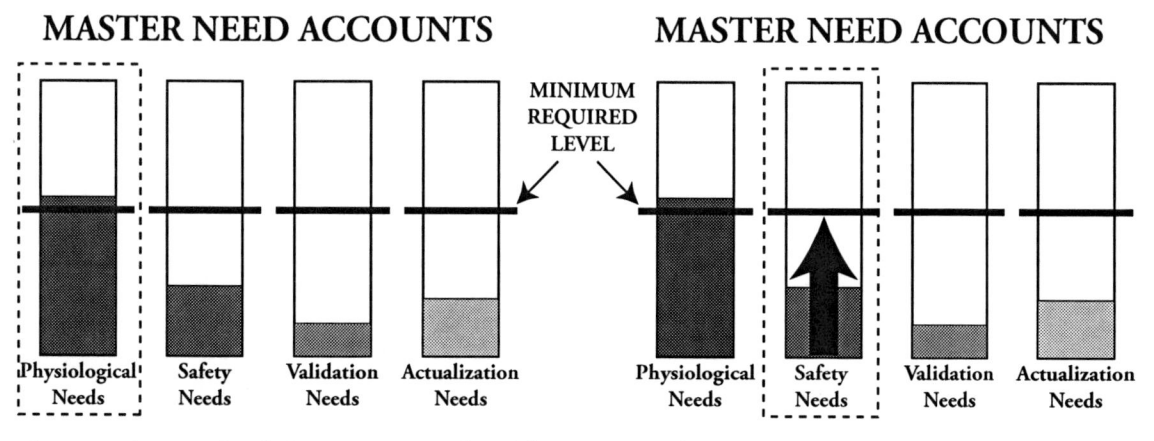

Once we've reached the minimum level for our physiological needs…

…we focus our attention on bringing our safety needs up to the minimum level.

Figure 2: Maintaining the Minimum Balance in our Need Accounts

It is possible for a surplus in one of the higher need accounts to compensate for a deficit in one of the lower need accounts—at least for a short time. The reason that falling in love can make us do so many foolish things is that when we fall in love, our Validation Needs are being met so well that our Validation Account is bursting at the seams. We're then able to ignore any deficits in our Safety Account in order to be with the object of our affections. We can even overcome deficits in our most basic, Physiological Needs when a higher need account is full. When we're consumed with completing a project—usually one that requires a certain degree of skill and creativity—we're meeting our Self-Actualization Needs in a big way, and we're able to go without food or sleep while we're immersed in that activity. As soon as we take a break, however, our Physiological Needs will demand to be met, and we'll suddenly realize just how hungry and/or tired we are.

Relationship Needs Bank Accounts

Our Master Safety and Validation Accounts motivate us in every aspect of our lives, and we are responsible for maintaining a minimum daily balance in these accounts on our own. In addition to these master accounts, we also have individual Safety and Validation Accounts for each relationship in our lives (see Figure 3). Each of these relationship accounts has its own minimum balance requirements of safety and validation. When a relationship account exceeds the minimum balance of safety or validation, we're able to make a deposit in our master accounts.

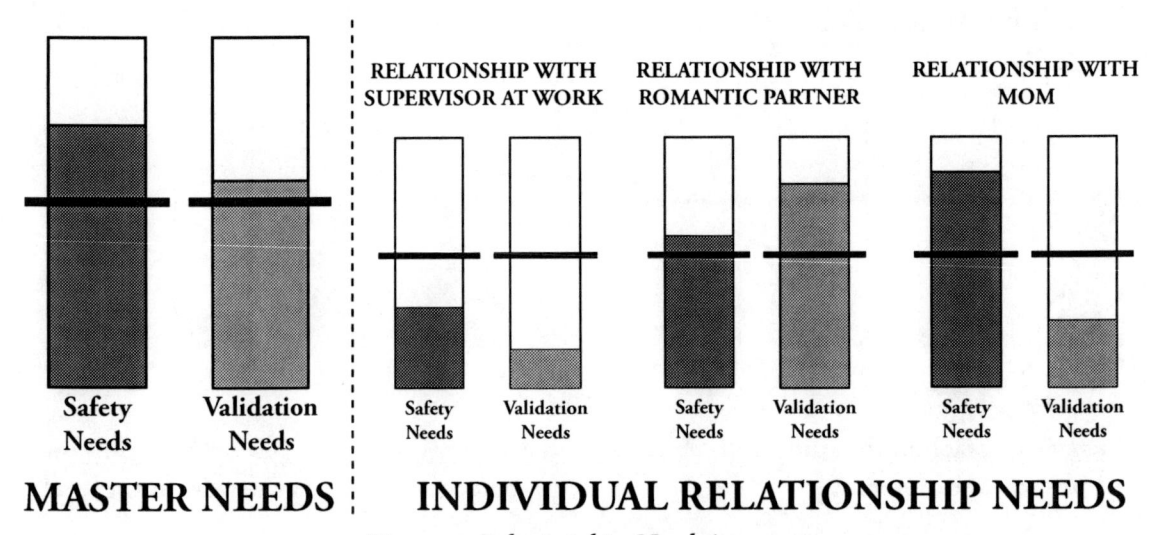

Figure 3: Relationship Need Accounts

However, if the balance of the Safety or Validation Accounts in one of our Relationship Accounts falls below the minimum level, we will make a withdrawal from our Master Accounts to cover the deficit. This can create challenges for us. Unless we are aware enough to monitor the balance in our various Need Accounts, one unsupportive relationship can adversely affect every area of our lives by making us feel generally unsafe and invalid.

We must remember that *we are responsible for maintaining our daily balance of safety and validation in our Master Accounts!* When our Safety and Validation Needs are met in a relationship, not only are we happy in the context of that relationship, but we're *also* more safe and more validated in general. Healthy balances in our individual Relationship Accounts contribute to the balance in our Master Accounts. Our relationships can help us to feel *more* safe and *more* validated. However, in order to function as a healthy individual, we must be able to meet our minimum requirements for safety and validation on our own. It's very easy for us to forget this, and to rely on other people to meet our Safety and Validation Needs.

Anytime one of our accounts drops below the minimum daily balance, it sets off internal alarms. The "lower" the account, the louder the alarms, and the more likely that our egos will get involved. We may not even hear the alarm when our Self-Actualization Account is running low, but when our Safety Account drops below the minimum balance, our egos will go on full alert. This applies both to our Master Safety Account, and to each of our Individual Safety Accounts.

The more involved our egos are in attempting to replenish our reserves, the more likely we will look to other people to meet those needs. When we listen to our egos, we forget the truth that we are responsible for meeting our own needs. More importantly, we *also* forget the truth that since we are individualized aspects of All That Is, our needs are automatically met. All we need do to experience complete safety and complete validation is to step into that truth and recognize that in this moment, we are whole, complete and perfect.

Relationship Checklists

So, how do we know when our needs are being met? What are the kinds of things that make deposits into our Need Accounts? We have checklists that detail the conditions that have to occur in order for us to feel that our needs are being met. The more successfully the conditions on our checklists are fulfilled, the greater the balance in our need accounts. Each checklist also has a set of emergency conditions: if any of the emergency conditions occurs, that tells us that our needs are *not* being met, and prompts us to take immediate action to change this.

We have *General* Safety and *General* Validation Checklists that define the *kinds* of things that will meet our Safety or Validation Needs. We also have *Specific* Safety and *Specific* Validation Checklists for each relationship in our lives that contain the specific things that we expect to happen in order for us to feel safe and validated in the context of the relationship.

Our fundamental needs to feel safe and to feel validated are constant in every relationship, but the *ways* in which we expect to meet those needs varies. The more intimate the relationship, the more we expect from our partners. We need to feel safe and validated in our professional relationships, but we don't expect the same kind of behavior from our co-workers that we do from our romantic partners. We certainly don't expect our employers to show their appreciation for our work by baking us a cake. We'd probably prefer that Mom express her love for us with a card rather than with a back rub. But a handshake from our romantic partner may not be enough to meet our needs.

Wants vs. Needs

Let's take a moment to clarify the relationship between our *expectations* (the things that we *want*) and our *needs*. Everything that we *want* is connected to one or more of our core *needs*. Our *wants* and our *expectations* are simply items on our checklists. We believe that if we get what we *want*, it will meet one of our *needs*. For example, many of us *want* to win the lottery and have millions of dollars in our bank accounts. For most of us, this *want* has to do with our *need* to feel safe. We believe that if we had millions of dollars, we would be self-sufficient, whole and complete. Our *Safety Needs* would be met, so we would be free to pursue our higher needs. If we didn't have to worry about money (Safety Needs), we could explore our creative passions (Self-Actualization Needs). We may *want* an expensive new car because it's a symbol of our status, and our status is one aspect of our *Validation* Needs. An expensive car would make us feel admired, powerful, prosperous or desirable—a small sampling of experiences that make deposits in our Validation Account.

It's important to remember, however, that we can meet our safety and validation needs in a number of different ways. We do not need to get the specific things that we *want* in order to meet our *needs*. We don't need to win the lottery to feel safe, and we don't need a Porsche to feel validated. However, the more attached we become to a specific *want*, the more difficult it is for us to meet our *needs* in other ways.

Relationship Checklist Languages

Understanding our own checklists is only half the challenge. Our checklists help us to define the kinds of things that make *us* feel safe or loved. We naturally assume that if something makes *us* feel safe or loved, then it must make *everyone* feel the same way.

We couldn't be more wrong.

Our checklists are specific to our own needs and expectations, and they're written in the languages that we speak—our Safety Language and our Validation Language. Quite often we speak one language for our Safety Needs and a different one for our Validation Needs. Whenever we review a situation to see if it meets the requirements of our checklists, we first translate it to our language and then evaluate what it means to us. We need to become conscious of what languages we speak when it comes to meeting our Safety Needs and our Validation Needs—and then recognize that our partners may speak different languages. We must also recognize that we may speak one language for our Safety Needs and an entirely different one for our Validation Needs. The things that make us feel validated may not make us feel safe.

There are four major types of languages we speak to meet our needs, one for each of the four elements. Each elemental style has a different focus on what makes them feel safe or validated. (We'll explore each elemental checklist language in greater detail in Chapter 3 and Chapter 4.)

- *Fire* needs to be active.
- *Earth* needs boundaries and structure.
- *Air* needs communication and social interaction.
- *Water* needs emotional connections.

We can't communicate effectively with our partners if we don't speak each other's languages. And if we can't communicate with our partners, we can't meet their needs—or expect that they will be able to meet our needs. Most of the time when we communicate with others, we translate everything on an unconscious level. We say or do something that expresses our feelings and intentions. Our partners receive this message and immediately translate it into their language. As is frequently the case, much can be lost in the translation. In fact, our partners may not have received our message at all. Their response is based on how they translated our message—and we in turn translate their response.

We may be doing our best to make our partners feel safe and validated. But if we're speaking our language and they're listening in theirs, we could be missing the mark entirely. The solution is to learn how to speak our partner's language, so that when we have something truly important to convey—when we want to provide support, to make them feel safe or validated—we can be certain that they receive the message the way we intended it.

If, for example, we have a Water Validation Checklist, words simply aren't that important to us. We communicate through emotional and spiritual connections. We can feel loved and appreciated simply spending time with our partners watching television. As long as we experience the emotional connections, our needs are being met. If our partner, on the other hand, has an Air Validation Checklist, they *do* need to hear the words. If we want to make sure that our partner is feeling loved and appreciated, we need to *tell* them. It doesn't matter that we're expressing our esteem and affection through our emotional connections; we must use words—even though the words don't matter very much to us. We have to speak *their* language to make sure that we're meeting their needs.

Relationship Blueprints

Relationships are some of the most important and the most powerful experiences in our lives. Our relationships can make us aware of the best in each of us, and they can make us confront our worst fears and our most painful beliefs. The possibilities of any given relationship are infinite. In truth, each relationship in our lives is unique, because each relationship we have is with a unique individual. Relationships are unpredictable, and have the potential to take us to entirely unexpected places.

Of course, our egos have a thing or two to say about that.

Our egos *hate* to be caught unprepared. Our egos believe that it's their job to protect us from anything that has the potential to cause us the least bit of pain. Well, relationships have the potential to create quite a lot of pain. In order to protect us, the ego creates frames of reference and sets of expectations about our relationships so that it can know what to expect. The challenge for the ego is that since each relationship is entirely unique, it's not technically possible to base our expectations of future relationships on our past relationships. This doesn't stop our egos from creating frames for our relationships, of course.

What makes our relationship frames different from the rest of our frames is that our relationship frames are created from observation only, and not from direct experience. We create our relationship frames as infants and children, long before we understand the nature of relationships. These frames become the plans that we use to build our future relationships. We unconsciously build our relationships to the specifications of the frame. This way, our egos can know what to expect from the relationship. The frames we create about our relationships are more than just frames: they're Relationship Blueprints.

Our egos need to know what to expect in order for us to feel safe (or so they believe). Relationships as a rule, defy expectations. In any given relationship, too many variables exist. The expectations that we create based on our experience in one relationship may not apply to another relationship. However, our egos have discovered that if we build a relationship based on our Relationship Blueprints, we can reliably predict the kinds of experiences we will have in the relationship.

The challenge is that each relationship that we build from a given blueprint shares the same fundamental structure. Any differences between relationships are cosmetic—the color of the paint, the landscaping, the window treatments, and so on. The floor plan, the amount of space, the structural style will remain consistent. The structure of our relationships is what matters, because the structure of the relationship determines how easily our needs can be met in that relationship.

To continue with the architectural metaphor, we may need a great deal of space in order to feel safe in a romantic relationship—at least a six-bedroom ranch style, for example. If the blueprint we use to create our romantic relationships is for a two-bedroom townhouse, we will never be happy with our romantic relationships because the romantic relationships we build from this blueprint don't allow us enough space to feel safe. And if we can't feel safe in a relationship, we won't continue with the relationship.

We have four significant Relationship Blueprints in our lives.

The **Soul Blueprint** is based on our experience of our relationship to the Creator, and governs our relationship with ourselves.

The **Authority Blueprint** is based on our experience of our relationship to our parents, and governs our relationship to authority figures, as well as our relationships when we are in a position of authority. We have a **Male Authority Blueprint** (based on our relationship to our father) that governs our interactions with male authority figures, and a **Female Authority Blueprint** (based on our relationship to our mother) that governs our interactions with female authority figures. When we are in a position of authority, we usually follow the blueprint of our same-gender parent.

The **Sibling Blueprint** is based on our experience of our relationship with our siblings. This blueprint is essential because it eventually governs our relationships with our co-workers in our professional relationships.

Finally, the **Marriage Blueprint** is the *only* blueprint we have for *any* romantic or sexual relationship of *any* kind. This blueprint is based on our experiences and perceptions of our parent's marriage. (If you feel the urge to scream, please feel free to do so.) We will revisit the Marriage Blueprint in Chapter 9.

The most important thing to remember about our Relationship Blueprints is that they are nothing more than beliefs, and their power lies in the fact that we're usually unconscious of them. As soon as we become aware of our Relationship Blueprints, they lose their power over us. It's silly to believe that our experience in one relationship will have anything to do with our experience in a different relationship with a different individual.

While we are free to redesign our Relationship Blueprints at any time, the process is not quite as straightforward as it might seem. The *real* power of our Relationship Blueprints lies in the assumptions we hold about the items on our blueprints, not in the items themselves. Becoming aware of what's actually contained in our Relationship Blueprints is often a challenging and lengthy process—hindered by the fact that our egos believe that our Relationship Blueprints protect us, and so our egos do not want us messing with them.

☦3☦
Using Classical Astrology to Create a Context to Find the Relationship in the Natal Chart

Before we can begin to look at relationship patterns in the natal chart, we must first create a context to find the relationship in the natal chart. This chapter covers the approach that I take to creating a context for understanding any natal chart. It includes an overview of how I evaluate an individual's temperament, and an introduction to Essential Dignities and Dispositor Trees, two classical astrology techniques that are exceptionally powerful tools for unlocking the secrets of the natal chart.

Elements and Modalities

Those of you familiar with my approach to natal chart interpretation (from *Astrology: Understanding the Birth Chart*) know that I always begin by analyzing the overall elemental balance and temperament of the chart. I place the greatest significance on the inner planets (Sun through Saturn). Occasionally, I will consider the placement of the angles and personal points. However, I do not consider the outer planets at all. The outer planets do not have any influence over an individual's temperament.

Elements

The elemental balance of the zodiac comes from the ancient Greek philosophical concept of the Universe: that everything was made up of a combination of the four basic elements of Fire, Earth, Air, and Water. Each element has qualities associated with it that are unique to that element. The qualities of each symbolic element are very much derived from the qualities of the physical manifestation of that element.

Fire

The Fire signs are Aries, Leo, and Sagittarius. The element of Fire represents the energy of life, and of spirit. Fire is outgoing, energizing and transforming, and is the most self-motivated of the elements. Fire signs are concerned with the question of identity. Fire signs also tend to be more action-oriented than the other elements. Fire signs are very intense: They usually radiate great warmth and light, but in close quarters, they can also burn.

Fire signs are very focused in the moment, although in the same way that a fire will spread quickly from one place to another, Fire signs have a tendency to follow a train of thought rather than to stick with one idea or concept and see it through to completion. One quality of Fire that is usually overlooked in the Western traditions (but is a fundamental quality of the Eastern element of Fire) is that Fire is clinging and dependent. Fire can only exist as long as there is fuel; once the fuel has been consumed, the Fire dies.

When we think of the word "fire" we also think of terms like "passionate" and Fire signs are very prone to intense emotions; however, the emotions that Fire signs are the most comfortable with are either intense joy or intense anger. Fire signs must learn how to experience the full range of emotions and not to limit themselves to these two extremes.

Fire is also a very masculine, one-pointed energy in that it has a strong "all or nothing" tendency. When a Fire sign takes action it instantaneously runs on all eight cylinders. When Fire signs go, they GO! By the same token, when they stop, it's usually a dead stop: They run out of fuel and drop from exhaustion. Another important lesson for Fire signs is moderation.

Fire signs are extremely honest; it never occurs to them to appear to be anything other than their true nature, and they have little tolerance for dishonesty in others.

Fire signs recharge through physical activity, especially physical activity outdoors and in the Sun, which is ultimately the strongest representation of the element of Fire. People with an emphasis in Fire in their charts may also find that they enjoy sitting in front of their fireplace, tending to campfires, or dining by candlelight. Short of direct physical exertion or intense emotional outbursts, simply being near actual flames can be a very nurturing and energizing experience.

Earth

The Earth signs are Taurus, Virgo and Capricorn. The element of Earth represents substance and physical form. Earth does not move: it stays in one place. Earth is practical, substantial, and material, and concerned with matter and our need to deal with it. Earth is passive and receptive: it must be acted on and formed by external energies. Earth is the most stable of the elements. Earth signs are concerned with the physical, the material and with issues of worth and value.

Earth is the slowest-moving of the elements; in fact, Earth almost seems not to move at all. Earth signs have the most even temperaments, and are the most difficult to provoke to take action. But don't forget that inertia works both ways! Yes, it takes a lot to get Earth signs moving, and yes, they tend to move rather slowly when they do, but the sheer weight and mass that Earth signs carry with them can be a formidable power to experience. Steamrollers don't have to be particularly fast, but they aren't to be trifled with.

Earth signs are first and foremost concerned with what is practical. Earth signs relate primarily on the physical, tangible level, and often struggle with understanding of more abstract concepts. Individuals with a strong emphasis in Earth tend to be very sensual, and very anchored in the physical. These individuals communicate best through their sense of touch, taste and hearing. They are far more likely to rely on what their physical bodies tell them, than on any information they receive on the mental, intellectual, or verbal levels. Earth signs experience the full range of emotions, although they are frequently so grounded that they do not appear to be feeling much of anything.

Earth signs have a tendency to become addicted to the illusions of the physical plane. It is a very short step from simply enjoying the material world and the creature comforts and pleasures that come with it, to identifying with these trappings and losing sight of our true, spiritual purposes. Earth signs can become so grounded that they have difficulty accepting that the unseen, spiritual world has any validity at all. The lesson of Earth signs is to discover how to ground the spiritual energy in the material world.

Earth signs recharge through connecting with the earth. Individuals with a strong emphasis in Earth in their charts often find that they enjoy gardening, caring for their lawns, and anything that puts them in direct contact with nature.

Air

The Air signs are Gemini, Libra and Aquarius. The element of Air represents the mental and social realms. Air moves horizontally across the surface, and with great speed, forming connections between all that it encounters. Air signs are the most comfortable in the realm of abstract ideas and concepts, symbols, and communication.

Air signs are the most objective, and capable of having the greatest amount of perspective of all of the signs. The element of Air is a member of the "masculine" polarity and is therefore more extroverted and active, and operates on the conscious, external level. All of the Air signs are double signs, rooted in duality, and able to understand and appreciate all sides of an issue simultaneously. Air signs are also fundamentally concerned with relationships and understanding our place in the universe. Gemini relates the individual to his or her environment; Libra relates the individual to other individuals; and Aquarius relates the individual to society.

Because Air is the element that relates to the mental plane, the element of Air is rational and logical. This also means that Air signs are not very comfortable with emotions in general, and with intense emotions in particular. Air signs will always try to distance themselves from emotions, and retreat to the mental, abstract realms where they are the most comfortable. Remember, Air moves along the surface; it does not like to go too deep.

Individuals with a strong emphasis in Air often have extremely vivid imaginations. They are so attuned to the energies of the mental plane that they are able to discover new ideas and concepts, and build on old ones by discovering new connections or different perspectives. While Air signs are full of wonderful ideas, they are not terribly successful at actually implementing these ideas. Air signs are thinkers, not doers—they leave the implementation of their ideas to the Earth signs.

Air signs recharge through social and mental activity, but also through direct experience of air. This can include everything from deep breathing, to kite flying, to riding a motorcycle or roller coaster and feeling the rush of the wind. Air signs enjoy abstract challenges, and can energize through working puzzles and riddles, through research or debate, or simply by socializing with friends and meeting new people.

Water

The Water signs are Cancer, Scorpio and Pisces. The element of Water relates to the emotional and spiritual plane. Water signs operate entirely on the level of feelings—but not just any feelings. The element of Water relates to our deepest, most primal emotions, as well as to the needs and longings of our soul. These feelings are buried deep in our unconscious and subconscious minds, and many times we would like to keep them locked up there and even forget that they exist, because we are frightened by the power and intensity that they carry.

Water is a "feminine" energy, receptive, responsive, and fluid. Water sinks, always seeking the lowest and deepest point, and Water will continue to flow until it is contained. Water has no shape or structure of its own, and instead takes on the characteristics and form of its container. The element of Water is irrational, instinctive, emotional, and entirely right-brained.

Like Air signs, Water signs also seek to make connections; however, Water seeks to connect on deep, transformational levels that Air would never consider exploring. Water signs are concerned with healing, and with the power of emotional release, and Water signs are the most comfortable with any kind of emotion, so long as it is intense. Something that Water shares with Fire is a tendency to exaggerate and to be overly dramatic.

Water signs are perhaps the most retentive of all of the elements. Water remembers each and every emotional experience, no matter how painful. At times, it almost seems that Water enjoys exploring the painful memories and emotions the most of all, as they are frequently the most intense. One of the hardest lessons for Water signs is learning how to let go, to truly release the pain and the negativity and allow the true healing process to complete.

Water signs feel the most deeply of any of the elements. They may not always be able to communicate the depth of their feelings, the extent of their pain and joy, because words do not come easily to Water signs. Water signs have an ongoing struggle with finding ways of communicating and expressing their feelings that truly encompass the intensity of the experience. Ultimately words are always inadequate; some things can only be communicated through direct emotional energetic connections.

Because the element of Water has no structure of its own and must be contained, Water signs tend to have the most difficulty accepting and respecting interpersonal boundaries, particularly emotional ones. Water signs must learn to respect the emotions and the comfort level of others; and that not everyone is able to bare their soul and share their deepest feelings five minutes after being introduced. This can be a very difficult and painful lesson.

Water signs recharge through intense emotional connections, as well as through proximity to water. Individuals with an emphasis in Water in their charts can clear their emotional bodies of the accumulated negativity by spending time in and near water. These individuals often find that they are happiest living near lakes, rivers or oceans in the first place; otherwise, they may be attracted to rainy climates. But even if no easy access to a body of water is available, taking long, hot showers, or soaking in a warm bath can have the same energizing and clearing effect.

The Modalities

The modalities are Cardinal, Fixed and Mutable. Each modality has its own core issue, and governs the ways in which the elements express.

Cardinal

The Cardinal signs are Aries, Cancer, Libra and Capricorn, and in the Tropical Zodiac, they correspond to the beginnings of the seasons of Spring, Summer, Fall, and Winter in the

Northern Hemisphere. Cardinal signs are initiating, and focused on new beginnings. Cardinal signs are also fundamentally concerned with the question of identity.

Cardinal signs are trailblazers and pioneers. They have a tremendous amount of initiative, and are extremely self-motivated. Cardinal signs are often associated with leadership, although mostly they come by this accidentally; they don't have any fundamental desire to lead, per se, but they do not want to be led themselves. If people follow them, or learn from their examples, that's fine, but it's not their primary motivation for acting.

Cardinal signs always seek to express and define individual identity; their tremendous energy and drive is necessary to break free of the collective and establish a sense of individuality. Each Cardinal sign is concerned with a different aspect of identity, depending on the element involved. Aries, the Cardinal Fire sign, is concerned with simply creating and expressing an individual identity; Cancer, the Cardinal Water sign, is concerned with establishing and expressing an emotional identity; Libra, the Cardinal Air sign, is concerned with one's social and intellectual identity; and Capricorn, the Cardinal Earth sign, is concerned with creating a physical and tangible manifestation of identity.

While Cardinal signs tend to be very dynamic, charismatic, direct, and impulsive, they have some lessons to learn as well. First and foremost, Cardinal signs are only concerned with starting new things: They care little for seeing a new venture through to completion, and tend to lose interest very quickly. As soon as something becomes routine, Cardinal signs become bored and begin looking for something new to start. Cardinal signs must also learn the art of impulse control. Cardinal signs tend to act as soon as they get a new idea, and rarely if ever take the time to think things through, or create an organized plan of action.

When pressured, the first reaction of a Cardinal sign is to defend itself by counter-attacking. Cardinal signs are the embodiment of the phrase, "Shoot first, ask questions later."

Fixed

The Fixed signs are Taurus, Leo, Scorpio and Aquarius. The Fixed signs correspond to the middle of each season, when the changes in the weather are well established, and the steady rhythm of life has reasserted itself. Fixed signs follow the Cardinal signs, and are concerned with sustaining and maintaining what was initiated by the Cardinal signs. Fixed signs are fundamentally concerned with the question of self-worth.

Fixed signs are concerned with stability and with structure; they want things to last. Fixed signs generally possess tremendous stamina and reserves—they aren't known for their speed (Cardinal signs are the sprinters of the Zodiac), but Fixed signs are the marathon runners.

Fixed signs, much like the element of Earth, represent slow-moving but incredibly powerful forces. Fixed signs do not like change, and they will tend to hold onto and follow their original course of action regardless of whether or not this is the wisest choice at the time.

Fixed signs are always concerned with the question of self-worth; they build on the identity issues established through the Cardinal signs, and are concerned not simply with expressing an identity, but with making sure that that identity has value and substance. Taurus, the Fixed Earth sign, is concerned with our material and physical worth; Leo, the Fixed Fire sign, is concerned with our value and worth as an individual; Scorpio, the Fixed Water sign, is concerned with our emotional and spiritual worth; and Aquarius, the Fixed Air sign, is concerned with our social worthiness.

Fixed signs have stamina and persistence, and this makes them very formidable to deal with. They are also, as you might guess, exceedingly stubborn, and one of the most important lessons for Fixed signs is flexibility and openness to change. Because Fixed signs are focused on issues of self-worth, they have a tendency to become invested in their ideas and actions—any suggestions that changes should be made are instinctively perceived as a personal affront and attack on our worth as individuals. The first response of Fixed signs when confronted is to dig in their heels and resist. This is not to say that Fixed signs abhor any kind of change; however, the idea to make a change has to come from within, not from without.

Mutable

The Mutable signs are Gemini, Virgo, Sagittarius, and Pisces. Mutable signs correspond to the end of each season, when the weather is preparing to change and transform into the next step in the cycle. Mutable signs are flexible and adaptable, and are concerned with change and with the completion of one cycle and the start of the next cycle. Mutable signs are all about adaptation, adjustments, and tying up loose ends. In Classical Astrology, Mutable signs were also known as "common" signs; they fall in between the haste of the Cardinal signs, and the methodical plodding of the Fixed signs, and generally represent events happening in the natural flow and in their own time. Mutable signs are the most aware of the dynamics of the complete cycle of birth, growth, death, and rebirth, and they strive to keep events moving smoothly along the wheel.

Mutable signs are fundamentally concerned with completion, healing and becoming whole. They follow and build on the work sustained and maintained by the Fixed signs, and represent the Universal Law that in order for one cycle to begin, the previous one must end. Gemini, the Mutable Air sign, is concerned with completing our social and intellectual self; Virgo, the Mutable Earth sign, is concerned with completing and perfecting the physical plane;

Sagittarius, the Mutable Fire sign, is concerned with completing our individual identity; and Pisces, the Mutable Water sign, is concerned with completing and healing our emotional and spiritual natures.

Mutable signs are known for their flexibility and their ability to adapt to and handle just about any situation in order to keep events moving towards their ultimate completion. Mutable signs, however, also have a tendency to be too flexible, too easily influenced by external forces, and too scattered to effect any kind of change. When a Mutable sign is confronted, its first response is to change its nature, to adapt, to avoid, to do anything it can in fact to avoid the actual confrontation. What Mutable signs must learn more than anything is focus: They tend to be concerned with so many different details at one time, that as a result their energy dissipates and becomes ineffective.

Temperament: Quadrants and Hemispheres

Much as the signs have elements and modalities, the houses have hemispheres and quadrants, as seen in Figure 4.

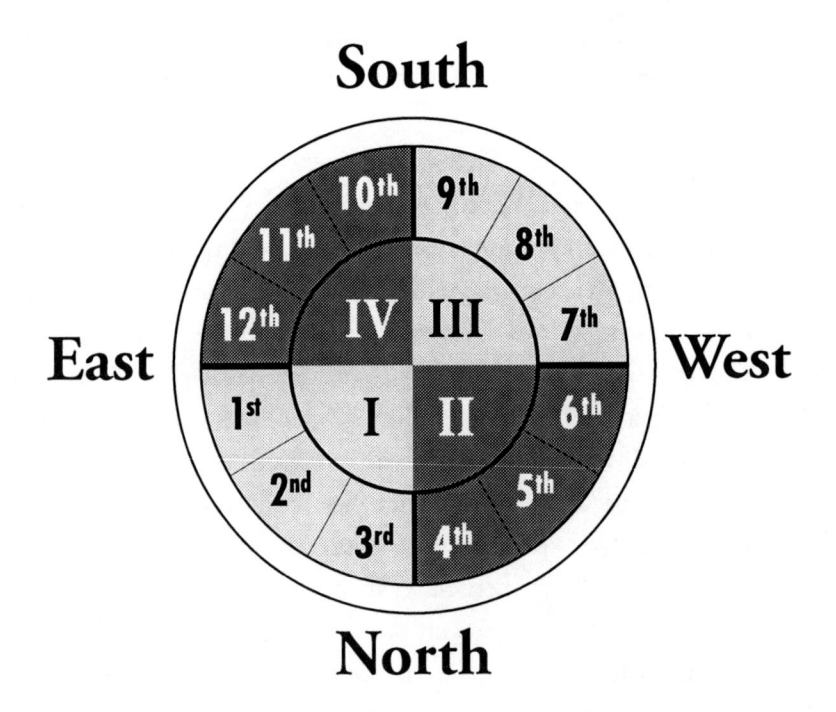

Figure 4. Quadrants and Hemispheres

The first thing you're likely to notice about the houses and quadrants is that the Cardinal directions aren't where you would expect to see them. The top hemisphere of the chart is the Southern hemisphere, while the bottom hemisphere is the Northern hemisphere. Likewise, the left hemisphere of the chart is the Eastern hemisphere while the right hemisphere is the Western hemisphere.

The Southern Hemisphere

The Southern Hemisphere of the chart includes houses 7 through 12. These houses are above the horizon; planets in these houses can be seen in the sky (assuming, of course, that the Sun isn't also in these houses!). The Southern Hemisphere then tends to be more visible, more extroverted in its expression. The houses in the Southern Hemisphere are meant to be seen by other people, and planets in these houses tend to express more openly.

The Northern Hemisphere

The Northern Hemisphere of the chart, which includes houses 1 through 6, is below the horizon, and can't be seen. Planets in the Northern Hemisphere of the chart are hidden from view. The Northern houses then tend to be more introverted and private in their expression. These houses are more personal, and aren't meant to be shared with everybody.

The Eastern Hemisphere

The Eastern Hemisphere of the chart includes houses 1, 2, 3, 10, 11 and 12. These houses surround the Ascendant, the point in the chart where we are the most focused on our individual expression. The Eastern houses tend to be more self-reliant, self-initiating and active.

The Western Hemisphere

The Western Hemisphere of the chart includes houses 4, 5, 6, 7, 8 and 9. These houses surround the Descendant, the point in the chart where we are the most focused on relating to other individuals. The Western houses tend to be more receptive and focused on taking others into consideration.

The Quadrants

Each quadrant combines the qualities of two hemispheres. Quadrant I (Houses 1, 2, and 3) is both introverted (Northern) and self-reliant (Eastern). Quadrant II (Houses 4, 5 and 6) is introverted (Northern) and reactive (Western). Quadrant III (Houses 7, 8, and 9) is extroverted

(Southern) and reactive (Western). Quadrant IV (Houses 10, 11, and 12) is extroverted (Southern) and self-reliant (Eastern).

Introducing Classical Astrology

Let's use the analogy that the planets are the actors, and the signs are the roles that they play. Needless to say, actors are far more comfortable and convincing in certain roles than they are in others. The more a given role fits an actor's "type" the more comfortable the actor is playing that role, and the more effective and compelling the performance.

Unlike actors (at least the best actors), the planets will never lose themselves in their roles. Mars is always Mars, no matter what sign it is in, or where it is placed in the chart. No amount of makeup and costuming could ever make us mistake Jupiter for Saturn. For example, take Sylvester Stallone, the action hero actor. He's the most convincing when he's doing Rambo, blowing things up and saving the day—that's the type of role that best fits his image, and he's by far the most comfortable in those roles. To cast Stallone as Hamlet, for example, or even worse, as Juliet, would be a grave mistake. (O.K., I know that *I'd* buy a ticket to see him play Juliet, but that's not the point.) By the same token, you wouldn't expect to see Shirley Temple playing an action hero. Most actors are lucky enough to only play roles that suit them and that will allow them to show off their strengths. The planets, on the other hand, aren't nearly as lucky.

In Astrology, we have 12 different roles: the 12 signs of the zodiac. And eventually each and every planet has to step into each and every role, no matter how miserable they may be playing the part, or how terribly miscast they may seem to be.

So how can we tell how convincing a planet will be in a given role? We evaluate that planet's overall strength or Essential Dignity.

Introduction to Essential Dignities

Essential Dignities were a fundamental part of classical astrology—one that has been largely forgotten or misunderstood by most modern astrologers. Thanks largely to the work of Project Hindsight, ARHAT (the Archive for the Retrieval of Historical Astrological Texts), and in particular to classical astrologers like Rob Hand and Dr. J. Lee Lehman, Ph.D., modern astrologers can now begin to understand the nature and quality of the Dignities, and discover how working with them makes interpreting and delineating the planets both much easier and far more accurate.

A table of Essential Dignities is shown in Figure 5.

ASTROLOGICAL RELATIONSHIP HANDBOOK

SIGNS	RULERSHIP	EXALTATION	TRIPLICITY DAY	TRIPLICITY NIGHT	TERM					FACE			DETRIMENT	FALL
♈	♂	☉	☉	♃	♃ 6	♀ 14	☿ 21	♂ 26	♄ 30	♂ 10	☉ 20	♀ 30	♀	♄
♉	♀	☽	♀	☽	♀ 8	☿ 15	♃ 22	♄ 26	♂ 30	☿ 10	☽ 20	♄ 30	♂	
♊	☿	☊	♄	☿	☿ 7	♃ 14	♀ 21	♄ 25	♂ 30	♃ 10	♂ 20	☉ 30	♃	☋
♋	☽	♃	♂	♂	♂ 6	♃ 13	☿ 20	♀ 27	♄ 30	♀ 10	☿ 20	☽ 30	♄	♂
♌	☉		☉	♃	♄ 6	☿ 13	♀ 19	♃ 25	♂ 30	♄ 10	♃ 20	♂ 30	♄	
♍	☿	☿	♀	☽	☿ 7	♀ 13	♃ 18	♄ 24	♂ 30	☉ 10	♀ 20	☿ 30	♃	♀
♎	♀	♄	♄	☿	♄ 6	♀ 11	♃ 19	☿ 24	♂ 30	☽ 10	♄ 20	♃ 30	♂	☉
♏	♂		♂	♂	♂ 6	♃ 14	♀ 21	☿ 27	♄ 30	♂ 10	☉ 20	♀ 30	♀	☽
♐	♃	☋	☉	♃	♃ 8	♀ 14	☿ 19	♄ 25	♂ 30	☿ 10	☽ 20	♄ 30	☿	☊
♑	♄	♂	♀	☽	♀ 6	☿ 12	♃ 19	♂ 25	♄ 30	♃ 10	♂ 20	☉ 30	☽	♃
♒	♄		♄	☿	♄ 6	☿ 12	♀ 20	♃ 25	♂ 30	♀ 10	☿ 20	☽ 30	☉	
♓	♃	♀	♂	♂	♀ 8	♃ 14	☿ 20	♂ 26	♄ 30	♄ 10	♃ 20	♂ 30	☿	☿
	+5	+4	+3		+2					+1			-5	-4

Ruler ▢   Exaltation ▢   Detriment ▢   Fall ▢

Figure 5: Ptolemy's Table of Essential Dignities and Debilities as shown in Essential Dignities *by J. Lee Lehman, Ph.D.*

As you will notice, there are five Essential Dignities (Rulership or House, Exaltation, Triplicity, Term, Face), and two essential debilities (Detriment, Fall). You may also notice that only the "inner" planets through Saturn are included in the table. The use of Essential Dignities predated the discovery of the outer planets by almost two thousand years. The outer planets can have no Essential Dignity or debility. Some of these terms may be very familiar to you. The concepts of "Rulership," "Exaltation," "Detriment," and "Fall" have survived into modern astrology, although few astrologers seem to understand exactly what they mean or how to work with them.

All degrees indicated in the table are rounded to the next whole degree: that is, 12°01′ would be rounded up to 13°. The degrees also represent the last degree that a planet rules. For example, Jupiter in Aries is in Term from 0°00′ Aries to 5°59′ Aries, but at 6°00′ Aries, Venus takes over.

Rulership

The definition of Rulership is the single biggest difference between Classical Astrology and Modern Astrology, and the cause of more verbal brawls at astrology conferences than I even want to think about. In Classical Astrology, there were only the seven planets, and the sign rulers were neatly divided with each planet ruling a pair of signs, and the Sun and Moon each ruling one. This was perfectly acceptable until 1781 when Uranus was discovered and, true to its nature, shook everything up. No longer did the planets and the signs match up neatly. And the subsequent discoveries of Neptune and Pluto made things even more messy. Modern astrologers decided to change the system of sign Rulerships to include these new planets.

This was only possible because at the time, the link between classical techniques and modern astrology had already been severed, and few astrologers either used or understood the true meaning of the Essential Dignities. Instead, they reassigned the Rulerships based not on how strong a planet was in a given sign, but on how much they felt a planet was like a given sign. Aquarius was taken away from Saturn and assigned to Uranus; Pisces was taken away from Jupiter and assigned to Neptune; and after a long dispute between Aries and Scorpio, the general consensus decided that Scorpio ruled by Pluto, not Mars. The modern usage of the Term "Rulership" is really a system of "affinities" and has nothing whatsoever to do with "Rulership" as an Essential Dignity.

When we talk about a planet in a sign that it rules, it is an evaluation of that planet's strength in that sign. How well can that planet play the role that it's been given? Well, a planet in a sign that it rules is playing the role that it is most famous for—the signature part that turned it into a $20 Million Plus A-List star. This is a planet that can do whatever it wants, and that doesn't have to answer to anyone or anything. It is the master of its own destiny. This is wonderful for the planet, but it's not always the best thing for the individual! Just like an A-List Hollywood star, no one is going to say "no" to a planet in Rulership—no matter how stupid, self-centered, dangerous, or potentially destructive their ideas happen to be.

On an esoteric level, planets in the signs of their Rulership are operating on the highest plane of existence: the level of pure being. In their own sign, planets are able to express their true nature, their highest purpose in its purest form. We have the opportunity to begin to understand and work with the planet on this level after the age of 60.

We will be working extensively with planets in Rulership.

Exaltation

Exaltation is a term that has more or less survived into the modern literature, but with little or no information on exactly what it means. Planets in the sign of their Exaltation are treated like honored guests: Things are done on their behalf by others, and with the best of intentions; but no matter how comfortable and pampered these planets may be, they ultimately do not get to choose their own agenda. They are bound by certain standards of acceptable behavior, and kept in check.

Planets in Exaltation are very strong—and in many ways much easier to deal with than planets in the signs that they rule. As honored guests, planets in Exaltation tend to be on their best behavior; they strive to be gracious and to express their higher nature. On an esoteric level, planets in Exaltation are operating on what we would call the Spirit or Soul level (what the Greeks called "*Nous*"), which is where we connect with our higher selves and our guides. We are able to access and experience planets in Exaltation on this level from the ages of 45–60.

When considering a planet in Exaltation, keep in mind the fact that other planets go out of their way to do things for the exalted planet on its behalf. The houses and areas of life ruled by the exalted planet may be very harmonious and fortunate. However, this also means that an exalted planet could become lazy or manipulative. It's quite easy to take for granted the fact that other people are always around to take care of our needs.

Triplicity

Triplicity is a moderately strong Essential Dignity; it is not nearly as strong a placement as Exaltation or Rulership, but a planet with dignity by Triplicity is still quite fortunate. In fact, "fortune" and "luck" seem to be the best ways to describe a planet in Triplicity. These planets just seem to be lucky. They have a knack for being in the right place at the right time, and receiving benefits because of this. Their strength, then, does not seem to come from any inherent talent or ability, merely from good timing. Think of Triplicity as an actor who comes off well in a performance because of strong direction, good production, and outstanding material—in other words, an actor in a role that would be very difficult to screw up. Luck is a very tricky thing, though, and with planets in Triplicity (as with so many other things), luck has a nasty habit of running out just when you begin to rely on it. To some extent, we can relate this to the fact that Triplicity is usually determined by the sect of the chart: a planet that would be dignified by Triplicity in a diurnal (day) chart, may have no dignity at all at the same position in a nocturnal (night) chart.

When considering a planet with dignity by Triplicity, always remember the keyword "Luck."

Term

A planet with dignity by Term is one that makes a valiant effort at the part that it's playing, but is simply out of its league. William Lilly described Term as representing a planet that was in very declining fortunes; someone who was struggling to make ends meet, and was perhaps only a short while from being turned out onto the street. Planets with dignity only by Term have an interest in the matter, but not enough strength, skill or luck to have much of an impact or to accomplish their goals. More than any other quality or dignity, William Lilly used Term to assign physical descriptions to people. Specifically, Lilly looked to the planet that ruled the Term of the Ascendant as the significator of physical appearance.

We will not be paying too much attention to a planet's Term in natal interpretations.

Face

Face is by far the weakest of the Essential Dignities: in fact it is hardly a dignity at all. A planet that only has dignity by Face has a great deal of anxiety about its situation. Because fear and anxiety about something give it focus, planets in Face at least have an interest in the situation. Unfortunately, they are in no position to have any kind of an impact on it whatsoever. This is an actor who probably stepped into the part at the last minute, had no time to prepare, and knows that his career depends on his performance. The only thing that can be said about Face is that it will keep a planet from being classified as Peregrine (without any Essential Dignity at all). The fear and anxiety keeps the planet focused on the goal, but in no way gives the planet the resources or ability to reach the goal.

When a planet only has dignity by Face, always remember the keyword "fear" when considering how that planet expresses.

Detriment

A planet in a sign opposite of a sign of its Rulership is in the sign of its Detriment. Planets in Detriment are classified as debilitated, but this does not mean that they are necessarily weak. In fact, planets in Detriment are actually quite strong; however, they tend to use their strength in ways that are inappropriate to their current situation, and as a result, end up in some very difficult positions. Planets in Detriment are in poor condition because of their own actions. A planet in Detriment is like Sylvester Stallone playing Juliet on Broadway because he insists that playing Juliet will be the best thing for his career. No one is going to tell him that he can't do it, but this doesn't mean that he'll do well in the part.

On an esoteric level, planets in Detriment are operating on the mental/emotional plane, and are most challenging to us between the ages of 15–45. In practice, individuals with planets in Detriment tend to worry too much about the affairs of that planet, and are often exceedingly self-conscious about how they express the energy of that planet.

Planets in Detriment are extremely important in natal interpretations. Whenever we see a planet in Detriment, we must always remember the keyword "worry." Planets in Detriment are always worried about how they express. Planets in Detriment are often involved in key behavior patterns.

Fall

A planet in the sign opposite the sign of its Exaltation is said to be in Fall. Planets in Fall are not in quite as bad a situation as planets in Detriment. Planets in Fall are weak because they are in a place where they have no influence—sort of like being stranded in a foreign country where you don't speak the language and don't understand the local customs. Planets in Fall are debilitated through no fault of their own. To continue with the actor analogy, a planet in Fall is Sylvester Stallone playing Juliet on Broadway because his agent got him into the contract, and he can't break it.

On an esoteric level, planets in Fall are operating on the physical plane, and are most prominent from birth to age 15. When we are not able to express the energy of a planet in Fall, when we experience difficulties and challenges with the planet, these will tend to manifest in our physical bodies as illnesses and injuries.

Planets in Fall are always worth noticing in natal interpretations. When considering a planet in Fall, look for the ways in which that planet can express on the physical plane, often in the physical body. One of the most common examples is that individuals with the Moon in Scorpio often experience physical discomfort—usually in their stomachs—when they're not able to express their true feelings.

Peregrine

A planet with no Essential Dignity is Peregrine, which means "wandering." Peregrine planets have no affinity, strength, talent or resources; but at the same time, they do not necessarily have any essential debility (although Peregrine is, in itself, considered a debility). Peregrine planets in natal charts are very different from Peregrine planets in other forms of astrology. In Horary and Electional Astrology, a Peregrine planet is in very bad shape; in Natal Astrology, where we have the ability to work with our understanding of the planets over the course of our lives, Peregrine planets are simply less predictable and less typical in their expression. This is not necessarily a bad thing, and it also does not mean that Peregrine planets can't express themselves. However, Peregrine planets do seem to take a very round about way of getting from point A to point B. A Peregrine planet in a natal chart is like an actor who has been cast against type in a role; the actor's approach to the part is unusual, and not at all what we would expect, and it takes some time to get used to it and to accept the actor's performance. But the actor still has a fighting chance of turning in an acceptable performance in the end.

A Word About Classical Interpretations

One adjustment that modern astrologers who use classical techniques must often make involves translating the very fatalistic and frequently negative interpretations assigned to the planets to a more supportive, enlightened, and empowering format. A planet in debility is not a bad thing. It does not mean that the individual will have a bad experience with that planet, nor does it limit what that individual can accomplish with his or her life—including the areas of life impacted by the debilitated planet. Essential Dignities are so valuable in Natal interpretations because they can help us to understand how a planet is likely to express in a given sign; and more than how, why. The challenges presented to a debilitated planet represent some of the most important growth and life experiences for the individual. By the same token, having a natal chart filled with strongly dignified planets presents its own set of challenges. The more strongly a planet is allowed to express its own nature, the more essential it becomes that we learn how to master that planet and keep it in its proper perspective in our charts and in our lives.

How the Outer Planets Fit In

One of the fundamental differences between "modern" astrology and "traditional" astrology boils down to how the newly-discovered outer planets fit in with the traditional systems of Rulership and dignity. True to its nature, when Uranus was discovered in 1781, the very neat and symmetrical system of Essential Dignities was challenged and upset for the first time in history. Here was a planet that didn't have a place in the scheme of things as they existed at the time. Astrologers scrambled to understand the energy of this new planet, and also to reevaluate the fundamental tools of astrology.

The fact that new planets were discovered (Neptune in 1846, and Pluto in 1931) at a time when the practice of astrology (and formal instruction in astrology) was in serious decline opened the door to the modern "Rulerships" which are not evaluations of a planet's strength, but instead are indications of how alike the planet and the sign seem to be. Other than in horary astrology, Essential Dignities fell out of favor in general practice until very recently, so the new system of Rulerships was not challenged too frequently (beyond the lingering debate about what the modern Rulership of Pluto should be: some astrologers still insist that Pluto rules Aries, not Scorpio).

In her book, *Cosmic Astrology,* June Wakefield proposes what I believe to be the most elegant solution, one that not only takes into account the outer planets, but that also, by extension, takes into account the modern Rulerships associated with Uranus, Neptune and Pluto. Wakefield sets up her theory by establishing a few key assumptions.

- ❖ The Sun as we use it in the chart is not the true Sun; instead, it is the Earth/Moon dyad.
- ❖ The true Sun is the source of all life, energy and light; its energy is expressed on the material plane through all of the planets and all of the signs.
- ❖ The outer planets, Uranus, Neptune and Pluto operate on a higher plane than the visible planets. These three planets act as "Secondary Suns" and bring the energy of the true Sun closer to the material plane. Each of the three Outer planets rules a different plane of existence: Uranus rules the Plane of Matter, Neptune rules the Plane of the Mind, and Pluto rules the Plane of Life. Each of these "Secondary Suns" in turn expresses through a pair of visible planets, and each of those planets rules and expresses through two signs.

I find this system to be exceptionally elegant—and it answers the question of the Modern "Rulerships" very nicely. Uranus rules Aquarius? It sure does: since Uranus, the ruler of the Plane of Matter expresses through Saturn and the Earth/Moon dyad, Uranus not only ultimately rules Aquarius, but also Capricorn, Cancer and Leo. Does Pluto rule Scorpio or Aries? Why quibble! Because Pluto, the ruler of the Plane of Life expresses through Mars and Venus, Pluto rules both Scorpio and Aries, as well as Taurus and Libra. And Neptune, the ruler of the Plane of Mind, expresses though Mercury (lower mind) and Jupiter (higher mind) and rules not only Pisces, but also Sagittarius, Gemini and Virgo. And since in order to manifest on the physical plane, all four elements are needed, isn't it nice that each of the outer planets "rules" four signs: one each of Fire, Earth, Air and Water.

Now, I still don't teach that the outer planets directly "rule" any signs: that is, they don't have any Essential Dignity or debility. But I certainly believe that they must somehow fit into the overall scheme of things. Since there's no question about the fact that the outer planets do not operate in the same way as the visible planets do, I'm very open to the idea that they even operate on a higher plane, and express, at least in part, through the visible planets.

Dispositor Trees

The simplest way of working with the Essential Dignities involves looking at the hierarchy of Rulerships in a natal chart. Rulership means just what it sounds like it means—the planet that rules a sign actually rules or governs any planets that are in that sign. When a planet rules another planet, it is said to be the dispositor of that planet's energy. The Moon, for example, rules all planets in Cancer—it is the *dispositor* of any planet in the chart in Cancer. Planets in Cancer will look to the Moon for guidance on how they can express themselves. The ruling planet is thought to impose form and structure on the expression of the planet ruled. Of course, the quality of the guidance and the nature of the form and structure imposed will depend entirely on the location, position, and Essential Dignity of the ruling planet. Mars in Cancer, for example, will tend to be more grounded and practical in its expression if the Moon (the Ruler of Cancer) is in Taurus, and more scattered and quick to react if the Moon is instead in Gemini.

We can create a diagram of how the planets in the chart relate to each other based on their Rulerships, called a Dispositor Tree. Dispositor Trees are extremely helpful in uncovering the themes of a natal chart because they quickly and obviously reveal which planets are the bosses, and which planets must do the bidding of the ruling planets.

When creating a Dispositor Tree, we always begin with planets in their own Rulership: these planets will be at the top of the tree because they are their own rulers. We then work through the rest of the planets in the tree, starting with the planets that are directly ruled by the planet in Rulership, then moving down to the next level by looking for the planets ruled by these planets, and so on. Although the outer planets will be included in the Dispositor Tree, they do not rule anything themselves; they are only ruled.

Here are the step-by-step instructions on how to create a Dispositor Tree for any chart.

Step 1: Find any planets in their own sign (Rulership). Each one of these planets will be the top of its own tree.

We'll use Liza Minnelli's chart (Figure 6) as an example.

We start with the Moon in Cancer (the only planet in Rulership), which goes at the top of the tree. The Moon in Cancer rules all planets in Cancer—in this case, Mars and Saturn. Mars and Saturn get placed in the second tier, reporting directly to the Moon.

Saturn rules any planets in Capricorn or Aquarius, but as Minnelli has none, this branch of the tree ends here.

Mars rules all planets in Aries and Scorpio. Minnelli has Mercury in Aries and Venus in Aries, and they get placed on the third tier, reporting directly to Mars.

Mercury rules all planets in Gemini and Virgo. Minnelli has Uranus in Gemini, and Uranus goes on the fourth tier, reporting directly to Mercury.

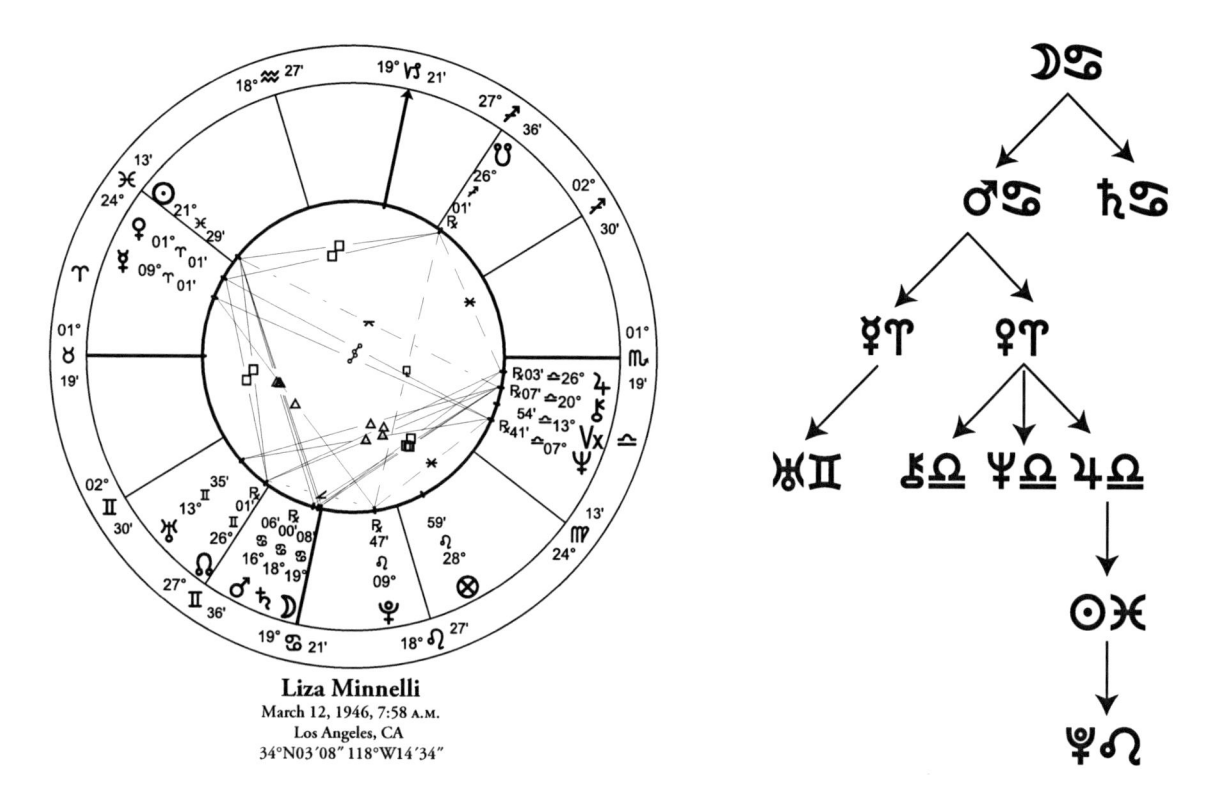

Liza Minnelli
March 12, 1946, 7:58 A.M.
Los Angeles, CA
34°N03'08" 118°W14'34"

Figure 6: Liza Minnelli's Natal Chart and Dispositor Tree

Venus rules all planets in Taurus and Libra. Minnelli has Chiron, Neptune and Jupiter in Libra, and they all go on the fourth tier, reporting directly to Venus.

Jupiter rules all planets in Sagittarius and Pisces. Minnelli has the Sun in Pisces, which goes on the fifth tier, reporting directly to Jupiter.

The Sun rules all planets in Leo. Minnelli has Pluto in Leo, which goes on the sixth tier, reporting directly to the Sun.

Every single planet in Minnelli's chart can be traced back to her Moon in Cancer. Because her Moon in Cancer effectively rules or disposes her entire chart, it is called the Sole Dispositor or Final Dispositor, which in interpretation would mean that just about everything in her life gets filtered through her Moon. In other words, the boss of Liza Minnelli's chart is her Moon.

Step 2: Find any planets in mutual reception by Rulership. Each pair of planets in mutual reception will be at the top of its own tree.

Let's look at Meryl Streep's Chart now (Figure 7). We begin with Step 1 and look for any planets in Rulership. Streep has Mercury in Gemini, which goes at the top of its own tree. Mercury in

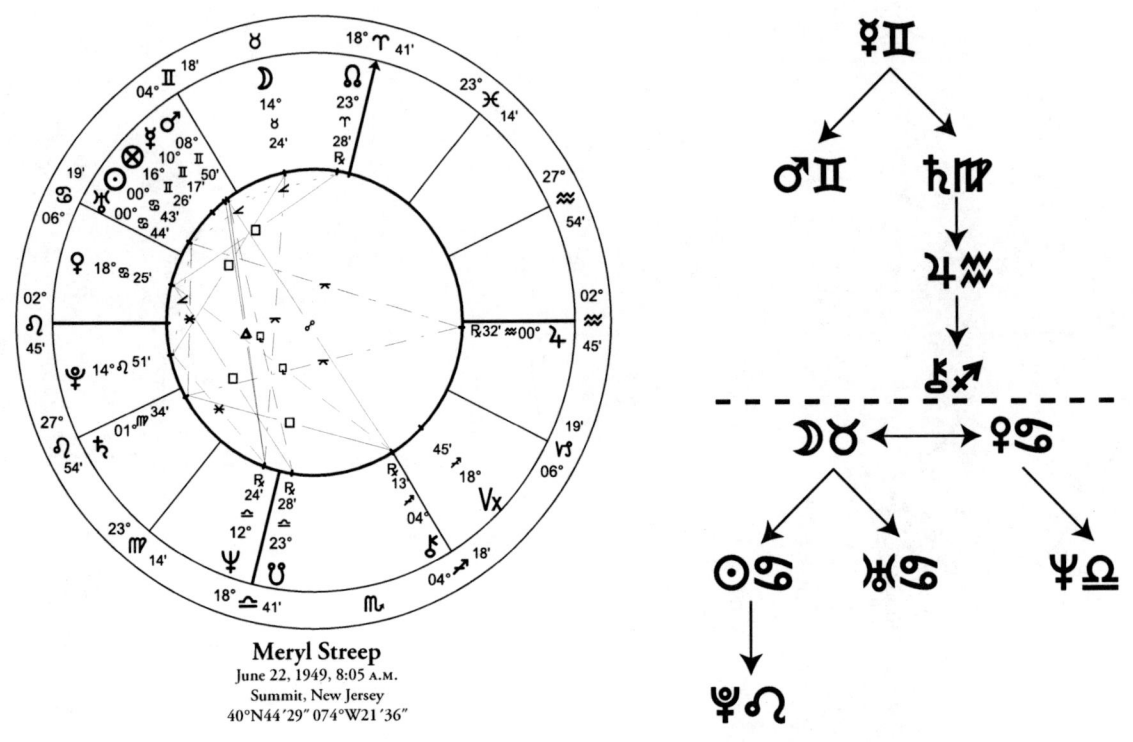

Figure 7: Meryl Streep's Natal Chart and Dispositor Tree

Gemini rules all planets in Gemini and Virgo. Streep has Mars in Gemini and Saturn in Virgo, and they go on the second tier, reporting directly to Mercury.

Mars rules all planets in Aries and Scorpio; Streep has none, so this branch ends here.

Saturn rules all planets in Capricorn and Aquarius. Streep has Jupiter in Aquarius, and that goes on the third tier, reporting to Saturn.

Jupiter rules all planets in Sagittarius and Pisces. Streep has Chiron in Sagittarius, and that goes on the fourth tier reporting to Jupiter.

This is the end of the Mercury tree in Meryl Streep's chart. Since we're still missing a few planets, and there are no other planets in Rulership in her chart, we move on to the next step.

Meryl Streep's Moon in Taurus and Venus in Gemini are in mutual reception, so they go to the top of a new tree, with a double-arrow showing that they receive each other.

The Moon rules all planets in Cancer. In addition to Venus, Streep has Sun and Uranus in Cancer. The Sun and Uranus go on the 2nd tier, reporting directly to the Moon.

The Sun rules all planets in Leo. Streep has Pluto in Leo, which goes on the third tier, reporting directly to the Sun.

This completes the Moon's branch—now we go back to the top and look at Venus.

Venus rules all planets in Taurus and Libra. Streep has Neptune in Libra, which goes on the 2nd tier, reporting directly to Venus.

Between the two trees, we have accounted for all eleven planets.

Notice how Streep's chart is split between the planets that "report" to her Mercury in Gemini and the planets that "report" to her Moon-Venus mutual reception? Right away we can tell that Streep has a very clear division between her emotional and feeling nature and her intellectual approach to the world, something that will prove to be a key theme in her chart.

Sometimes, you'll come across a chart with no planets in rulership and no mutual receptions. In these cases, we have to move on to Step 3.

Step 3: Look for a committee of rulers.

It is possible for a committee of three or more planets to be at the top of the Dispositor Tree. To find the committee, you have to work your way through all of the dispositors until you come full circle. As an example, we'll look at Sylvester Stallone's chart (Figure 8). He has no planets

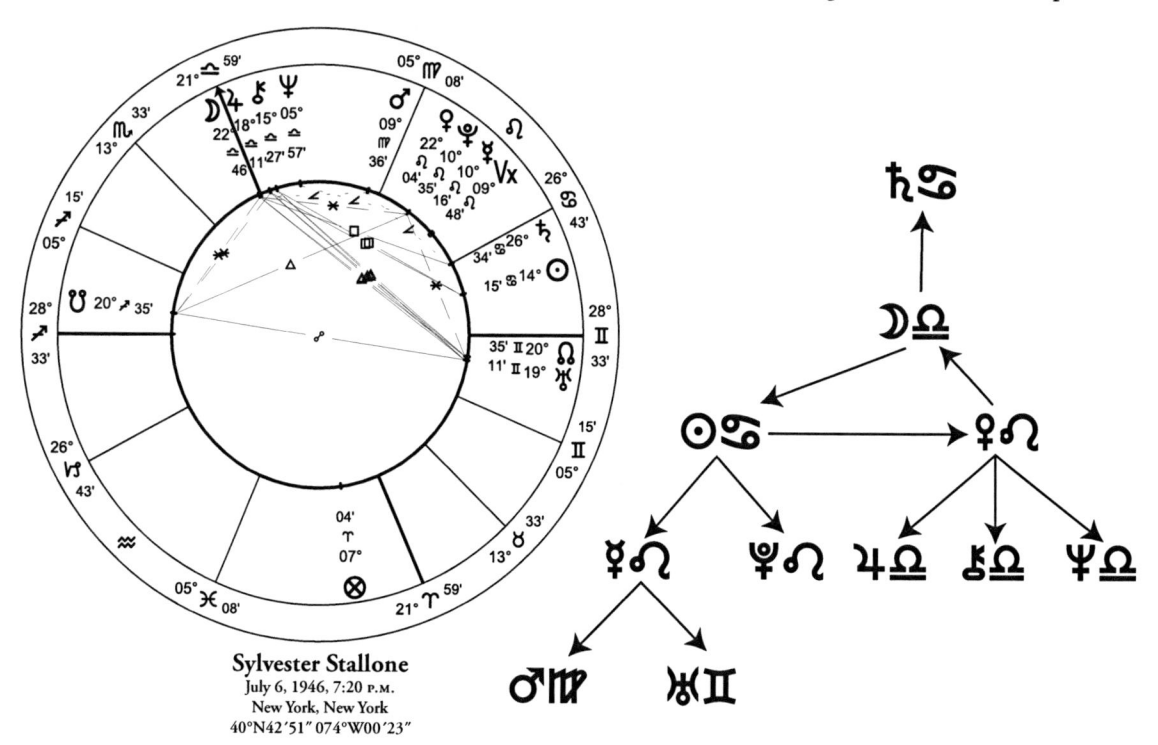

Figure 8: Sylvester Stallone's Natal Chart and Dispositor Tree

in Rulership and no mutual receptions. Picking a planet at random, we'll start with his Jupiter in Leo. Jupiter in Leo is ruled by the Sun in Cancer; the Sun in Cancer is ruled by the Moon in Libra; the Moon is in Libra is ruled by Venus in Leo; Venus is in Leo is ruled by the Sun in Cancer—and we now have a closed loop. The Sun, Moon and Venus form a committee that will be at the top of a Dispositor Tree. As you can see in Figure 8, every other planet in his chart reports to one of the three members of the committee.

Stallone's chart is not ruled by a single planet, but rather by a committee made up of the Sun, Moon and Venus. And because none of these three planets has any real autonomy in the chart since they each answer to the others, this has the potential to set up an inherent struggle for Stallone. Every choice, every action, every decision that he makes will first have to meet with the approval of the committee. And like any governing body, each member of the committee has its own agenda. Since each member of this particular committee is also Peregrine, we're not looking at a terribly efficient process.

It is possible for three, four, or even five planes to rule the Dispositor Tree in committee. In order to find the committee, you must start with one planet at random and work your way through the dispositors until you return to a planet you've already covered.

Creating a Context to Find the Relationship: Elizabeth Taylor

Let's take a moment and put all of this information together and see how it works in practice. We'll begin with looking at the first of our celebrity charts, Elizabeth Taylor.

When working with natal charts, I exclusively use the Koch house system. This is somewhat of a departure from strict classical astrology (which would use whole sign houses). However, in my practice, I've found that the Koch houses provide the most accurate interpretations, particularly when we explore the rulers of the different relationship houses and look at the relationship between the 5th house (love affairs) the 7th house (spouses) and the 11th house (friends). The information I get when working with other house systems is not nearly as accurate. You are welcome (and invited) to experiment on your own. I simply wanted to point out that every chart used in this handbook uses the Koch house system.

You'll notice that each chart we interpret will follow the same steps and the same process, and we'll build on each chart as we go. The entire process (and the entire Relationship Astrology Worksheet) is included in Appendix A.

Elizabeth Taylor's chart is pictured in Figure 9.

Elizabeth Taylor
February 27, 1932, 2:00 A.M.
Golders Green, England
51°N34 000°W12′

Figure 9: Elizabeth Taylor's Natal Chart

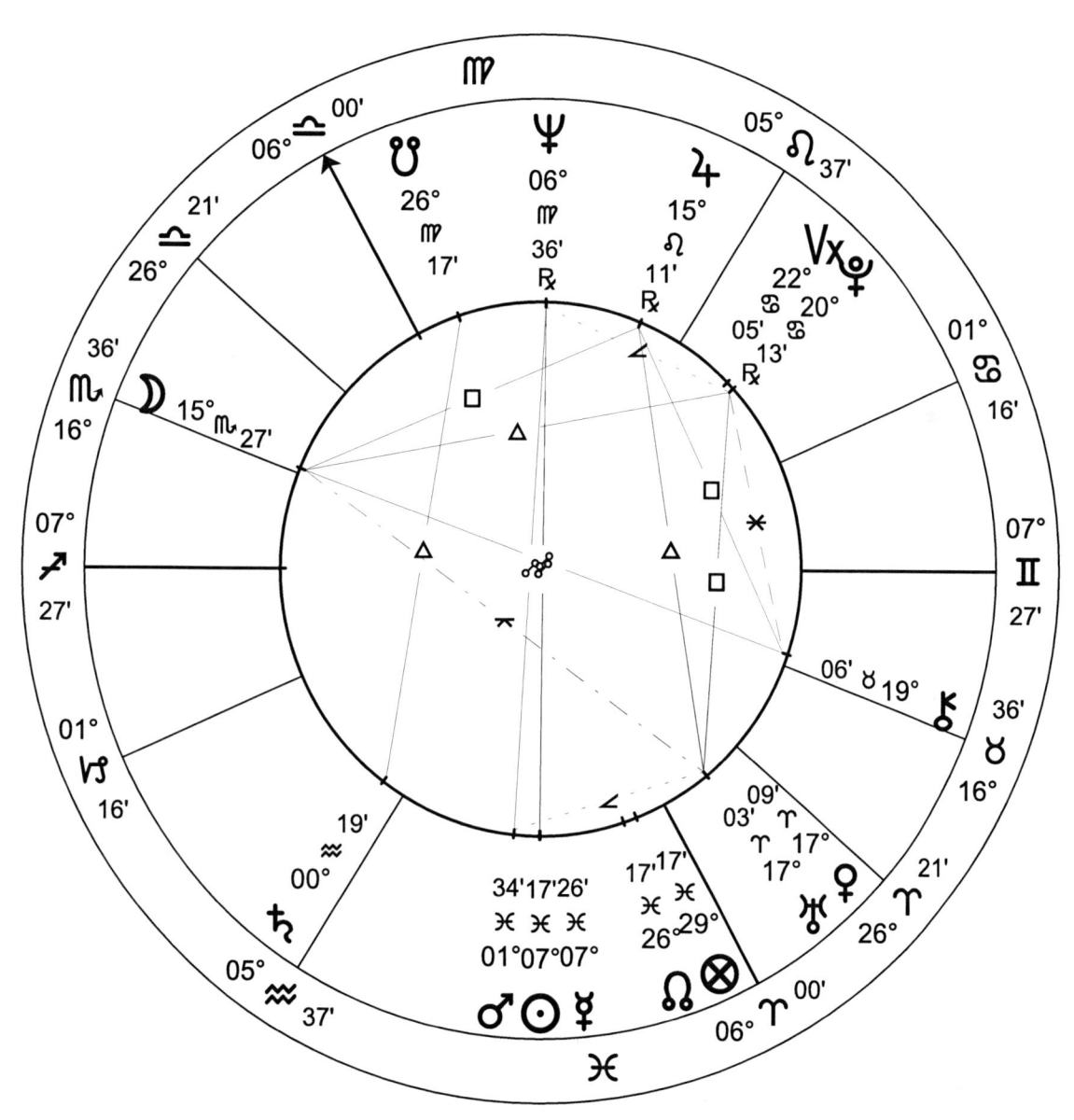

Part 1: Elements and Modalities

Element/Modality	Personal Planets	Personal Points	Outer Planets
Fire	♀ ♃	As	♅
Earth		☋	⚷ ♆
Air	♄	Mc	
Water	☉ ☽ ☿ ♂	⊗ ☊ Vx	♇
Cardinal	♀	Mc Vx	♅ ♇
Fixed	☽ ♃ ♄		⚷
Mutable	☉ ☿ ♂	As ⊗ ☊ ☋	♆

Part 2: Temperament

Hemisphere	Planets	Quadrant	Planets
Northern (House 1–6)	☉ ☿ ♀ ♂ ♄ ⚷ ♅	I (House 1–3)	☉ ☿ ♂ ♄
Southern (House 7–12)	☽ ♃ ♆ ♇	II (House 4–6)	♀ ⚷ ♅
Eastern (House 10–12, 1–3)	☉ ☽ ☿ ♂ ♄	III (House 7–9)	♃ ♆ ♇
Western (House 4–9)	♀ ♃ ⚷ ♅ ♆ ♇	IV (House 10–12)	☽

The first thing to notice about Elizabeth Taylor's chart is that she has four personal planets in water—including the Sun, Moon and Mercury. Emotions and spiritual connections will be exceptionally important to her. She also has two planets in Fire; next to water, Fire is the most emotional of the elements. She has no planets in Earth, and so she's likely to overcompensate, making a conscious effort to be grounded, practical and stable. She may seek security in the material plane. She has only one planet in Air: Saturn. From an elemental standpoint, she is apt to be influenced by her emotions and her intuition; logic, reason and practical issues are not likely to be well-developed skills.

Her core issues have to do with self-worth (three Fixed planets) and with healing and completion (three Mutable planets). Her only Cardinal planet is Venus in Aries—her identity concerns are expressed through her relationships.

Temperamentally, she has a good balance between introvert and extrovert, and between self-reliance and need for relationships.

Part 3: Essential Dignities

Pt	Ruler	Exalt	Trip	Term	Face	Detri	Fall	Score
☽	♂	--	♂	♀	☉	♀	☽ -	-9 p
☉	♃ m	♀ m	♂	♀	♄	☿	☿	-5 p
☿	♃	♀	♂	♀ m	♄	♀ -	☿ -	-14 p
♀	♂	☉ m	♃	☿ m	☉	♀ -	♄	-10 p
♂	♃	♀	♂ +	♀	♄	☿	☿	+3
♃	☉ m	--	♃ +	♀	♃ +	♄	--	+4
♄	♄ +	--	☿	♄ +	♀	☉	--	+7
♅	♂	☉	♃	☿	☉	♀	♄	--
♆	☿	☿	☽	☿	☉	♃	♀	--
♇	☽	♃	♂	♀	☽	♄	♂	--
⚷	♀	☽	☽	♃	☽	♂	--	--
☊	♃	♀	♂	♄	♂	☿	☿	--
☋	☿	☿	☽	♂	☿	♃	♀	--
As	♃	☋	♃	♃	☿	☿	☊	--
Mc	♀	♄	☿	♀	☽	♂	☉	--
Vx	☽	♃	♂	♀	☽	♄	♂	--
⊗	♃	♀	♂	♄	♂	☿	☿	--

Part 4: Dispositor Tree Diagram

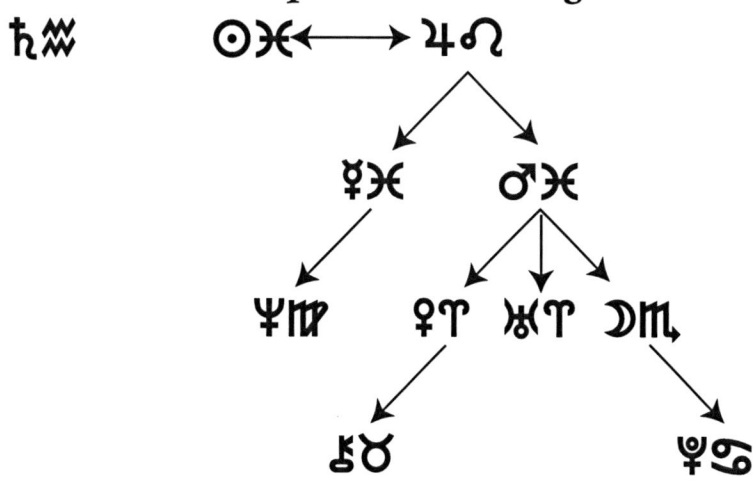

♄♒   ☉♓ ←→ ♃♌
                ↙   ↘
           ☿♓   ♂♓
           ↓   ↙ ↓ ↘
         ♆♍   ♀♈ ♅♈ ☽♏
                 ↓   ↓
                ⚷♉   ♇♋

Taylor has a split in her Dispositor Tree. Saturn in Aquarius, the only air she has in her chart, is off on its own. More importantly, Saturn makes no major aspects to any other planet in her chart. Her internal authority figure, then, is largely ineffective. She may be very aware of appropriate boundaries and personal responsibility in her life, but these skills may only manifest in very limited, specific areas. Saturn is in her 2nd house, and rules her 2nd house, which indicates that she is likely to manage her personal resources exceptionally well. This, however, may be the only area of her life that benefits from Saturn's advice and guidance.

The rest of her chart answers to Jupiter in Leo, in mutual reception with her Peregrine Sun in Pisces. While her Sun is Peregrine, her Jupiter is reasonably dignified (Triplicity and Face). Jupiter in Leo embodies the energy of the movie star: larger than life, gracious, fun-loving, warm, generous, and underneath it all, desperate for validation, appreciation and attention. The planet that sets the agenda for the rest of her chart is primarily concerned with the question, "What do I have to do in order for people to love and validate me?"

We will look at Elizabeth Taylor's chart again, along with her two-time husband, Richard Burton, in Chapter 8. Now, however, it's time for us to take a closer look at the planets that rule our relationship needs: the Moon (safety) and Venus (validation).

⁂4⁂
Safety Needs (The Moon)

Let's take a few moments to consider the concept of safety. We rarely consider our Safety Needs in general, let alone in terms of our relationships. We take our safety for granted when we think about it at all. But, we're about to see that our Safety Needs play a very important role in our lives and in our relationships.

Exploring our Safety Needs

Our Safety Needs can be grouped in three major categories: survival needs, emotional connections, and boundaries.

Survival Needs

In Maslow's hierarchy of needs, Safety Needs become important once our Physiological Needs are met. Our Physiological Needs include our core survival needs—air, food, water, shelter, sleep, etc. Once those needs are met, we become concerned with our safety, and our most fundamental Safety Need is to know that our Physiological Needs will *continue* to be met. Anything that has the potential to threaten our physical bodies and our ability to survive is a fundamental threat to our safety. Our autonomic nervous system is specifically designed to help us survive threats to our physical bodies. Even though we rarely face actual life-or-death situations in modern society, we still have the core programming to switch to survival mode at the slightest hint of danger.

The fight-or-flight response exists to help us to escape from predators and to survive truly dangerous life-threatening situations. It's intended for emergencies only. Think of it as a biological cash advance on a credit card. We only get cash advances as a last resort because the costs are so high. Not only do most credit card companies charge an up-front fee for the advance, but the interest rate on the cash advance is also significantly higher than the standard interest rate for purchases. In terms of our biology, the fight-or-flight response has very similar costs. When our autonomic nervous system is triggered, it takes a significant toll on our bodies. Our normal biological functions are either shut down or diminished, and all of our resources are devoted to finding the strength and the energy to either overcome (fight) or outrun the predator (flight). Once we've survived the threat, we need to be able to rest and recover for a period of time. We need to replenish our reserves, and we need time and resources to repair the short-term damage we did to our bodies with the sudden rush of adrenalin.

The challenge is that our egos have taken over most of the fight-or-flight control, and we switch into this mode anytime we feel the least bit threatened on *any* level. Anywhere the ego senses the potential for pain, it sends a signal to our nervous systems that we're not safe and then it steps in to try to protect us. We're so used to this response that we don't even notice it most of the time. The ego has us well trained, and whenever it senses danger, it pushes our buttons and we act out our old patterns to avoid the pain, either by defending ourselves, or by running away from the situation.

Whenever we feel unsafe in a relationship, we react as if our lives are in danger. We become emotional and defensive. In short, we become unfit to sit down to have a reasonable discussion with our partners about what may be bothering us. This, of course, is likely to trigger our partner and make *them* feel unsafe. And then, *their* reaction to *our* reaction may make us feel even *more* unsafe.

Fight or flight. Or frequently, fight *then* flight.

Need to Know What to Expect

In order to feel safe, we need to believe that our core survival needs will continue to be met. This means that another aspect of our Safety Needs is the need to know what to expect. As we discovered in Chapter 2, the ego creates frames of reference based on our past experiences, so that we can anticipate and evaluate future experiences to ensure that we can continue to survive. Unfamiliar experiences and situations can feel fundamentally unsafe because we do not know what to expect, and our egos do not know how to protect us.

The irony is that the more we project into the future to identify and defend against potential threats, *the less safe we actually feel*. We simply can't anticipate every possible scenario. Our egos believe that the way to feel safe is to anticipate the future. However, the only *true* way to feel safe is to stay centered in the present moment.

Emotional Connections

Emotional connections are another key aspect of our Safety Needs. Emotional connections are closely related to our core survival needs. Once we feel comfortable that we're able to survive, we begin to experience the illusion that we are separated from the Source. We feel isolated and alone, and the emotional connections that we create and share with others help us to remember the truth that we are *not* alone.

Our earliest experience of nurturing emotional connections occurs as infants when we're fed, held and loved by our mothers and fathers. Many theories of child development suggest that as infants, we don't truly comprehend that we are separate from our parents; as we begin to recognize that we are not part of our parents, we cling to the emotional connections we share with our parents for safety and security. For the rest of our lives, sharing emotional connections with other individuals can make us feel safe, nurtured and protected once more.

Boundaries and Personal Space

Boundaries are necessary to define our sense of individual identity while we have our human experiences. Boundaries, like the ego, are entirely part of the third dimension. Boundaries help us to maintain the illusion that we are separated from the Source. Part of the game we play while we're on Earth has to do with our relationship to boundaries. On the one hand, we need to believe that boundaries exist so we can explore the world from an individual perspective. On the other hand, we need to remember the truth that the boundaries are illusions, and that there *is* no separation. We have to walk a very fine line here—if our boundaries are either too weak or too strong, we will feel unsafe. Our egos see boundaries as essential to our sense of safety, because our boundaries define the parameters of what our egos believe we should be able to control. Our ego strengthens our boundaries to protect us from the pain of the outside world. As long as we believe that our walls protect us, we feel safe. Of course, if our boundaries are *too* strong, we won't be able to experience any emotional connections with other people; we'll feel isolated and alone—trapped (and essentially unsafe) in our fortress.

Our boundaries operate on many different levels. On a physical level, our boundaries have to do with our need for personal space. We have emotional boundaries that determine the kinds of emotional connections we share with others. The more intimate and trusting the relationship, the more we're likely to share with our partners. When strangers or professional acquaintances ask personal questions, for example, we feel threatened and unsafe because these questions are not appropriate—they represent boundary violations. Our fundamental right to privacy, in fact, is an effort to assert our individual boundaries and to help us feel safer as individuals.

How Do We Know We're Feeling Unsafe?

Many of us spend so much of our lives in a low-grade state of fight-or-flight response that we aren't even aware that we don't feel safe. Anytime we experience anxiety, stress, fear, worry, tension, and any of the hundreds of physical and psychological side-effects of these emotions, we're feeling unsafe. These emotions, these experiences only occur because we don't feel safe; they are either triggers for or results of the fight-or-flight response being activated.

In relationships, we can look for additional cues to make us aware that we're feeling unsafe. Anytime we feel defensive, we're reacting to a safety violation. Our egos have stepped in and are trying to protect us from an attack. A need for personal space, or a desire to escape or to be alone can also be an indication that we're feeling unsafe. Most often, we feel these urges because of a boundary violation.

If we feel angry, that's another sign that we feel unsafe. Of course, for many of us, feeling angry in itself will make us feel unsafe. See *The Relationship Handbook* for a detailed exploration of the true nature of anger, and the "Present Moment Safety Exercise," which restores the minimum balance in our Safety Accounts.

Safety Checklists: The Moon

There are four major categories of Safety Checklists, each one corresponding to a different element. When we understand the kinds of things that all of the items on our Safety Checklist will have in common, it's easier to identify the specific items on our checklist. Each elemental style has a different focus on what makes them feel safe.

- *Fire* needs to be able to take action to feel safe.
- *Earth* needs boundaries and structure to feel safe.
- *Air* needs communication and social interaction to feel safe.
- *Water* needs emotional connections to feel safe.

So how do we determine which Safety Checklist we have? Simply look at the Moon in the natal chart. The sign (and element) of the Moon identifies our Safety Checklist. We'll take a look at each of the four elemental Safety Checklist Languages, and explore the three dialects of each language in turn.

Fire Safety Checklists

The element of Fire is about taking action. Fire is passionate and intense, and very concerned with self-expression and individual identity. If your Moon is in Aries, Leo or Sagittarius, you have a Fire Safety Checklist.

Feels Safe When: If you have a Fire Safety Checklist, you feel safest when you are able to take action. You need to be free to express yourself, and to follow your dreams and desires. Fire is the most active element, and the most passionate. Maintaining and defining your identity is very important to you. You need to experience the truth of who you are as an individual, and you need to be able to take action based on that truth.

Feels Threatened When: Anytime you feel that you are being limited and prevented from expressing your true nature, you will feel threatened. This can take many forms. You won't be comfortable with strong boundaries, particularly when other people impose them. You need to feel free to take immediate action—when others insist that you wait, that you think things through, or that you only act when it's practical or appropriate, you will become very frustrated. You may find the need to compromise to be threatening to you, especially when you feel pressured to modify how you want to express yourself.

Instinctive Reaction When Threatened: When you feel threatened, your instinctive reaction is to shoot first and ask questions later. You have a very low tolerance for feeling unsafe, and you will always try to do something to eliminate the threat. You may argue, you may throw a fit, or you may simply leave the hostile environment. You may even do all three. But whatever you do, the point is that you will do *something*. You will address each threatening situation as it occurs.

Expresses Emotions: Fire is the most passionate of all of the elements, and you're likely to express your emotions with great intensity. You're apt to be the most comfortable with the extremes of joy and anger, however. The more subtle emotions hold less interest for you. You express your emotions immediately and completely—you do not like holding your feelings inside. It's very important that you feel that you've honestly expressed yourself in the moment. Once you've expressed your emotions, however, you're done. You don't hold on to old feelings and you don't nurse old wounds.

Nurtures and Protects Others: You nurture and protect others by doing things for them. You show that you care by giving of yourself—your time, your energy, and your essence.

Feels Protected When: For you, actions will always speak louder than words. You feel protected when others take action and do things on your behalf. Of course, you'd much prefer to do things yourself, but if you find that you need to rely on others, they need to prove that they're up to the task.

The Moon in Aries

Dignity/Debility: The Moon is Peregrine in Aries. While the Moon in Aries is free to express itself, the impulsive nature of Aries means that the Moon tends to act and react indiscriminately, and without direction or focus.

Core Needs: To be free to act impulsively and without restrictions.

Core Lessons: To learn to accept and recognize inter-personal boundaries; to learn to accept responsibility for its actions; to learn self-control and self-discipline.

Feels Safe When: Able to express emotions freely and impulsively. Able to take action based on feelings and instincts.

Feels Threatened When: Limited, restricted, controlled or otherwise hindered from being able to express itself freely.

Instinctive Reaction When Threatened: Counter-attack. Lashing out impulsively and instinctively. Anger and aggression.

Expresses Emotions: Most comfortable with extreme emotions, specifically with extreme joy and extreme anger. Emotional responses are impulsive, immediate, passionate, intense, and over quickly. The Moon in Aries does not hold onto old emotions—they are expressed and released.

Aries is by far the most impulsive energy in the zodiac. Aries is about taking immediate action with no forethought or concerns about how that action may affect others. Aries is so focused on expressing the self that it is completely unaware of other individuals.

The core need of the Moon in Aries is to be free to act impulsively and without restrictions. This is not always possible, of course. Individuals with the Moon in Aries have to make a conscious effort to be aware of how their actions affect others. For that matter, they have to make a conscious effort to even *recognize* that there are other people around. They must learn self control (and above all, impulse control!) and self-discipline.

If you have your Moon in Aries, you feel safe when you can express your emotions, and when you can take action based on your feelings. Since Aries is a Fire sign, your feelings are likely to be very passionate. Fire signs tend to like joy or anger the most out of all of the possible emotions. In other words, when you're happy or when you're upset, everyone knows it! The good part of this is that you most likely don't carry around old emotions with you. You express what you're feeling, and when you're done, you're done.

What will feel threatening to you, however, are any kind of limitations or restrictions. If you don't feel like you can be yourself and express what you're feeling, you will go into defensive mode. The more threatened you feel, the more likely you will instinctively lash out, venting your anger and frustration.

If your Moon is in Aries, it's very important for you to feel that you're being true to yourself. You will feel threatened in any situation where you feel pressured to compromise.

The Safety Checklist for the Moon in Aries is very much a "to do" list. It consists almost entirely of action items. It's also very short because the Moon in Aries feels safest in the present moment.

One of the best indicators that your Safety Checklist has been triggered is that you're feeling angry about something—or more specifically, you're feeling angry *at* someone. Since your emotions and your reactions are usually so quick, it may be easier for you to understand your checklist in hindsight. Ultimately, all of your Safety Needs will to relate to your ability to feel like an individual. You need to feel that you are able to express who you are. You *don't* need anyone else to recognize you or acknowledge you. In fact, you even prefer to be independent on many levels.

Now, obviously, you won't be able to be completely independent all the time. But in relationships, your Safety Checklist will have a lot to do with how much personal space and personal freedom you expect in any given relationship.

Moon in Leo

Dignity/Debility: The Moon is Peregrine in Leo.

Core Needs: To be validated and appreciated by others for its core essence and identity; to open the heart and express love and warmth.

Core Lessons: To no longer rely on the validation of others and to base self-image and self-worth on self-knowledge, rather than on what others think.

Feels Safe When: Receiving attention in any form; ideally wants to be acknowledged and appreciated by others for its warmth, generosity and love.

Feels Threatened When:	Ignored and taken for granted; not appreciated for its warmth, generosity and creativity.
Instinctive Reaction When Threatened:	Acting out to become the focus of attention. When threatened, the Moon in Leo's primary concern is to be noticed; negative attention is better than no attention at all.
Expresses Emotions:	The Moon in Leo is the most comfortable with the passionate, fiery emotions of joy and anger, and is less familiar with the more subtle emotions. Moon in Leo tends to express emotions dramatically.

Leo energy seeks to sustain and maintain our sense of individuality. Leo seeks approval from others to validate our sense of self and our self-worth as individuals.

The core needs of the Moon in Leo are to be validated and appreciated by others for our core essence and identity. The Moon in Leo needs to be able to open the heart and express love and warmth and generosity—and to be acknowledged by others for their love, warmth and generosity. It's worth noting that Moon in Leo individuals feel safe when their Validation Needs are met.

If your Moon is in Leo, you probably enjoy being in the spotlight. In fact, you feel the safest when you are the center of attention. And while it's one thing to enjoy the attention of other people, it's important that you don't become dependent on it. Ultimately, what you're looking for from other people is validation of your own self-worth. You need to recognize that the only opinion that matters is your own. If you know that you are a good, decent, warm and loving person, that's enough. While it's nice when other people recognize you and acknowledge how wonderful you are, if you become too attached to what other people think, you will be very unhappy. And remember that other people are our mirrors—the more you are able to validate yourself, the more you'll see that validation reflected back to you in your relationships.

But even so, the Moon in Leo does crave attention—any kind of attention. Ideally, you want to be appreciated, but with the Moon in Leo, any attention is better than none. If you feel like you are being ignored, taken for granted, or otherwise overlooked, you will feel threatened. And when you feel threatened, your instincts are to act out. Whatever you may do on the outside, on the *inside*, you're throwing a temper tantrum. When your Moon in Leo is triggered, your inner child starts kicking and screaming. Ultimately, you don't care if people appreciate you or are upset with you—what matters is that you're not overlooked.

Leo is a Fire Sign, and if your Moon is in Leo, you are likely to express your emotions with great passion and intensity. Fire signs, remember, tend to be the most comfortable with joy and anger. Leo's love of the spotlight is apt to give you a flare for the dramatic when it comes time to express your feelings.

The Moon in Leo checklist is very straightforward. As long as you're the center of attention, you're perfectly happy and safe. It's nice if you're able to share your warmth and generosity with others, but the essence of the Moon in Leo checklist is "Me! Me! Me!"

In a perfect world, everything *would* revolve around you. Unfortunately, we do not live in a perfect world, and this means that it's not always appropriate for you to be the center of attention. With the Moon in Leo, the challenge is less discovering what's on your checklist and more making sure that the items on your checklist are actually appropriate. The more responsibility you take for your own sense of self-worth and validation, the easier it will be for you to keep your Moon in Leo checklists under control.

What you must do is look at each relationship and each checklist and determine when and how it is appropriate for you to be the center of attention. You my have to accept that you will have to give up the spotlight from time to time, or that you may have to wait your turn. You will also need to keep your reactions in check when you are triggered because you're not getting the attention you want. These are the times when you can draw on your reserve of self-worth and validate yourself instead of looking for others to validate you.

Moon in Sagittarius

Dignity/Debility: The Moon has dignity by Face from 10–20 degrees of Sagittarius, and is Peregrine the rest of the sign.

Core Needs: Honesty and truth, freedom and trust.

Core Lessons: Tolerance of others, tact—not everyone appreciates brutal honesty the way the Moon in Sagittarius does.

Feels Safe When: Able to explore new ideas and have fun; able to be generous and expansive, sharing with others.

Feels Threatened When: Lied to or betrayed in any way; freedom is curtailed or limited in any way.

Instinctive Reaction When Threatened: Escape. Sagittarius will avoid conflict by leaving and going off on its own. Personal freedom becomes the top priority for the Moon in Sagittarius; when this freedom is restricted, or they feel betrayed, the Moon in Sagittarius will not stick around to repair the damage.

Expresses Emotions: Jupiter's influence tends to make the Moon in Sagittarius prone to over-reacting, and the passionate Fire influence once again indicates a preference of joy or anger along the emotional spectrum. Mutable quality means that once emotions are expressed, they're released. The only issues that the Moon in Sagittarius won't easily forgive are lies and betrayals of trust.

Sagittarius energy seeks to complete our sense of identity by discovering how we fit into the universe and how we as individuals relate to all of creation. The core needs of the Moon in Sagittarius are honesty, truth, freedom and trust. Sagittarius is always on a quest for discovering the Truth, and needs the freedom to do so.

If your Moon is in Sagittarius, you're likely to appreciate honesty. You want the truth, the whole truth, and nothing but the truth. You don't want it sugar coated or dressed up in any way. It's important to recognize, however, that not everyone appreciates brutal honesty the way that you do! You need to make a conscious effort to be tolerant of others. And while you can still speak your truth, you would do well to learn how to speak it with tact. You're not likely to hold onto old emotional baggage. You express your feelings and then you're done. Even when someone hurts your feelings by being brutally honest with you, the moment passes quickly. You value the truth too much to have it any other way. Your emotions are transitory—the truth endures. In fact, you can forgive just about any kind of emotional slight except for dishonesty or betrayal.

You will feel safe when you're free to explore, to expand your horizons, and most of all, to have fun. Sagittarius is a Fire sign, so you enjoy being active. You're likely to be very passionate, and to enjoy sharing your feelings with others. Sagittarius is ruled by Jupiter, the planet of growth and expansion. While this means that you love to have a good time, it also means that you may have a tendency to do everything in a big way—and that you may tend to overdo things. Moderation is an important skill to learn. Ultimately, you will feel safe when you are able to explore your identity. You like to feel alive and active, and to interact with other people, places, and philosophies. You're always up for an adventure, and you're always open to learning something new.

The single biggest threat for you is dishonesty. Even the smallest lie is a very big deal to you, because the search for the ultimate Truth is such an integral part of your sense of safety. You can forgive anything but betrayal and lies. The other thing that threatens you is being limited or restricted. You need to feel that you have enough freedom to explore your own path and discover your own Truth.

When you feel threatened, your immediate reaction is to try to escape. If you're not happy (or safe) in a situation, you will set out on your own. Your sense of freedom and your sense of truth are the single most important aspects of your security. As soon as either has been breached, you will want to abandon the situation—or leave the relationship. You may not leave for good, of course. But as long as your Safety Needs are triggered, you will need to go off on your own until you feel safe again. You won't want to stick around and try to resolve the conflict.

Your Safety Checklist with the Moon in Sagittarius is concerned with how much freedom you have, and how much honesty and truth you perceive. It's not only important that you feel that people are being honest with you at all times, it's also important that you feel that people recognize that *you're* being completely honest with them. Ultimately, you need to be true to yourself, and feel that you can express yourself freely. As long as you can say that you're standing in your integrity and expressing your truth, you will feel safe.

Earth Safety Checklists

The element of Earth is about the physical and material plane. Earth is grounded, stable, and practical. You have an Earth Safety Checklist if your Moon is in Taurus, Virgo or Capricorn.

Feels Safe When: If you have an Earth Safety Checklist, you feel safest when you have clearly-defined boundaries. You prefer things to be practical and concrete. You enjoy the physical world, and draw comfort from your senses, particularly your sense of touch. Words do not matter to you: Words do not endure. What matters to you are results, things that can be seen and felt, things that are practical and tangible and that will last. You need to be able to take your time, and to consider the consequences of your actions and your choices. You value loyalty, and always try to live up to your promises and responsibilities. You are the most comfortable when life is stable, reliable and somewhat predictable. Physical contact is important to you, particularly in intimate relationships.

Feels Threatened When: You find situations that are abstract, impractical or unclear to be very uncomfortable. You do not like to be rushed, and you feel threatened when others pressure you to take action or make a decision before you're ready to do so on your own. You expect other people to do what they say they will do. Loyalty is very important, and when others don't follow through with their commitments to you, it is a very big deal. You rely on the established structures, boundaries and rules to make you feel safe. When these structures are missing, or when others ignore them, you feel very threatened.

Instinctive Reaction When Threatened: When you feel threatened, you turn to the physical and material realms for protection and comfort. You do whatever you can to ground yourself once more. You search for familiar boundaries and structures. You may look to authority figures and established precedent to support your reactions and your choices. You may batten down the hatches and dig in your trenches so that you can wait out any attack.

Expresses Emotions: You're very comfortable expressing and experiencing emotions, and you have a very even temper—mainly because you think before you react. You experience the full range of emotions. You are, however, concerned that you express your emotions in a practical, responsible manner.

Nurtures and Protects Others: You nurture and protect others through the physical and material plane. You enjoy giving gifts to others to show that you care about them. Because physical comfort is so important to you, you like to make sure that other people are comfortable.

Feels Protected When: You feel the most protected when you are surrounded by familiar, comfortable, sensual things. In romantic and intimate relationships, it's important for you to be physically close to your partner. The physical connection helps you to feel that your life will be constant, steady, and unchanging. In other words, it makes you feel safe.

Moon in Taurus

Dignity/Debility:	The Moon is Exalted in Taurus and also has dignity by Triplicity in a night chart. The Moon in Taurus is very strong and grounded.
Core Needs:	To experience physical security and safety; to explore the pleasures of the physical plane.
Core Lessons:	To learn to release attachments to the physical plane; to learn to accept the necessity of change and the cycles of death and rebirth.
Feels Safe When:	Experiencing physical comfort and pleasure. When in familiar surroundings with a stable and predictable routine.
Feels Threatened When:	In unfamiliar surroundings or faced with a disruption in the normal, expected routine. Fear of change.
Instinctive Reaction When Threatened:	Resistance and denial. Clinging to the physical. Digging trenches (figuratively and literally) to protect territory and position.
Expresses Emotions:	Experiences full range of emotions, in a rather practical, grounded manner. Nurtures through touch and physical contact. The Moon in Taurus is somewhat slow and considered when it comes to emotional responses, and generally very even-tempered.

Taurus sustains and maintains on the physical plane. Taurus is concerned with the question of our physical and material sense of self worth.

The Moon is very happy in Taurus. The Moon in Taurus is in the sign of its Exaltation—a dignity that is both very comfortable for the planet and at the same time much easier for the individual because the planet doesn't set its own agenda. The grounded, practical and sensual energy of Taurus provides an excellent container for the emotional nature of the Moon. The Moon can express the full range of emotions, and Taurus' slow and plodding nature means that individuals with the Moon in Taurus aren't driven by the heat of the moment. They tend to be more practical with their emotions, and are more aware of appropriate boundaries.

If your Moon is in Taurus, physical contact is very important to you. You share your feelings through touch, and you feel safest when your surroundings are comfortable and very solid. You need to be careful how attached you become to your material possessions, however. You can sometimes rely too much on the physical world to feel safe. Your possessions help you to stay in contact with your past, and let you feel that you're always surrounded by familiar things and unchanging surroundings. Change is very threatening to you, and when you're threatened, you will tend to look to the material world to protect you. Ultimately, you have to learn to accept that the cycles of death and rebirth are a necessary part of life.

Even so, you will feel the safest when you're physically comfortable. While you may not have expensive tastes, you could get used to the finer things in life very easily! Individuals with the Moon in Taurus truly appreciate physical pleasure. In a very real sense, the Moon in Taurus needs to have its security blanket. Old, familiar sensations, and long-standing routines and rituals will make you feel safe and secure. The creature comforts in your life are very important to you, and without them, you may feel vulnerable and unstable.

What threatens you the most is change. Any disruption in your routines, any unexpected events, particularly when they are outside of your control, make you feel very unsafe. Taurus moves very slowly, and it takes time for you to be able to make adjustments to new situations. Think of Taurus energy as a steamroller: It's slow-moving and very powerful, but it has a lousy turning radius. When you feel threatened, your first reaction is to try to keep things the way that they are. You instinctively resist any pressure to change or adapt, especially when it seems to come from other people. The only time that change is acceptable to you is when you are the one who made the decision to change.

If your Moon is in Taurus, your Safety Checklist has to do with routines, with familiar sensations, and with slow, steady, and continuous progress. Loyalty is a very important issue for you. Your emotional connections are enduring, and when you make a commitment to someone, you tend to see it through to the end. You expect the same level of commitment and loyalty from others as well. If you've made plans with someone who cancels at the last minute and you get upset, it's because you're experiencing a safety violation. Your routine has been disrupted, and you may even feel betrayed on some level.

When you feel threatened, you will dig in your heels and resist. As long as you feel threatened, as long as you feel unsafe, you're not going to be terribly reasonable. It's important that you learn to recognize when your ego has been triggered because you feel threatened, and move past your initial defensive reaction. If you can take a few steps back and give yourself some space (and time) to consider the situation, you will be better able to evaluate it. Your initial reactions don't leave you any room to consider your partner's requests. If you can learn to keep your immediate "Hell, no!" response to yourself, you'll find it easier to explore your options. The longer you're able to consider a new idea, the easier it will be for you to be open to making a change.

Moon in Virgo

Dignity/Debility: The Moon in Virgo has dignity by Triplicity in a night chart. The Moon is Peregrine in Virgo by day.

Core Needs: To be of service and of use; to improve the physical plane.

Core Lessons: To move beyond the physical and the literal and connect with the spiritual; to gain a greater sense of perspective.

Feels Safe When: Taking care of details; nurturing others through little gifts and favors; being of use.

Feels Threatened When: Details are being overlooked or ignored; things are out of place; they are not able to do something to improve a situation or be of use.

Instinctive Reaction When Threatened: Becomes overly critical of self and others. The more threatened the Moon in Virgo feels, the more focused it becomes on the smallest details and imperfections and the less perspective it is able to maintain.

Expresses Emotions: The Moon in Virgo is comfortable with the full range of emotional expression, and tends to experience emotions in a stable, grounded manner. The Moon in Virgo is acutely aware of distinct emotions and emotional nuances.

Virgo is motivated to perfect and complete on the physical plane. Virgo's talent is discrimination and analysis, and Virgo is motivated to be of use and of service to others.

The core need of the Moon in Virgo is to be of service and of use, and to improve and perfect the physical plane. The core lesson of the Moon in Virgo is to learn to move beyond the physical and the literal and to connect with the spiritual. The Moon in Virgo must learn to gain a greater sense of perspective.

If your Moon is in Virgo, you feel safe when you're being helpful. You're always looking for ways that you can improve the world around you. You're also always aware of any imperfections that need to be addressed. You're likely to enjoy taking care of others, and you do this through little gifts or favors. You want to feel that you're making a difference in every aspect of your life. Virgo is all about the details, and you will always sweat the little things. On an emotional level, you're apt to be very sensitive to subtle emotional nuances. Emotional connections are important to you, but you're likely to have a healthy sense of boundaries and be skilled at expressing and communicating exactly what you're feeling.

One of the most important lessons for you is to accept that perfection is a *process*, not a *destination*. There will always be ways that you can improve, but you have to recognize and appreciate your progress and what you've accomplished as well. This can be challenging, because you find imperfections to be very threatening. Anytime you see something that is out of place, you will feel the need to fix it. The longer you're not able to fix it, the more unsafe you will feel. You may find that you will focus on the slightest imperfection, and the more you focus on it, the bigger it seems to become. It's very easy for you to lose all sense of perspective.

What threatens you is discovering imperfections that you're not able to fix. When you're feeling threatened, your instinctive reaction is to become overly critical—both of yourself and of others. Your ego believes that if you make a big enough deal of the thing that needs fixing, that eventually someone will have to do something about it. Often, someone does something about it simply to stop you from complaining. Needless to say, this is a pattern that you would do well to control.

If your Moon is in Virgo, your Safety Checklist is all about the details. What's interesting about Virgo is that it's only concerned about the things that it believes it can influence. If you encounter a situation that is entirely and completely out of your control (the United States Foreign Policy, for example), it won't bother you no matter how many problems you may see there. What *does* matter to you is that you're able to take care of every little detail of the things that you *can* influence. In any given situation, you'll be aware of what you can influence, and what you can improve. You're always looking for ways that you can make a contribution and be of service to the world.

It's important to recognize that when you feel threatened, you will begin to focus on even smaller and more insignificant details. In a very real sense, if you're not able to fix something that you feel that you *should* be able to fix, you'll focus on some aspect of it that you *can* fix. The content of your checklist won't change, but the magnification of it will. You will tend to narrow the scope until you can feel that you've made an improvement.

Moon in Capricorn

Dignity/Debility: The Moon is in Detriment in Capricorn, and is also Peregrine in a day chart. The Moon has dignity by Triplicity in a night chart. The Moon in Capricorn operates on the mental/emotional plane. Individuals with the Moon in Capricorn tend to worry about how they can express their emotions in a responsible, appropriate manner; this worrying is what often makes it difficult for these individuals to open up emotionally.

Core Needs: To create structure and boundaries to define sense of individuality. To protect and be responsible.

Core Lessons: To learn how to accept help from others; to learn how to be receptive emotionally.

Feels Safe When: Acting in a mature, responsible manner; when setting boundaries, and protecting others.

Feels Threatened When: Lacking structure or definition; pressured to let go of responsibility and experience emotions in unstructured, undefined manner.

Instinctive Reaction When Threatened: Close down emotionally, put up walls, reinforce boundaries and impose structures and limitations. Attempt to assume position of authority and responsibility to impose order and control, either self-imposed, or on others.

Expresses Emotions: The Moon in Capricorn experiences the full range of emotions. However, being in Detriment, the Moon in Capricorn worries about how to express these emotions, and often individuals with the Moon in Capricorn appear to be cold and reserved. This does not mean that they're not experiencing emotions, only that they're having trouble finding an acceptable way of expressing them.

The Moon in Capricorn is in the sign of its Detriment. Capricorn is opposite the sign of Cancer, the sign of the Moon's Rulership. When planets are in the sign of their debility, they must learn to use their strength in very different ways than they normally would. The Moon in Cancer (Rulership) can express emotions freely, but must learn self-reliance and good boundaries. The Moon in Capricorn (Detriment) finds self-reliance and good boundaries to come quite naturally—expressing emotions, on the other hand, is an unexpected challenge.

If your Moon is in Capricorn, you feel safest when you can create structure and boundaries that help to define yourself as an individual. You have a natural understanding of responsibility, and a very strong drive towards self-reliance. You have to learn that it's okay to accept help from other people, however. Emotional connections are not signs of weakness. You are very protective of the people you love, and you try to make them feel safe by creating very clear boundaries. Since these boundaries also serve to create a certain amount of emotional distance between you and your loved ones, you may not be creating the safe environment for them that you hoped to.

You feel the most threatened when you are in a situation that has no clear structure or definition. If you don't know how you are supposed to behave or to react, you will feel very uneasy. You also feel threatened when you're being pressured to simply express your feelings freely. You much prefer to find an appropriate, responsible way to express your feelings.

Planets in Detriment operate on the mental/emotional plane, and individuals with the Moon in Capricorn often find that they *worry* constantly about whether or not their emotions are appropriate, and about how they can express their feelings in a manner that meets with the approval of their internalized authority figure.

When you feel threatened, you instinctively put up walls. You will automatically look for an authority figure, and if you can't find one, you will take on that role yourself and try to impose order and control.

It's important to point out to people *without* the Moon in Capricorn, that you *do* experience the full range of emotions. In fact, you experience emotions in a very powerful way. However, you are continually worried about finding a responsible way to express you emotions. You may appear to be cold and reserved to others, but this does not mean you're not feeling anything. It just means that you're trying to keep your feelings from expressing in inappropriate ways. The more you worry, the more threatened you feel, and the more threatened you feel, the more walls you put up to contain your emotions.

The Moon in Capricorn Safety Checklist is usually very well organized, and always very specific. Everything has its own designated procedure that must be followed to the letter. If your Moon is in Capricorn, you can often identify what's on your checklist by asking yourself

"What are my responsibilities in this situation?" because ultimately, you feel safe when you're fulfilling your responsibilities.

It's important that you become well acquainted with your inner parent—the voice in your head that tells you what you *should* be doing in any given situation, because your inner parent will have a lot to do with your Safety Checklists. Sometimes it may feel like you've got an inner *drill sergeant* instead of an inner parent. Most of your Safety Checklists will be concerned with evaluating how self-reliant you are. The more you can do on your own, the safer you feel. This also means that it may be difficult for you to feel safe forming emotional connections with other people, because emotional connections require us to accept support and love from someone else.

Air Safety Checklists

The element of Air operates on the social, mental and intellectual plane. Air functions on the surface, exploring and making connections. If your Moon is in Gemini, Libra or Aquarius, you have an Air Safety Checklist.

Feels Safe When: If you have an Air Safety Checklist, words are extremely important to you. You feel safe when you can understand and make sense of a situation. You appreciate reason, logic, and intellect. Air is the most social of all of the elements, and therefore Air is the most concerned with relationships. You feel safest when you are able to make connections with other people, and experience your environment. You need to be able to exchange ideas and explore different perspectives and points of view. You thrive on the exchange of ideas and information. You need to feel free, and you need to be able to keep moving.

Feels Threatened When: You feel the most threatened when you are faced with limitations restrictions or strong boundaries. Safety to you has to do with the freedom to move and to explore, and the ability to experience new ideas and perspectives. Anything that slows you down or forces you to focus too long on any one idea will make you feel unsafe. You feel threatened when others force you to consider the practical applications of your ideas. You also feel threatened when you are forced to explore or express deep emotions. Finally, you will feel threatened when you are denied social contact, or are not being mentally or intellectually stimulated.

Instinctive Reaction When Threatened: Whenever you feel threatened, you will go into your head to think, reason, or talk yourself back into a safer situation. For you, safety is always about freedom—particularly the freedom to explore with your mind, your intellect, and your imagination. Words and ideas are always your first line of defense. You will use charm, diplomacy, and wit to negotiate your way to freedom. If this doesn't work, you will take refuge in your own mind, distancing yourself from the situation at hand.

Expresses Emotions: Air is the least comfortable with emotions. Emotions are, by their nature, irrational and unpredictable. Air is far more comfortable with things that are logical and easily understood. Because Air is entirely focused on the surface, you are the most comfortable with the more pleasant emotions, and prefer to ignore any deeper, more disruptive feelings.

Nurtures and Protects Others: Words are your first choice when it comes to nurturing others. You want to help others to understand that they are safe and protected. You prefer to tell others that you are there for them, that you care about them, and that you will keep them safe. For you, speaking the words is enough to make it so.

Feels Protected When: You feel protected and nurtured when others tell you that they care about you and reassure you that you are indeed safe. When you feel vulnerable, you want a logical explanation of the situation so that you can at least understand your position on an intellectual level. You rely on and believe what you are told, because the words can help you to feel safe.

Moon in Gemini

Dignity/Debility: The Moon is Peregrine in Gemini. Air signs are not comfortable with deep emotions, and Gemini in particular moves so quickly that sustained emotional bonds are somewhat difficult.

Core Needs: To be free to explore duality; to be able to sample the full range of emotional experience, and to freely move between opposite ends of the emotional spectrum.

Core Lessons: To learn how to focus and form deeper emotional connections rather than only surface connections.

Feels Safe When: Exploring new ideas and social situations; able to keep moving, forming new connections and sampling different emotional connections and experiences. The Moon in Gemini likes to play.

Feels Threatened When: Forced to make a choice and focus on one concept, idea, or emotion exclusively; when forced to explore deeper, slower-moving emotions. The Moon in Gemini feels threatened when forced to "grow up" and take responsibility.

Instinctive Reaction When Threatened: Avoidance and adaptation. The Moon in Gemini will instinctively retreat to the mental/social realm where Gemini is by far the most elusive and quick energy. Charm, humor, and verbal sparring can all be used in order to change the subject and escape the threat.

EXPRESSES EMOTIONS: The Moon in Gemini prefers to express and experience the more playful emotions. While the full range of emotions are available to the Moon in Gemini, they are usually expressed in brief flashes and accompanied by sudden and unexpected shifts in mood.

Gemini is motivated to explore duality, to move quickly and to make connections and draw conclusions. Because Gemini is an Air sign, it is not comfortable with deeper emotions and prefers to operate on the mental and social realm. The Moon in Gemini tends to move so quickly that sustained emotional bonds are somewhat difficult.

The Moon in Gemini needs to be free to explore duality and to be able to sample and experience the full range of emotional experience, moving freely between opposite ends of the spectrum. While individuals with the Moon in Gemini are capable of experiencing the full range of emotions, they tend to move quickly from one emotion to another.

If your Moon is in Gemini, you feel safest when you're exploring new ideas and enjoying social interaction with other people. You like to keep moving, and to sample a wide range of different emotions and emotional experiences. You like to play, and appreciate wit, charm, intelligence and style. Gemini is an Air sign, and so you're the most comfortable operating on the surface. You're not terribly interested in probing the emotional depths. Even when you do express or experience more powerful emotions, you tend to do so very quickly and then move on. Ultimately, you will need to learn how to enlarge your attention span. You have to be able to focus on things for longer periods of time, and you will need to become more comfortable with sustained emotional connections.

This will take some practice, because what you find the most threatening is being forced to focus on only one idea, concept or emotion exclusively. Gemini is about duality—you need to be able to explore both sides of any issue and move between them freely. When you're not able to see both sides of any issue, when you don't feel like you have the ability to change your mind and your direction at any time, you're likely to feel trapped and threatened.

One of the most common ways that you may experience this is when other people tell you that you need to "grow up" or "take responsibility" in your life. Many people view your need to explore all of the options and your ability to take either side of any issue as a sign of immaturity. This is not immaturity, however: it's innocence. You have a tremendous curiosity about the world, and your ability to feel safe depends on your ability to be able to explore.

When you do feel threatened, you're likely to adapt very quickly. Gemini is the fastest energy in the zodiac, and you may instinctively use your charm, humor and wit to diffuse any tension. When faced with uncomfortable emotions, you'll tend to retreat to the mental and social realm and try to defend yourself using your intelligence and logic (left brain) rather than try to cope with the situation from an emotional (right brain) perspective.

When threatened, you instinctively avoid and adapt; you retreat to the mental/social realm where Gemini is by far the most elusive and quick energy. Charm, humor, and verbal sparring can all be used in order to change the subject and escape the threat.

If your Moon is in Gemini, your Safety Checklist has a lot to do with keeping your options open. You need to feel that you have the freedom to explore, to play, and to create your own understanding of the different elements in any situation. You'll be the most comfortable when you can focus on the abstract and intellectual arena. Ideas and theories are your element. Once you start worrying about practical applications, you start to eliminate your options, and the fewer options you have available, the less safe you may feel.

Words and language are particularly important to you. All of your safety concerns ultimately involve how you communicate any given situation to yourself.

Moon in Libra

Dignity/Debility: The Moon has dignity by Face for the first 10 degrees of Libra and is Peregrine for the rest of the sign.

Core Needs: Create emotional connections with others that maintain balance and harmony.

Core Lessons: Learn how to maintain harmony while enforcing individual needs, feelings, and boundaries; learn not to automatically capitulate to resolve conflict.

Feels Safe When: Everyone is getting along, when things are balanced and harmonious, and beautiful. Able to focus on outward appearances and avoid looking too far beneath the surface.

Feels Threatened When: Confronted, faced with disharmony and imbalance; forced to take a stand or make a choice, particularly when unsure of the long-term repercussions of that choice. Forced to explore deeper emotions and explore below the surface and appearances.

Instinctive Reaction When Threatened: Immediately attempts to restore a sense of balance through diplomacy and tact; may capitulate and deny own needs in order to avoid or end confrontation and resolve conflict.

Expresses Emotions: Moon in Libra is the most comfortable with pleasant, comfortable emotions. The deeper, more disturbing emotions are inherently disruptive, and tend to be threatening to the Moon in Libra.

Libra energy is motivated to express our intellectual and social identity through one-to-one relationships. Libra is concerned with balance, beauty, and harmony in all things. Libra is an Air sign, and all Air signs operate on the surface and are most comfortable with abstract, intellectual concepts. The Moon in Libra is not comfortable with intense emotions because intense emotions tend to disrupt balance and harmony.

If your Moon is in Libra, you need to create balanced and harmonious emotional connections with others. Your key lesson, however, is that you still have to express your own needs, feelings and boundaries while you're maintaining balance and harmony. Sure, it's much easier to simply defer to other people, and always do whatever they want to do. That's certainly a way to avoid conflict, but it's not the way to achieve true balance.

You are likely to feel safe when everyone is getting along, when things are balanced, harmonious and beautiful. Appearances are very important to you—you don't want to look too far beneath the surface. Emotions are messy and disruptive, and unless they're strong enough to make a visible show, you're more than happy to focus on how things look.

Any kind of conflict is very threatening to you. You can always understand both sides of any situation (which is one of the reasons that you make such a good moderator). But having to take a definitive stand—especially if you haven't had time to explore the long-term effects of your choices—is terrifying. You much prefer to make your choices with a cool head. This is one of the reasons that you're uncomfortable with intense emotions: Emotions lead to snap judgments and rash choices, which lead to disruptions in the harmony and balance that you so desperately crave.

Your immediate response when you feel threatened is to try to resolve the conflict and restore a sense of harmony. You may use diplomacy and tact (and you are likely to have quite a lot of both at your disposal). You may also simply surrender, letting the other person have his or her way, and denying your own needs. Ultimately, this is not the best course of action. You have to learn how to assert your own needs and stand up for your own rights. Compromise is one thing—but giving up the things that you're entitled to is quite another.

If your Moon is in Libra, your Safety Checklist will focus on harmony, balance, and fairness. You are naturally aware of boundaries, and so long as you're meeting *your* responsibilities, and your partners are meeting *their* responsibilities, you'll feel safe. An emotional connection is important to you, because that helps you to know that you're participating in a relationship.

What you need to discover is exactly how much emotion is enough, because too much emotion will make you feel threatened.

You will certainly not like to fight with your partners. When you feel yourself getting upset, when emotions are starting to run high, your best course of action is to step back and cool down. As long as you can keep your emotions under control, you can use diplomacy and tact and resolve the issue fairly. If you're forced to stay and fight, however, you'll feel increasingly threatened, until finally, you'll give in because you have to get out of the conflict and restore a sense of balance.

Moon in Aquarius

Dignity/Debility: The Moon is Peregrine for the first 20 degrees of Aquarius, and has dignity by Face for the last 10 degrees.

Core Needs: To feel accepted as a rightful and equal member of the group.

Core Lessons: To learn to appreciate the value of the individual, and to recognize that sometimes an individual's needs are more important than the needs of the group.

Feels Safe When: Surrounded by others who share common beliefs, opinions, ideals and social standing; accepted as a member of the group.

Feels Threatened When: Group identity is in question and others do not seem to share feelings and beliefs; when forced to apply emotions in specific and focused manner, to individual situations.

Instinctive Reaction When Threatened: Retreats further into mental/social/theoretical realm and avoids emotional expression. Protects itself by hiding behind rules, conventions, theories, and ideals. Operates in abstract terms rather than applying these to the specific situation at hand.

Expresses Emotions: Aquarius is perhaps the most abstract and theoretical of the Air signs. While the Moon in Aquarius has a great deal of compassion, it has difficulty in expressing this on an individual basis. The Moon in Aquarius has a great love of humanity, but difficulty loving individual humans.

Aquarius energy is motivated to sustain and maintain our sense of social and intellectual self worth through identifying with groups of our own choosing. Aquarius energy is entirely group oriented and has great difficulty in focusing on individuals and individual needs.

The Moon in Aquarius needs to feel accepted and an equal member of the group. The sense of group acceptance is the single most important Safety Need for individuals with the Moon in Aquarius.

If your Moon is in Aquarius, you will feel safest when you are surrounded by other people that share your beliefs, opinions, ideals and social standing. The group dynamic is very important to you, and it is where you feel the most secure. However, you have to learn to accept that sometimes an individual's needs are legitimately more important than the needs of the group.

Aquarius energy does not understand the concept of an individual. Aquarius energy is all about the group. What's important to Aquarius is that everyone in the group be equal, and that everyone has absolute freedom within the definitions of the group.

If your Moon is in Aquarius, you will instinctively look for what you have in common with others. The things that you have in common with others are what define the group. Now, bear in mind that the group can have as few as one member (you). The group can also be defined by absolutely anything. You're not just considering the larger beliefs and obvious groups (religion, race, social status, etc.). A group can be defined as people who wear tennis shoes, or people with brown hair. The more things the members of the group have in common, the stronger the group identity, of course, but the point is that anything at all can define a group as far as Aquarius is concerned.

The Moon in Aquarius is looking for validation of self-worth through being an accepted member of a group. Just like the Moon in Leo, if your Moon is in Aquarius, it's essential that you learn to take responsibility for your own sense of self worth. Whether you rely on other individuals for validation or for group acceptance for validation, anytime you look outside for validation, you're asking to be disappointed.

So, if your Moon is in Aquarius, you'll feel safe as long as you feel like you belong, and so long as everyone in your group shares the same core ideals and perceptions.

In every situation, and in every relationship, you'll search for the things that you have in common with other people so that you can maintain a sense of the group. Each group contains many sub groups, each of which is defined by a different core idea, belief or quality. You will feel safe as long as everyone seems to behave within the definition of the group. Anytime someone breaks out of the group and reveals that they are not actually a member of the group, you will feel threatened because you fear that you may not be in the group you thought you were in.

For example, let's consider that you loved the movie *Titanic*, and your love of this film is one of the foundations of your group. You feel safe when you're with people who also love

Titanic. As long as you all agree on *Titanic*, it doesn't matter if you don't have any other films in common. You can discuss and debate the merits of *Citizen Kane* or *Halloween* and never find any common ground at all, but you'll still be safe in the knowledge that you're both members of the *Titanic* fan club. If, however, you find that a fellow member of your group can't stand Leonardo DiCaprio, that may feel threatening to you because it conflicts with your core definition of the group. You no longer feel that you share the same values as the rest of the group, and you may begin to question if you deserve to be included in the group at all.

Remember that the Moon in Aquarius equates safety with social acceptance.

Aquarius is an Air sign, and Air signs are not particularly interested in the emotional side of things. If your Moon is in Aquarius, you may find that you prefer to approach your emotions from a logical perspective (and yes, that's as difficult to do as it sounds). Ultimately, you're not too comfortable with exploring your emotions on a deep and probing level—and when you're pressured to do this, you will feel threatened. You much prefer to explore your emotions in a more abstract and theoretical way.

It's been said that Aquarius has a great love of humanity—but difficulty loving individual humans. This does not mean that with the Moon in Aquarius you're incapable of love! It does, however, mean that you're more comfortable with abstract emotions than you are with specific ones. You would be far more comfortable volunteering at a charity where your efforts will go to help many people that you will never personally meet, than you would be with helping an individual in need—especially when that individual is not a member of your group.

If your Moon is in Aquarius, your Safety Checklist is all about how much you have in common with other people. You need to feel that you have a clear understanding of the rules and structures that define your group, so that you can feel free to explore within those boundaries. Aquarius energy has a reputation for being unpredictable, but that's simply because it's not always obvious what defines the group.

You may also not be aware of what defines each group in your relationships. Pay attention to the times when you find yourself defending your ideas and taking a stand. What are the things that you're not willing to accept or tolerate? These are the things that help to define your ideas of the group.

Ultimately, the only group that matters is humanity, and we're all equal members of that group. When you can accept and validate yourself and others for simply being human, it matters less if we also share the same points of view.

Water Safety Checklists

The element of Water operates on the emotional and spiritual plane. Water needs to form emotional connections and to explore our spiritual and unconscious depths. You have a Water Safety Checklist if your Moon is in Cancer, Scorpio or Pisces.

Feels Safe When: If you have a Water Safety Checklist, you feel safe when you share emotional connections with other people. You're very in tune with your feelings, and you rely on your emotions and your intuition. Appearances don't matter to you; what matters is how you *feel*. You need to share your feelings, and you need other people to share theirs with you. Words are not important to you—what matters to you are the feelings behind the words. Much of your Safety Checklist may involve asking the question, "Is this familiar?" The more familiar and comfortable your surroundings, the safer you are likely to feel.

Feels Threatened When: You feel the most threatened when you're unable to create or maintain emotional and energetic bonds with other people. In particular, when people cut you off and shut you out, you will feel extremely unsafe. Water's primary motivation is to reconnect with the Source and to experience the truth that we are all part of All That Is. Good boundaries are very important, particularly when it comes to emotional connections. However, you need boundaries to enhance the safety and strength of these connections, not to prevent them.

Instinctive Reaction When Threatened: When threatened, your instinctive reaction is to create new emotional connections. Depending on the nature of the threat, you may also retreat inside yourself to nurse your wounds.

Expresses Emotions: If you have a Water Safety Checklist, you experience emotions more deeply and intensely than any other element. You are likely to hold on to your emotions and feelings longer than any other element.

Nurtures and Protects Others: The element of Water often carries a very motherly and protective quality. You want to provide emotional support and comfort to the people you love. You try to make others feel safe by sharing your feelings and emotions with them, and by encouraging them to share their emotions, their hopes and their fears with you. You may tend to take responsibility for others in an effort to protect them. This is a "mothering" instinct to keep your loved ones out of harm's way, and even to bear their pain and burdens for them. You must be very careful about this: it is rarely appropriate to take on this kind of responsibility for others.

Feels Protected When: You feel protected and nurtured when other people initiate supportive emotional connections with you. The closer the emotional bond, the more protected you feel.

You may also feel protected when other people actively try to shield you from the burdens, responsibilities and pain of the world. On a core level, you may actually want to return to the womb, where you were warm, safe, protected, and above all, completely connected to your mother and the Source. On a more practical level, you are likely to feel protected when other people try to spare you pain or discomfort.

Moon in Cancer

Dignity/Debility: The Moon in Cancer is in the sign of its Rulership. This means that the Moon is able to express and explore emotions whenever and however it chooses.

Core Needs: To form emotional connections and express emotional identity.

Core Lessons: To learn how to be self-sufficient and to meet its own needs.

Feels Safe When: Able to form nurturing emotional connections with others; emotional needs are being met; feels supported, protected and nurtured, or is able to nurture and protect others.

Feels Threatened When: Denied emotional connections with others; prevented from forming emotional bonds; emotional needs are not being met.

Instinctive Reaction When Threatened: Simultaneously attempts to protect itself by crawling back into its shell, and to form new, nurturing emotional connections intended to protect, heal, and make sure that the core needs are being met.

Expresses Emotions: Experiences the full range of emotions, and expresses emotions freely and openly. Feels and experiences emotions on a very deep level. Actively seeks to form emotional connections with others.

Cancer energy is motivated to express our emotional identity through forming emotional bonds and connections with others. Cancer is perhaps the most emotional sign, operating entirely on the level of feeling and intuition.

The Moon in Cancer is in the sign of its Rulership. This means that the Moon in Cancer is able to express and explore emotions whenever and however it chooses. This is wonderful for the Moon, but not always good for the individual with the Moon in Cancer who often finds that they are at the mercy of their emotions and that they struggle with keeping their feelings and emotional sensitivity in check.

If your Moon is in Cancer, emotional connections are tremendously important to you. In fact, in a very real sense, you need to feel emotional and spiritual connections with other people in order to survive. The bonds you share with others help to remind you that you are not alone, and the longing for emotional support is the longing to return to the Source, where we remember that we are a part of All That Is. You want to care for other people, and you want to be cared for in return. The emotional bonds that you create with others help you to feel safe. It's important, however, that you lean how to take care of your own needs as well. You can easily become too dependent on the emotional support of other people.

You will feel safest when you can form emotional and nurturing bonds with other people. You need to be able to express your feelings. The Moon in Cancer has a very strong mothering instinct, and you feel safest when you know that you and the people you care about are protected.

What threatens you the most is not being able to share an emotional bond with others. If you can't create an emotional connection with someone, this immediately tells you that your emotional needs aren't being met, and you simply can't survive without meeting those needs. Your ego will go into a complete panic, because your deepest, darkest fear is that you are alone in the world.

When you're threatened, your instinctive reaction is simultaneously to hide and to try to reestablish the emotional connections. Cancer is represented by the crab because Cancer energy needs the protection of its shell.

If your Moon is in Cancer, you're probably very aware of the things that make you feel safe. Safety and protection are, after all, very important to Cancer! Habits and routines are likely to be very comforting to you. Much of your Safety Checklist is concerned with asking the question, "Is this familiar?" The more familiar and comfortable your surroundings, the safer you're likely to feel.

In relationships, you feel safest when you feel a deep emotional connection with your partner. You need to be able to express your feelings, and you need to believe that your partner will take your feelings into consideration. You also need to feel that you know what your partner is feeling. Anytime anyone pulls away from you, you will feel threatened. This is important to recognize, because it's not always appropriate to maintain strong emotional connections in every relationship. At any given time, you have a minimum level of emotional contact that you need to experience in order to feel like you can survive. These emotional connections can be spread across multiple different relationships. However, it's important to recognize that if one relationship cuts you off emotionally, you will unconsciously start to expect more from your other relationships to make up for the loss.

The more aware you can become of your need for emotional connections, the easier it will be for you to begin to meet your own emotional needs. When you truly recognize that you can meet your own core survival needs without the support of others, you can make better choices about the kinds of emotional connections you share with the people in your life.

Until then, you will want to keep a close eye on your Safety Checklists in each relationship. You will have to be aware of whether your expectations and desire for emotional support are appropriate at any given time.

Moon in Scorpio

Dignity/Debility: The Moon in Scorpio is both Peregrine and in Fall. Individuals with the Moon in Scorpio tend to experience their emotions on a very visceral and physical level. If they are not able to express their emotions, they will experience physical discomfort, usually in the form of stomach cramps or nausea (the Moon rules the stomach).

Core Needs: To connect with other individuals on a core, primal, soul level, experiencing the death (and rebirth) of the ego.

Core Lessons: To learn to trust others enough to experience emotional connections; to gain control over the ego and overcome the ego-based fears of emotional intimacy and spiritual union.

Feels Safe When: Experiencing deep, transformational emotional connections.

Feels Threatened When: Experiencing deep, transformational emotional connections. The Moon in Scorpio can never truly feel safe because the very emotional connections that it needs are by their nature, threatening and frightening to the ego.

Instinctive Reaction When Threatened: An eye for an eye. Once the Moon in Scorpio is backed into a corner and forced to defend itself, it will lash out with the deadly scorpion sting and attempt to inflict the same amount of pain on its attacker that it's experiencing. The Moon in Scorpio has great difficulty in releasing old anger and healing old wounds.

Expresses Emotions: The Moon in Scorpio experiences emotions on an extremely deep and powerful level. Scorpio is a very slow-moving energy, and it takes time for the deep emotions to make their way to the surface, so often times, individuals with the Moon in Scorpio find it difficult to communicate and express their feelings

Scorpio energy seeks to sustain and maintain our sense of emotional self worth through forming intense and deep emotional connections with other individuals. Scorpio energy wants to merge completely with another individual, and to experience the death of the ego—remembering, for a moment, what it was like before we took on physical form, and when we truly understood that we are connected to all of creation. From this experience, Scorpio then is reborn.

The fundamental needs of the Moon in Scorpio are to connect with other individuals on a core, primal, soul level, and to experience the death and rebirth of the ego. The key lessons are to learn to trust others enough to experience these emotional connections and to gain control over the ego in order to overcome the ego-based fears of emotional intensity and spiritual union.

If your Moon is in Scorpio, you feel safe when you're experiencing deep, transformational emotional connections. Unfortunately, you also feel *threatened* when you're experiencing deep, transformational emotional connections, because the ego is petrified of deep, transformational emotional connections.

In other words, if your Moon is in Scorpio, you may never truly feel safe, because the emotional connections that you need in order to feel safe trigger your ego. Only when you have mastered your ego can you truly experience safety. In the meantime, you are likely to be very careful about sharing your emotions and creating emotional bonds with other people. You need to feel a tremendous level of trust and feel exceptionally supported and protected in a relationship before you will be comfortable enough to truly open up and share your feelings.

Our egos, remember, believe that they are our only defense against a dangerous and frightening Universe. Anytime we experience the kinds of emotional connections that the Moon in Scorpio needs, we have to give up the "protection" of our ego. This makes us very vulnerable, and we're in great danger of being hurt. When you feel threatened, you will try to protect yourself by pulling away, but if you're backed into a corner, you will defend yourself with deadly force. With the Moon in Scorpio, you're very familiar with emotional pain, and if you have to, you know how to inflict it.

You are also likely to have a very difficult time letting go of old emotional wounds. Your ego will tend to hold onto these ancient scars and pick at them, so they stay fresh in our mind. If you can still feel the pain of the last time you tried to form an emotional connection with someone, you're more likely to think twice before you do it again. Remember, the ego is not doing you any favors at this point—it's trying to protect itself. Should you actually experience a true emotional and spiritual bond, the ego would be completely destroyed. Sure, the ego would come back from the dead—we can't sustain those kinds of connections for more than a few moments at a time—but the ego doesn't understand this.

If your Moon is in Scorpio, you may tend to experience emotions on an extremely deep and powerful level. Scorpio is a very slow-moving energy, and it takes time for the deep emotions to make their way to the surface, so you may often find it difficult to communicate and express your feelings. It's important that you do find ways to let your feelings out—if you keep them bottled up, you will experience them in your physical body. Typically, you'll experience discomfort in your stomach, as cramps or nausea.

Since the Moon in Scorpio already knows it will have trouble feeling safe, the Moon in Scorpio Safety Checklist usually contains the things that let us know that we could possibly consider making ourselves vulnerable to another person and forming an emotional bond with them. One thing that definitely contributes to a feeling of safety is when other people seem to understand your emotions without your having to communicate them directly.

You need to be able to build up trust in your relationships, and privacy is very important to you. Certain things you're happy to share with anyone, but other feelings or areas of your life can only be shared with people who earn that right. You will feel threatened when people come too close to your private areas, or when they seem to be prying. It's important for you to recognize, however, that they may not be doing this on purpose. You're entitled to your privacy, but you may have to gently let others know that they have crossed a line with you, and ask that they respect that boundary in the future. It's not a betrayal of trust if someone accidentally crosses a line, particularly if they didn't know the line was there in the first place.

Moon in Pisces

Dignity/Debility: The Moon is Peregrine in Pisces.

Core Needs: Explore emotional and spiritual connections to other individuals and to all of creation; to merge with others and return to the source.

Core Lessons: To establish and maintain good emotional and energetic boundaries; to learn to release and transmute the accumulated negative energy.

Feels Safe When: Sharing emotional and spiritual connections with others; expressing compassion, healing others by absorbing their negativity.

Feels Threatened When: Denied emotional connections with others, and confronted with strong boundaries. Experiencing significant and intentional energetic attacks/extreme boundary violations.

INSTINCTIVE REACTION WHEN THREATENED:	Generally, the Moon in Pisces simply allows all energetic and emotional boundary violations; these individuals may tend to dissociate and leave their bodies depending on the severity of the violation. Pisces also dissociates when trapped by strong and well-defined boundaries.
EXPRESSES EMOTIONS:	The Moon in Pisces is extremely empathic and sensitive to other people's emotions. It can express the full range of emotions, although it tends to be strongly influenced by the emotions of the people around it

Pisces energy seeks to complete our emotional, soul and spiritual nature by merging once again with the Source. Part of the function of Pisces is to absorb negativity and pain, and to transmute this energy. Pisces seeks to heal the emotional wounds of the world.

If your Moon is in Pisces, you have a fundamental need to explore emotional and spiritual connections to other individuals and to all of creation. Ultimately, you are looking for a way to reconnect with the Source, and to let go of the illusions of separation that we experience while we're having our human experience. Needless to say, emotional connections are very important to you, and you're likely to be very much in tune with your feelings. One of the challenges, however, is that you're also likely to be very much in tune with everyone else's feelings as well.

While you feel safe when you're sharing emotional and spiritual connections with others, you must learn to create healthy emotional and energetic boundaries. On an unconscious level, you pick up negative emotions from everyone that you encounter—that's the entire purpose of Pisces. In the first place, you want to become aware of this so that you can take a more active role in choosing when you want to create these emotional connections and with whom. In the second place, you want to become aware of this because you need to recognize that not everything that you're feeling actually belongs to you. It's very easy to mistake the pain and negativity that you've absorbed from other people for your own.

With the Moon in Pisces, you do feel safe when you take on other people's pain, because you're healing them. You need to be able to make these connections. However, you also have to learn how to transmute and release these negative emotions! You're meant to be a healer, not a martyr. You do not need to suffer in order to ease the suffering of others. Your compassion is one of your greatest gifts, and you feel safe when you can share it with others.

You're so used to experiencing emotional connections that anytime they are cut off, or you're confronted with strong boundaries, you feel threatened. This can often be a case of "Safe

Doesn't Feel Safe," however (see Chapter 6). It's important that you learn how to create and maintain stronger boundaries and recognize that healthy boundaries are safe. In many cases, you're so used to experiencing energetic and emotional boundary violations that these feel safe to you. Even so, if you experience an intentional attack or an extreme boundary violation, you will feel threatened—and rightfully so.

When you're threatened, you're likely to try to leave your body. Pisces energy tends to dissociate when put under pressure. In fact, anytime you are in a situation where you feel threatened, either by very strong boundaries or by severe boundary violations, you're likely to try to escape.

The Moon in Pisces checklist has to do with how strong the emotional and spiritual connections are in any given situation. In many ways, you use your emotions to guide you through your life. You will tend to trust your intuition and follow your instincts. The more you can feel connected to the universe and the more in tune you feel with the people around you, the safer you will feel. It's often challenging to come up with specific words to identify what's on the Moon in Pisces checklist, because it's so much about how you feel.

When you're threatened and you feel yourself trying to escape, try to bring yourself back into your body. Visualizing a connection to the Earth is often helpful. You can also let your body relax, keep your feet in contact with the floor, and simply let yourself find your center. Most of the time you feel unsafe because you weren't able to maintain appropriate boundaries—but you can only strengthen your boundaries if you're in your body.

✧5✧
Validation Needs (Venus)

"I can live for two months on a good compliment."
—Mark Twain

The next set of relationship needs is our Validation Needs. Validation Needs have to do with defining and supporting our sense of individual identity. Validation Needs encompass a wide range of emotions and experiences, all of which are essentially different degrees and expressions of love. "Love," however, is a four-letter word that has very powerful and specific connotations for most of us. We can easily accept that in our romantic relationships we need to have our "love needs" met. But when we say that we need to have our "love needs" met in our professional relationships, it seems less appropriate—not to mention it could get us into a heap of trouble. Love is certainly the ultimate way to meet our Validation Needs, but it's not the only way. Let's take a few moments to get to know our Validation Needs.

Exploring our Validation Needs

Our Validation Needs fall broadly into two categories: *group acceptance* and *self-acceptance*. The group acceptance needs are the most closely related to our core Safety Needs, and have to do with our relationship to and status within the groups that help to define who we are as individuals. The self-acceptance needs are concerned with defining and supporting our sense of individual identity and our value as individuals. As we explore and meet our Validation Needs, we grow from group consciousness to individual consciousness. We develop a healthy sense of self, and a healthy sense of self-worth. As we reach the minimum balance in our Validation Accounts, we are able to shift our attention to exploring and meeting our self-actualization needs.

Group Acceptance Needs

The group acceptance needs involve our relationship as individuals to a social group. The group may be quite large (other individuals who share our religious faiths), or quite small (the members of our bridge club). We belong to hundreds of groups at any given time. In fact, the groups to which we belong help to define who we are as individuals. Almost everything we can say about ourselves to describe ourselves indicates our membership in a group. For example, I'm a *writer* and an *astrologer,* who currently lives in *San Diego*, and uses *Macintosh* computers (four different groups). As we will see, many of our basic Validation Needs are met through our group affiliations. Group acceptance needs correspond to Maslow's "Belongingness and Love" Needs.

Acceptance by the Group

Our Validation Needs begin where our Safety Needs end. Just as our most fundamental Safety Needs are concerned with our ability to continue to meet our Physiological Needs, our most fundamental Validation Needs are concerned with our ability to continue to meet our Safety Needs. The underlying belief here is that there is safety in numbers. If we are accepted as a member of a group, we have other individuals who can protect us, increasing our chances of survival. The experience of group acceptance is what makes the opening deposit in our Validation Account (as it were). Our membership in the group makes us feel safe enough to shift some of our attention to meeting our Validation Needs.

This first level of validation is fundamentally a tribal mentality. Everyone contributes to the good of the tribe, and the tribe protects its members. We identify entirely with the tribe, operating from a group perspective rather than an individual perspective. Any threat to the tribe is a threat to us as individuals, because the tribe constitutes our core sense of identity.

Even in modern times we still experience tribal connections. Consider, for example the tribes of sports fans. In the spring, Manhattan seems to consist of two warring tribes: the Yankee fans and the Mets fans. Tribal members wear clothing with the tribal insignia to announce their membership and identify themselves to other members of the tribe—and they will defend the honor of their tribe against any perceived attacks. The more devoted members of the tribe of sports fans feel tremendous joy and validation with each of their team's victories, and crushing depression and betrayal when their team is defeated. They will rearrange their lives to make sure that they can be a part of every single game, cheering and supporting their team either in person, or in their living rooms. And if for some reason, they are forced to miss a game, they often feel that they have let the team down in some way. More to the point, they feel less validated because they were not a part of the group watching the game.

Equality within the Group

The next set of Validation Needs builds on the experience of group acceptance. When we experience group acceptance, we feel safe enough to explore our individual identities. The first way we do this is by affirming our equality within the group. In a sense, we look for the ways in which we *deserve* to be a member of the group. We seek acknowledgement for our contributions to the group. When we are with other members of the group, we seek validation and confirmation that we are rightful members of the group by discussing our role in the group.

Discovering that we share a group affiliation with a person we've just met is called "breaking the ice." We often have a fundamental distrust of new people. If we make ourselves vulnerable by sharing who we are and the things that we love, we could be hurt. They might not value the same things we do, and this could have a negative impact on the balance of our Validation Accounts. When we discover that we share something in common with a new person, it makes a small deposit in our Validation Accounts. We belong to the same group, and therefore we can trust each other. We can meet each other's Validation Needs by discussing our equal membership in the group.

Prominence in the Group

Equality is a fine thing. Most of us believe in equal rights. However, while most of us believe that everyone was created equal, it's also clear to us that we didn't *stay* that way. *Equal* sounds too much like *average*, and no one wants to believe that they are just *average*. Oh, we may accept that we're just average at some things, but at the things that really *matter*, we're well *above* average. And we'd really appreciate it if more people would acknowledge that, thank you very much.

This next level of validation involves receiving attention from the group for our individual accomplishments or contributions to the group. We want to be admired, respected—even envied by our peers. What we're talking about here is *status*.

Many of us become trapped at this level of validation for periods of time in our lives. The first is most often during adolescence at school. The pecking order of the "in crowd" can be brutal, and it's almost always determined by some arbitrary rules of style. Certain brands or styles of clothing identify us as being "in" while others brand us as outcasts. We may find ourselves seeking this level of validation again in our twenties, as we try to find the newest, hottest clubs, restaurants and places to be seen before everyone knows about them and they've become passé. Later in life, we may find ourselves buying cars the size and weight of Sherman tanks because everyone else has one. Sure, we *tell* ourselves that we need a back seat you could park a Volkswagen in because we have to pick up the kids at soccer practice and we buy toilet paper in bulk, but the *real* reason is that it meets our Validation Needs to be seen driving it. (It's worth noting that the only way sales of SUVs have held strong is by changing their name from Sport Utility Vehicles to *Safety* Utility Vehicles. When we're feeling unsafe because of terror alerts, we won't spend money to meet our Validation Needs but we *will* spend money to meet our *Safety* Needs.)

Self Acceptance Needs

The next set of Validation Needs involves our experience of ourselves as individuals. We want to differentiate ourselves from the group and be seen as unique individuals. We are driven to support our sense of self-esteem and self-worth. Self acceptance needs correspond to Maslow's Esteem Needs.

Asserting Individuality

The first stage of self-acceptance follows directly from our desire for prominence in the group. We begin to look for ways that we can distance ourselves from the group. We want to be seen as an individual, not as a part of a group, no matter how influential our role in that group may be. We may make choices intended to shock the other members of the group, or even to alienate ourselves from the group. We believe that we no longer care what the group thinks of us—the only thing that matters is that we are free to be an individual. The irony, of course, is that we *do* care what the group thinks of us. We want the group to recognize that we're an individual and are no longer just a member of the group. There's no point in being an individual if we don't have a group of people to be an individual *at*.

Once again, the first time most of us encounter this energy is during our adolescence. We're torn between our need to be accepted by the group and our need to assert our individuality. The compromise is that we often assert our individuality by rebelling against our parents. We adopt styles of clothing and speech that offend and upset the adults in power, and at the same time give us status among our peers.

Many individuals continue to look for this kind of validation even as adults. When we see people on the street with fluorescent hair color, multiple body piercings, or really *interesting* body art, this is how they assert their individuality. They make deposits in their Validation Account because they look so *different* from the more conventionally dressed people they encounter, which reinforces their sense of being a unique individual. Other individuals express this energy in different ways. A wealthy and successful businessman might choose to drive a beat-up 1973 Chevy to make sure that others recognize that he isn't the *typical* corporate executive—he is an individual. Of course, the only people who would notice this choice would be *other* corporate executives—in other words, other members of the group.

Equality as an Individual

The next category of Validation Needs is met through our one-to-one relationships with other individuals. For the first time, we are truly interested in expressing our individual identity. We no longer need the group to recognize that we're individuals, but we *do* need other *individuals* to recognize that we are individuals. In particular, we seek the approval of individuals we admire and respect—individuals whose worth and value we perceive as greater than our own. These are the people whose opinions really matter to us. They may be our friends, our romantic partners, or our parents. When we're with these individuals, our esteem for them makes us question our own worth. We feel the need to earn the right to be in relationship to them. When they validate us, we feel that we do indeed belong in their lives.

Of course, we would do well to remember the truth that these individuals we so admire are our mirrors. The qualities that we find so worthy and attractive are in fact parts of us. We notice and envy these qualities so much in others because we have yet to recognize these qualities in ourselves. When we realize that we are admiring our own reflection in others and embrace these qualities in ourselves, we move to the final category of Validation Needs: self-esteem.

Self-Esteem

The highest level of Validation Needs is self-esteem. We can only meet these needs by validating ourselves. At this level, we begin to connect to the truth of who we are. We no longer question our value or worth as an individual, because we know that we are worthy. We do not need the approval or acceptance of the group, or of other individuals. We base our sense of self-worth on our own accomplishments and on our level of mastery.

Consider the drive to compete as an example. When we strive for prominence in the group, we compete with the other group members for status. When we strive for equality as an individual, we compete against another individual, hoping to be viewed as a worthy opponent. When we focus on our self-esteem, we only compete with ourselves. We measure our success and our accomplishments against personal progress, and not against the progress and achievements of others.

We can still receive validation from other people for our accomplishments, of course. But having self-esteem means that we do not *require* other people to validate us. We love and accept ourselves, and we are able to validate ourselves for our own accomplishments.

Praise, Gratitude and Love

On an emotional level, we experience validation through *praise, gratitude* and *love*. Any deposit in our Validation Accounts is the result of one of these three emotions. We can experience praise, gratitude or love in each and every stage of our Validation Needs, from the most basic level of group acceptance to the most advanced level of self-esteem.

Praise is the most basic form of validation. When we praise something or someone, we give it our attention. We notice it, and acknowledge it. Praise doesn't need to carry a great deal of emotion behind it, nor does it even need to be entirely sincere. Praise is about being noticed and being acknowledged. When we are praised, we are not being overlooked. Praise reinforces our sense of individual identity, and therefore makes a small deposit in our Validation Account.

Gratitude, on the other hand, requires more sincerity and emotional support. Because of this, gratitude is more powerful than praise, and will make a more significant deposit in our Validation Accounts. When we are truly grateful for something or someone, our hearts expand. In fact, when we experience gratitude, we also experience our Safety Needs being met because we also feel supported and nurtured. Because we feel safe, our egos are able to disengage, so we're more easily able to recognize the truth of who we are. We are able to sense the divine spark in ourselves—and to recognize that same spark in others as well.

Love is the most difficult emotion to experience. Love requires the greatest level of surrender, the greatest level of sincerity, the greatest level of vulnerability, and the greatest level of emotional commitment. Not surprisingly, love is the most powerful form of validation, and makes the largest possible deposits in our Validation Accounts. Of course, most of us have very specific and narrow definitions of love, which limit how and with whom we experience or express it. Often, we limit love to our families, our romantic partners, and our closest friends.

Love is so difficult to express because when we love someone, we accept and honor them completely. The Yogic greeting, *namaste* embodies the true nature of love: "The God in me greets and acknowledges the God in you." What is so difficult about this for most of us is that in order to love and accept the divine in others, we must also love and accept the divine in ourselves. We are only able to love others to the extent that we love ourselves. And we will only experience love from others to the extent that we love ourselves.

Validation Checklists

As with the Safety Checklists, there are four elemental styles of Validation Checklist. The Validation Checklist is entirely independent of the Safety Checklist. Quite often, we have different elemental styles for our Safety Checklists and our Validation Checklists. Venus is the planet that rules our Validation Checklists, and the element and sign of Venus in the natal chart reveals how we expect our Validation Needs to be met.

- ❖ *Fire* needs to be able to take action to feel validated.
- ❖ *Earth* needs boundaries and structure to feel validated.
- ❖ *Air* needs communication and social interaction to feel validated.
- ❖ *Water* needs emotional connections to feel validated.

We'll take a look at each of the four elemental Validation Checklist Languages, and explore the three dialects of each language in turn.

Fire Validation Checklists

If you have a Fire Validation Checklist, relationships are all about doing things with your partner. You need to feel active and involved, and it's very important that you're able to express yourself fully in your relationships. If your Venus is in Aries, Leo or Sagittarius, you have a Fire Validation Checklist.

Feels Validated When: You feel validated when you're free to do the things that you want to do, and your partner participates. You need to be recognized and appreciated as an individual. You need to be free to express yourself—and sometimes this means that you need the freedom to go off and do your own thing, whether your partner wants to accompany you or not. Trust is very important to you. You feel validated when you know that your partners trust you, and believe in your integrity and your commitment to the relationship.

Feels Rejected When: You feel rejected and unappreciated when you have to put your partner's needs and desires before your own. You need to feel that you're able to maintain and express your own individuality in relationships. Often, accommodating your partner's wishes can feel like you're compromising your own integrity. Any breech of trust, no matter how small, is an issue for you. If your partners don't trust you enough to allow you the freedom to express yourself and explore your identity within the relationship, then they don't truly love or value you in the first place.

Instinctive Reaction When Rejected: When you feel rejected or unappreciated, you will take immediate action to rectify the situation. You may confront your partner and ask (or demand) that you be recognized. You may act out so that you can no longer be ignored or overlooked. Or you may simply leave and set out on your own so that you can pursue your own path without any restrictions. Whether or not you choose to return to the relationship depends on the size of the violation. Breaches of trust are likely to provoke the strongest reactions from you.

Wants to be Recognized by Others: You want to be recognized by others for whom you are as an individual. It's important to you that your unique identity is noticed and acknowledged by your partners in relationships.

Expresses Affection: Actions speak louder than words for you. You express affection for others by inviting them to share in your life and to participate in the things that you enjoy the most. When you pursue the things that you love, you express your true nature. You want to show affection for others by sharing your true nature with them.

Venus in Aries

DIGNITY/DEBILITY:	Venus is in Detriment in Aries. Venus has dignity by Term from 6–14 Aries and by Face from 20–30 Aries.
CORE NEEDS:	To express individual identity in relationships.
CORE LESSONS:	Venus is the planet of relationships, and Aries is the sign that is the least focused on relationships because Aries is entirely focused on individual expression to the point that it's not even aware that other individuals exist. The core lessons involve learning how to take one's partner into account in relationships, and how to express one's self fully while maintaining balance and parity in the relationship.
FEELS LOVED WHEN:	Able to do one's own thing whether or not one's partner chooses to come along for the ride; able to pursue own desires and attractions freely and impulsively.
FEELS REJECTED WHEN:	Forced to take others into account (for example, their partners) and prevented from following their own desires.
INSTINCTIVE REACTION WHEN REJECTED:	Confront partner directly; argue to try and get their way; go off and do what they want anyway, regardless of how partner feels.
EXPRESSES AFFECTION:	Actions speak louder than words. Venus in Aries enjoys being active, going out and doing things with their partner.

If you have Venus in Aries, you have a somewhat unusual approach to relationships. You need to express your *individuality* in the context of your relationships. In essence, in relationships, your primary focus is on "me" not on "us."

Remember how I suggested you look at the planets as actors and the signs as the roles that they play? Well, Venus in Aries is a lot like Sylvester Stallone playing Juliet. It's an unusual casting choice to say the least, and he's going to have his work cut out for him in order to turn in a convincing performance.

This isn't nearly as bad as it sounds. Remember that in relationships, we're ultimately looking to find a way to balance two individuals. Most people approach relationships from the perspective of needing to find balance—they're ready to compromise and to take their partner's into account, but they have to learn to express their own needs in the relationship. With Venus in Aries, you have no problem with being an individual and asserting your needs. What *you* need to learn is how to take other people into account and learn how to find balance in the relationship.

You feel loved and appreciated when you get your own way and can do the things that you want to do, when you want to do them. Aries is active and impulsive and doesn't like to be kept waiting. If your partner wants to come along for the ride, so much the better—but ultimately, you'd rather be free to do what you want on your own than to have to compromise in order to be with your partner.

By the same token, when you're *not* allowed to do the things that you want to do, and when you feel like you have to give up your own desires in order to make someone else happy, you'll feel unappreciated and rejected.

When rejected, your first reaction is to confront your partner directly and to and argue until you get your own way. If that doesn't work, you're apt to go off and do your own thing *anyway*. Your degree of willingness to put up with your partner and to accommodate them depends on how full your Validation Account is. Every time you have to do something you don't want to do in order to make your partner happy, you make a withdrawal from your Validation Account. Once the account is empty, nothing will get you to compromise—you will simply go off and do what you want, and deal with any consequences later.

With Venus in Aries, actions speak louder than words. This is how you express affection and how you interpret it from others. You are likely to enjoy being active, and sharing activities with your partners. The more things that you can do with a partner that *you* want to do, the greater the balance in your Validation Account. When you do things together with your partner, you feel validated, appreciated and loved.

Venus in Leo

DIGNITY/DEBILITY:	Venus is Peregrine for most of Leo, only dignified by Term from 13–19 of Leo.
CORE NEEDS:	To express love and warmth and to have their partner appreciate and validate them for their unique creative self.
CORE LESSONS:	To no longer depend on validation from others to reinforce self-image and sense of self-worth.
FEELS LOVED WHEN:	Being appreciated, acknowledged, and generally validated by their partners for their warmth and generosity and love.
FEELS REJECTED WHEN:	Ignored and taken for granted. Not made to feel special by their partners. Not receiving validation and attention on a regular basis.
INSTINCTIVE REACTION WHEN REJECTED:	Act out in order to become the center of attention; any attention, even negative attention is better than being ignored.
EXPRESSES AFFECTION:	Extremely warm and generous, gives freely and openly of the self; genuinely wants to love and be loved in return.

Venus in Leo is motivated to relate to others in a completely heart-centered manner. With Venus in Leo, you have a natural warmth, love and generosity when you relate to others—and you truly have a tremendous amount of love to offer. Leo energy, however warm, expansive and generous, needs to be recognized and appreciated for its contributions. If you don't feel that you're being acknowledged for your love, if you don't feel that you're being adequately loved in return, then you may find that you are tempted to act out in less appropriate ways in order to receive the attention from others that you feel that you deserve.

Planets in Leo tend to believe that they are "stars" and deserve the "star treatment;" when they don't get it, they can become childish, petty and throw temper tantrums. When you stay in a heart space, however, this type of reaction doesn't happen, because when you are truly connected to your heart energy, Venus in Leo knows that there is more than enough love in the world to go around, and that when you truly give of yourself in a relationship, you can't help but receive love (and attention) in return.

In short, if you have Venus in Leo, you will feel loved and validated when you're being appreciated and acknowledged by your partner for being your own warm, generous self. Any time you feel ignored, overlooked or in any way taken for granted, however, you will feel completely rejected. While you would unquestionably enjoy being the center of attention in your relationships on an ongoing basis, that's not a reasonable expectation. You must learn how to validate yourself. If you are entirely dependent on other people to remind you of how special you are, you will give away all of your personal power. While it's always nice to have others pay attention to us, and make us feel special, you need to develop a healthy sense of self-worth and self-esteem in your relationships so that you don't *need* this from your partners.

With Venus in Leo, you express love and affection through giving of yourself. As Leo is a Fire sign, for you, actions speak louder than words. Sharing your time, your attention, your creativity, and your energy is your preferred way of showing people that you care about them. Conversely, you feel loved and appreciated when others give you their attention and focus. This can be a challenge in relationships, because of Leo's tendency to need continuous validation (as a Fixed sign, Leo's core issue is one of self-worth). In particular, with Venus in Leo, you may find that you look to others to validate your sense of self-worth, and this will only get you into trouble. When you feel that you are being ignored or taken for granted, you may tend to act out. You must make a conscious effort to remember that your self-worth comes from within, and that you can (and must) be the one to validate yourself.

Venus in Sagittarius

DIGNITY/DEBILITY: Venus is Peregrine for most of Sagittarius, only having dignity by Term from 8–14 degrees.

CORE NEEDS: To explore the higher truth of our individual identity through relationships.

CORE LESSONS: To become more flexible when it comes to accommodating partner's beliefs; to forgive breeches of trust.

FEELS LOVED WHEN: Exploring new ideas and experiences with partner; partner accompanies them on their quest for truth; having fun with partner, being physically active; doing things.

FEELS REJECTED WHEN: Partner displays lack of trust, jealousy, or deceives them in any way. Partner tries to set limitations or boundaries that curtail their freedom and ability to follow their own path.

INSTINCTIVE REACTION WHEN REJECTED:	Leave relationship. Trust and freedom are too important to Venus in Sagittarius, and if these are lacking, they won't put any more effort into the relationship.
EXPRESSES AFFECTION:	Taking partner on new adventures, exploring the unknown, having new and unfamiliar experiences. Sagittarius is a Fire sign and likes to be active.

Individuals with Venus in Sagittarius tend to view relationships as adventures and opportunities to grow and explore. Having the freedom to go wherever your fancy takes you is very important, as is mutual faith and trust. With Venus in Sagittarius you probably have little time or patience for jealous and controlling partners. Life is something to be experienced and enjoyed, and you will be happiest with a partner who feels the same way. Because Sagittarius is ruled by Jupiter, the planet of growth and expansion, Venus in Sagittarius is apt to enjoy things in a very big way. Venus in Sagittarius can tend towards the extravagant, and values and appreciates anything that is new, exciting, and most of all bigger and better than anything that has come before. Sagittarius is motivated to find the underlying truth in the universe, and with Venus in Sagittarius, you may find that you value honesty both in yourself and in others.

Ultimately, you will have to learn how to be more flexible in your relationships, particularly when it comes to accepting that your partners may not share your particular beliefs, philosophies, or idea of what path leads to the Truth. While it's nice when your partners share your ideals, if they don't, you must learn to support them in their own paths. So long as your partners allow you the freedom to explore your path, this should be relatively easy for you to do. You must also learn to be more flexible when it comes to forgiving the things that you interpret as violations of trust. It's important to distinguish between accidental violations and intentional ones, and to modify your reactions accordingly.

If you have Venus in Sagittarius, you will feel loved and validated when you're exploring new ideas and experiences with your partners, and when your partners accompany you on your quest for truth. Having fun and being active, physically *doing* things is extremely important to you.

You will feel rejected when your partners display a lack of trust, jealousy, or deceive you in any way. Truth, trust and honesty are exceptionally important to you in your relationships. You will also feel rejected when your partners try to set limitations or boundaries which curtail your freedom and ability to follow your own path—you're likely to view this as evidence that your partner's don't trust you.

When rejected, you immediately want leave the relationship. A breech of trust is the single most serious infraction you, and you simply can't tolerate it. Anytime you feel betrayed, or feel that your partner doesn't show the appropriate faith in you, you will need some time and space to yourself. Whether or not you choose to return to the relationship will depend on how serious the betrayal seemed to you. Trust and freedom are the two most important elements in any relationship for you, and if they're not present, you will not want to invest your time and energy in the relationship. You would rather be free and alone than restricted and in a relationship.

With Venus in Sagittarius, you will tend to express affection by taking your partners on new adventures, exploring the unknown, and sharing new and unfamiliar experiences with them. You enjoy being impulsive, and being surprised (and surprising). Last-minute plans, impromptu trips—these mean a lot to you, and you show that you care about others by wanting to include them on your adventures. Ultimately, you express affection by having *fun*, and you look for ways that you can share your fun with others.

Earth Validation Checklists

If you have an Earth Validation Checklist, you are willing to invest time and energy in building a strong and lasting relationship. You want to create a clear definition of the parameters and boundaries of your relationships. You have an Earth Validation Checklist if your Venus is in Taurus, Virgo or Capricorn.

Feels Validated When: You feel validated when your partners are willing to support and define the relationship with you. Commitment is very important to you, and you expect that your relationships will endure. Since Earth relates to the physical and the material plane, the more tangible elements of your relationship are very important. You feel validated when you receive gifts from your partner, and when appropriate, when you can share physical intimacy with your partner. In romantic relationships, holding hands and snuggling up to your partner is essential. In your professional relationships, you still prefer tangible expressions of appreciation in the form of salary increases and bonuses, or even token awards or certificates. What matters to you is that you have some kind of lasting reminder that you are valued and appreciated.

Feels Rejected When: You feel rejected and unappreciated when you do not receive tangible reminders that you are loved. It's important to you that your partners remember and commemorate the milestones in your relationship. Not only do the gifts embody the love and affection that you feel from your partner, but they also demonstrate to you that your partner is as committed to supporting and maintaining the relationship as you are. If your partner misses an anniversary, or your supervisor doesn't shake your hand to congratulate you on a job well done, you will feel rejected. Loyalty is extremely important to you in relationships, and if you feel that your partners aren't as committed to the relationship as you are, you will take it personally.

Instinctive Reaction When Rejected: When you feel rejected, you're likely to blame yourself for not doing enough to maintain and sustain the relationship. You may feel that you're not worthy of your partner's affection or appreciation. You may decide that you haven't taken enough responsibility for defining and supporting the structures of the relationship. Or you may decide that you need to change or improve yourself (or that your partner needs to improve!).

Wants to be Recognized by Others: You want to be recognized by others for your value and worth, and for the contributions you have made. You want to be loved because you are loyal and dedicated, and willing to work to create a loving, supportive, successful relationship.

Expresses Affection: You have a very strong preference for tangible expressions of affection. Buying gifts or even cards for the people you care about is very important to you. When appropriate, physical contact is another way you show affection for others. A pat on the back, an arm around the shoulder, or a hug shows that you care far better than words alone could ever convey.

Venus in Taurus

DIGNITY/DEBILITY:	Venus rules Taurus, has dignity by Triplicity during the day, and by Term for the first 8 degrees of Taurus.
CORE NEEDS:	To experience physical pleasure and stability in relationships.
CORE LESSONS:	To accept the necessity of change.
FEELS LOVED WHEN:	Experiencing physical intimacy with partner. Settling down in a comfortable, familiar routine with partner.
FEELS REJECTED WHEN:	Denied physical contact; faced with unexpected changes in routine or in the nature of the relationship.
INSTINCTIVE REACTION WHEN REJECTED:	Question self-worth, look to the physical plane for comfort and support; denial and resistance; slow to change and adapt.
EXPRESSES AFFECTION:	Physical contact is extremely important. Holding hands, cuddling, being close to their romantic partner. Gifts and tangible expressions of affection, particularly things of beauty or things that they have created themselves.

Taurus is one of the two signs ruled by Venus. Venus is particularly strong in Taurus—and once again, while this is great for Venus, it's not always easy for the individual. Taurus is an Earth sign, and so it operates on the physical and material plane. Taurus is the most sensual energy in all of astrology, and individuals with Venus in Taurus particularly enjoy physical pleasure, and tend to have a weakness for the finer things in life. As a Fixed Earth sign, Taurus is particularly concerned with stability and continuity. Individuals with Venus in Taurus do not approach relationships casually—to them, relationships are long-Term investments; they expect their relationships to endure.

While loyalty and stability are fine things, everything changes, and relationships will inevitably evolve, take unexpected turns, and eventually end. This is the most difficult lesson for individuals with Venus in Taurus to accept.

If you have Venus in Taurus, you feel loved and validated when you experience physical intimacy with your partner. Even in non-romantic relationships, touching is important. You define and experience the essence of your relationships through touch. Loyalty and trust are very important, and anything that demonstrates that your partner is committed to the relationship will mean a great deal to you. What you crave in relationships is a comfortable routine, filled with familiar sensations and casual intimacy. You find routines attractive because they seem to be insurance against change. You know what to expect, and when it happens, you feel validated and secure that the relationship is stable and enduring.

Any disruption in the routine, however, will make you feel rejected and abandoned. In fact, any change at all—unless you're the one initiating the change—will cause some concern and make you question how much you're being loved or appreciated. Likewise, when you're denied the kind of physical contact that you want and enjoy, you're apt to feel rejected and unappreciated.

When rejected, you will instinctively question your own self-worth. This is the central issue for all Fixed signs. You'll tend to look to the physical plane to provide comfort and support. When you're feeling unloved, you may find that you want to go out and buy yourself something to make yourself feel better. It's also possible that you may simply ignore and deny any changes in your relationships for as long as you possibly can. Adapting to change is not one of your more advanced skills.

With Venus in Taurus, you will tend to express affection through physical contact. Holding hands, cuddling, and being close to a romantic partner is fundamental to how you express love and feel loved. Taurus is an Earth sign, so gifts and tangible expressions of affection are also very popular. The most important thing to recognize with Venus in Taurus is that words are *not* enough. When you're told that you're loved and appreciated, it simply does not have any real impact. You need to *feel* it. You need some kind of physical contact or tangible proof to back up the words, or your Validation Needs will not be met.

Venus in Virgo

DIGNITY/DEBILITY: Venus is in Fall in Virgo. However, Venus has dignity by Triplicity in a day chart, by Term from 7–13 of Virgo, and by Face from 10–20 of Virgo. In a day chart, when Venus is at 10–13 Virgo, Venus can actually end up with a score of +2, even being in Fall.

CORE NEEDS: To work to improve and perfect the relationship through analysis, discrimination, attention to details, and service.

CORE LESSONS: To learn that perfection is a process, not an end result; to learn to accept self and others as is, and without criticism.

FEELS LOVED WHEN: Partner remembers details and special occasions; when receiving tangible expressions of affection—the amount of thought and care that goes into the choice of gift is far more important than the price tag; when partner demonstrates commitment to improving self and relationship.

FEELS REJECTED WHEN: Partner forgets details and important events; partner doesn't put enough thought into words or deeds.

INSTINCTIVE REACTION WHEN REJECTED: Identify critical flaws—both in one's self and in others—and attempt to improve them.

EXPRESSES AFFECTION: Remembers little occasions; buys little gifts, cards, etc. Pays attention to the details; likes to be of use, do favors, etc. Even though Virgo is an Earth sign, it's ruled by Mercury and is very mentally-oriented, so words are a very important means of expressing affection.

Individuals with Venus in Virgo are often very analytical in their approach to relationships and to the things that they value. Virgo's purpose is to be of service, perfecting the material plane for the benefit of everyone. If you have Venus in Virgo, it is often an indication that you're more than willing to put the effort and energy into a relationship to make it work; the Earthy nature of Virgo keeps you focused on the practical nature of relationships. The main challenge for you is that Virgo energy can often become too focused on the idea of perfection. You must be particularly aware of how you relate to others, and must be careful not to become overly-critical of your partners. The hardest lesson you is to accept that there is no such thing as a perfect relationship, and that perfection is about the commitment and the process of improving a relationship, not about the end result.

With Venus in Virgo, you feel loved and validated when others remember details and special occasions. You enjoy receiving tangible expressions of affection; however, the amount of thought and care that goes into the choice of gift is far more important than the price tag. You also feel loved when your partners demonstrate commitment to self-improvement, and to improving the relationship. Even though Virgo is an Earth sign, it's the most mental of all of the Earth signs, so words actually matter to you. You're not exclusively focused on the material aspects of your relationships: You can also feel validated and loved when your partners simply *tell* you that you're appreciated.

You will feel rejected and unappreciated when your partners overlook details or forget things or events that are important to you (don't *ever* forget the birthday of someone with Venus in Virgo!). You will also feel unappreciated if you perceive that your partners aren't putting enough care or thought into the relationship. Details are what matter to you the most.

When you're feeling rejected, you instinctively identify critical flaws and try to improve them. These can either be self-perceived "flaws" ("How can I improve so that I deserve the attention of my partner?") or flaws pointed out in their partner ("How can I help my partner to improve?"). Of course, your helpful suggestions and critiques may not always be welcome. Even though your intention is to find ways to improve the quality of your relationship (which would involve both of you having your needs met in more effective and fulfilling ways), other people may view your suggestions as personal attacks.

If you have Venus in Virgo, you will tend to express affection by remembering little occasions; you buy little gifts and cards. You pay attention to the details, and you like to be of use, so you often do favors for others. Virgo is all about finding the best way to express your thoughts. You feel that giving your time and attention to finding a way to make someone feel special means far more than simply writing a check. You're also likely to appreciate finding just the right words to express your feelings.

Venus in Virgo is in the sign of its Fall, which means that additionally, Venus in Virgo operates very specifically on the physical and material plane, most prominently during the first fifteen years of life. The experiences that individuals with Venus in Virgo have in their early lives—particularly those that involve their relationships with others, and how comforting, supportive and protective those relationships were—form the foundation and template for future relationships for these individuals. Because Venus in Virgo tends to focus so much on the physical and material plane, it is important for individuals with Venus in Virgo to consciously choose to explore and experience the higher, more spiritual aspects of relationships as well as the day-to-day routines that hold relationships together.

Venus in Capricorn

Dignity/Debility: Venus is dignified by Triplicity in Capricorn in a day chart; in a night chart, Venus is Peregrine for all but the first 6 degrees of Capricorn, where Venus is dignified by Term.

Core Needs: To define the relationship through creating and supporting strong boundaries, rituals, structures and traditions. To create a tangible expression of the relationship.

Core Lessons: Learning to be more flexible; learning to let down some of their walls and allow emotional connections.

Feels Loved When: Receiving expensive gifts; partner takes responsibility in the relationship and works to strengthen the commitment.

Feels Rejected When: Partner does not seem to take relationship seriously or is not willing to put the effort into working through differences and difficulties. Lack of tangible expressions of affection (i.e., no gifts).

Instinctive Reaction When Rejected: Take responsibility, reinforce boundaries and structures, work to overcome difficulties. Look for physical/tangible solution).

Expresses Affection: Buying expensive gifts. Capricorn operates on the physical/material plane, and on some level will always pay attention to the price and value of things.

With Venus in Capricorn, the structure and strength of the relationship is extremely important. Relationships are about sharing responsibility, and working with a partner to create an enduring and tangible expression of the connections you experience. It's important to know what the relationship is supposed to look like, and it's important to do the things that will strengthen and define the expression of the relationship. Anniversaries, rituals and traditions are only some of the ways that we can strengthen and reinforce the nature and endurance of a relationship.

The challenge with Venus in Capricorn is that if the boundaries become too strong and too rigid, they don't leave any room for the relationship to grow. Instead of feeling supportive, they start to become restrictive. If you have Venus in Capricorn, you're likely to be very aware of your own responsibilities in a relationship, and you're also likely to be conscious that you have to pull your own weight. What you may have to learn is that you can be responsible and still accept support from your partner. You also don't have to be the one that is always taking care of the obligations in the relationship (or taking care of your partner). Part of understanding your individual responsibilities in a relationship is recognizing where your responsibilities *end*. You have to let your partners do their part in the relationship, and if they aren't able to hold up their end, then you need to be willing to reconsider the whole relationship rather than taking on more than your fair share of the responsibility. Leaving a relationship that does not support you is the truly responsible thing to do.

If you have Venus in Capricorn, you feel loved and appreciated when you receive expensive gifts—the bigger, the better. Putting it another way, what you appreciate the most are tangible expressions of affection and appreciation. Remember, with Venus in Capricorn, it's all about amassing *tangible proof* of the value and strength of the relationship. You also feel validated when you see that your partners are making an effort to support and strengthen your relationship. You automatically assume that any relationship will require effort to make it work—but you truly feel loved when you find a partner who shares that perspective, and is willing to work as hard at the relationship as you are.

Of course, when you feel that your partners aren't taking the relationship as seriously as you are, you'll feel rejected and unappreciated. You're willing to stick it out and to work through whatever problems you may have. You're always looking to refine and strengthen your understanding of the relationship. When your partners aren't willing to put that same effort into the relationship, you tend to take it personally, and feel that your partners don't believe that *you're* worth the effort. You'll also feel unappreciated if you go too long without some kind of tangible expression of affection (i.e., lack of gifts).

Remember, if you have Venus in Capricorn, you need tangible expressions of appreciation in *all* of your relationships. In your professional life for example, bonuses and raises mean a lot to you: They make you feel appreciated. Likewise, awards and certificates, even inexpensive ones, will make you feel far more validated than a kind word and a pat on the back.

When you feel rejected, your instinctive reaction is to blame yourself for not doing enough. You will try to reinforce the boundaries and structures of the relationship, and you will do whatever it takes to overcome the difficulties in the relationship in a mature and practical fashion. You're most likely to look for a tangible or physical solution to any problem, since that's what means the most to you—in other words, you're not above throwing money at a problem to resolve it.

This is, after all, how you express affection and show appreciation for others: You buy them gifts. And on some level, you're apt to associate the price of the gift with the level of affection expressed or experienced. You don't always have to go for the grand gesture, though. Sharing resources, picking up the check, or generally trying to protect and look after the best interests of others are other ways that you express affection.

Air Validation Checklists

If you have an Air Validation Checklist, words are especially important to you. For you, relationships are about the social, mental and intellectual connections. If your Venus is in Gemini, Libra or Aquarius, you have an Air Validation Checklist.

Feels Validated When: Told that you are loved, valued and appreciated. It's not enough for you to feel emotional connections or for your partner to demonstrate their feelings in some way—you need to hear the words. You need the freedom to communicate and interact with many different people, and you feel validated when your partners understand this and allow you to go out and play. Relationships are very much a meeting of the minds for you, and when your partners share your ideas and beliefs, and approach the world from a similar point of view, you will feel validated and loved.

Feels Rejected When: When others feel that your words are not enough for them, you feel rejected and unappreciated. You are not comfortable with exploring or expressing your deeper emotions in your relationships. You are also apt to be uncomfortable when you and your partner disagree on topics that are fundamentally important to you. While you enjoy spirited debate, actual arguments are another matter entirely. When your partners do not acknowledge and accept your ideas, opinions and perspectives, you feel rejected. You require a certain amount of mental and social stimulation in your relationships. If your partner isn't challenging you, you may feel unappreciated.

Instinctive Reaction When Rejected: When you feel rejected or unappreciated in your relationships, your initial reaction is to engage your partner once more. Since the most important connections for you are the mental and social ones, you will want to talk with your partner, and discuss, debate, and negotiate until you have restored balance and harmony to the relationship.

Wants to be Recognized by Others: You want to be recognized by others for your ideas, thoughts, beliefs and insights. The part of you that you value the most is your mind.

Expresses Affection: You express affection with words, and you expect that words will be enough. You enjoy being playful with your partners, and you may tease, flatter, or banter with people to show that you value them. You expect others to recognize that if you didn't care for them, you wouldn't spend time talking with them. The fact that you feel that they are worthy of your attention, and that you want to understand their thoughts and dreams is the highest measure of your esteem.

Venus in Gemini

Dignity/Debility:	Venus has Term from 14–21 degrees, and is Peregrine the rest of the sign.
Core Needs:	To explore a variety of different social interactions and to learn about vastly different aspects of relationships; to be charming, social, and stimulated intellectually.
Core Lessons:	To learn to focus on one relationship at a time; to learn to discover and uncover the different facets of their partners and find more of their social and intellectual stimulation within the relationship.
Feels Loved When:	Encouraged to explore a variety of ideas, thoughts, experiences, and social interactions; playing with partner; presented with new ideas; expressing charm and poise in social situations.
Feels Rejected When:	Denied social stimulation; not challenged and entertained mentally and socially.
Instinctive Reaction When Rejected:	May lash out verbally; go into "game playing mode" and avoid contact with partner, evade questions, etc.
Expresses Affection:	Very verbal and skilled with finding the right things to say; playful bantering, charming compliments. Connects on mental/social realm.

Individuals with Venus in Gemini tend to be very social and enjoy interacting with a wide variety of individuals. Venus in Gemini is extremely charming and well-mannered, but individuals with Venus in Gemini also tend to want to keep in motion at all times. Gemini energy is not conducive to the focus, routine, and constancy that relationships often require. This does *not* mean that if you have Venus in Gemini you're incapable of a committed relationship. You do, however, need almost constant social stimulation.

What makes Venus in Gemini feel loved and validated is the freedom to explore a wide range of ideas, thoughts, experiences, and social interactions. You need to be able to satisfy your curiosity, and to always be allowed and encouraged to play. If you have Venus in Gemini, you're likely to enjoy flirting for what it is: a social interchange. Flirting does not need to lead to anything more serious, and indeed, you're more likely flirt for the sheer enjoyment of it than to attempt to initiate an illicit liaison. You do have to recognize that not everyone takes the same lighthearted approach to social intercourse. You have to learn to exercise some restraint—and, of course, if you happen to be in a relationship, your partner has to be willing to give you the freedom to meet and socialize with new people.

When you're not allowed to explore or to socialize in the ways that you want, you will feel rejected and unappreciated. You also feel unhappy if your partner doesn't challenge and entertain you, or stimulate you enough socially.

When you're feeling rejected or under stimulated you're likely to react verbally, using words (and wit) to attack. You may also begin to play games or to toy with your partner in a more malicious and less innocent manner—anything to generate some level of social or intellectual stimulation.

With Venus in Gemini, you express love and affection through the social and playful energy of Gemini. Words and ideas are very important to you, and you are far more comfortable expressing love and appreciation by saying something charming than you are with more physical and tangible expressions. By the same token, you much prefer to be told that you are loved and appreciated than to be shown. Relationships should be fun and playful for you. Gemini energy is not comfortable with intense emotions or indeed with maintaining any single focus for a long period of time. You need a partner who will share your curiosity and who is willing to go exploring with you.

Venus in Libra

DIGNITY/DEBILITY:	Venus rules Libra, and has additional dignity by Term from 6–11 of Libra. In a day chart, however, Saturn is usually the *almuten* of Libra (the planet with the most essential dignity at a given degree) with a minimum score of +7 for Exaltation and Triplicity.
CORE NEEDS:	To experience a truly balanced, equal, harmonious and beautiful relationship with a partner.
CORE LESSONS:	To maintain a strong individual identity while in relationship and not automatically deny or ignore individual needs to avoid conflict, accommodate their partner, and maintain balance in the relationship.
FEELS LOVED WHEN:	Spending time with a partner or engaged in activities that emphasize the relationship; respected and acknowledged as an equal by their partner; sharing artistic expression and appreciation of beauty.
FEELS REJECTED WHEN:	Faced with conflict or disagreements; blamed for imbalances in relationship or disharmony.
INSTINCTIVE REACTION WHEN REJECTED:	Restore balance and harmony or at least the appearance of balance and harmony at all costs.

Expresses Affection: Sharing things of beauty; words and language are very important because of the Air element.

Libra is one of the signs ruled by Venus, and Venus is very strong in Libra. Again, this is wonderful for Venus, but not necessarily wonderful for the individual.

Venus in Libra needs to experience true balance, harmony, equality and beauty through one-to-one relationships. The most important lesson, however, is to maintain an equal focus on your individual identity and on the balance and harmony in the relationship. *True* balance and harmony can only occur when you're being yourself completely, and your partner is doing the same. You discover how to balance when you're both coming from a position of completeness and strength. This is a very difficult lesson to learn, and while learning it, it's very easy to put too much emphasis on the *balance* aspect of the relationship and deny or ignore your own needs to avoid conflict and keep the relationship on an even keel.

If you have Venus in Libra, you feel loved and validated when you're in a relationship, and when you and your partner are doing things that *emphasize* the fact that you're in a relationship. You want to feel respected and acknowledged as an equal by your partner. You will also feel loved and validated when you're experiencing things of great beauty. Libra energy is associated with the fine arts.

It's worth noting that the *ultimate* relationship that Venus in Libra is about is our relationship to our higher self, and to the Creator/Universe/Spirit. Venus in Libra is the ultimate relationship mirror—what we see is only what we project. On a fundamental level, the balance, harmony and equality that Venus in Libra needs, is about self acceptance. We need to acknowledge ourselves as individuals, and validate ourselves for who we are.

Any kind of conflict, disagreement, or upset in the balance of your relationships will make you feel rejected and unworthy. Libra is an Air sign, and not especially comfortable with emotions. You prefer to take things at face value, and when people get upset, they tend to say thing that they don't truly mean.

When you feel rejected, you will try to restore balance and harmony (or at least the *appearance* of balance and harmony) at any cost. Your first line of defense is likely to be diplomacy, tact, and reason. Libra is very fair and just, and if you can resolve the situation through reason and logic, so much the better. If this doesn't work, however, your next choice is usually to give up, and do whatever it takes to make your partner happy so that you can end the conflict.

You're likely to express affection by sharing things of beauty. Words and language are very important to you because Libra is an Air sign. You enjoy being told that you are loved or appreciated, and you enjoy telling others how much you love and appreciate them.

Venus in Aquarius

DIGNITY/DEBILITY:	Venus has dignity for the first 12 degrees of Aquarius (Face from 0–10 degrees and Term from 6–12 degrees) and is Peregrine for the last 18 degrees of the sign.
CORE NEEDS:	To feel that they are relating to others who share their core beliefs and ideals.
CORE LESSONS:	To learn how to connect and relate on an individual, personal level, rather than on an objective, idealistic, group-identity level.
FEELS LOVED WHEN:	Sharing common goals and ideals with partner; being acknowledged and appreciated for ideas, beliefs, and ideals. Working with partner on shared goals.
FEELS REJECTED WHEN:	Partner expresses differences in opinion on core issues; partner puts individual needs before the needs of the group (or of the relationship). Forced to move out of the abstract mental realm and deal with specific emotions.
INSTINCTIVE REACTION WHEN REJECTED:	First response is to defend position and attempt to convert others back to their point of view. Seek out a new relationship that will reinforce group identity (and social value and worth) once again.
EXPRESSES AFFECTION:	Sharing ideas and ideals for the future that include the partner as an integral part of the group.

Individuals with Venus in Aquarius need to feel that they are relating to others who share their core beliefs and ideals. Even though Venus in Aquarius is still focused on one-to-one relationships, Aquarius is always a group-oriented energy. It's essential for Venus in Aquarius to feel that they are relating to people who belong to the same group as they do.

As always, the challenge with Aquarius energy is to learn how to move from the theoretical and group-oriented perspective where Aquarius is most comfortable to the specific and individual relationships where Aquarius is less skilled.

If you have Venus in Aquarius, you feel loved and appreciated when you're reminded that you and your partner share the same goals and ideals. Essentially, when you feel that you are a rightful and equal member of the group, you feel validated. You're likely to enjoy working together with your partners in activities where you're both moving towards a shared goal. The more your partner demonstrates that you share the same opinions and values, the more validated and loved you feel. The social and intellectual aspects of your relationships are what matter to you the most. Aquarius is an Air sign, and the fewer emotions that surface and disrupt your ideal perceptions, the happier you are.

You will feel rejected when your partner expresses differences in opinion on core issues, or when your partner puts individual needs before the needs of the group (or of the relationship). Venus in Aquarius prefers to operate on the abstract mental/social/intellectual realm, and can feel rejected when the logical aspects are ignored and the emotional aspects take precedence.

Again, it's important to make the distinction between general issues and "core" issues. The "core" issues are whatever beliefs or ideas define the group for Venus in Aquarius. When we covered the Moon in Aquarius, I used the example of the group of people who loved the film *Titanic*. In this case, the "core" issues would be everything associated with *Titanic*, including opinions on the stars and Celine Dion singing the theme song. As long as you always agree on these issues, you can disagree on absolutely everything else and it won't make a difference to you from a validation perspective. Within the definition of the group, you actually *enjoy* the freedom to disagree. The fact that you can disagree with your partners on so many things actually emphasizes the definition of the group for you, and makes you feel more loved and appreciated. As long as you never question the core issues, you will be fine.

Aquarius' instinctive identification with the group means that an attack on the group's ideals is viewed as a personal attack. Your first response when rejected or attacked is to defend your position vehemently and to attempt to convert your partners back to your point of view. If this is not possible, you will seek out a new relationship that will reinforce your group identity (and sense of social value and worth) once again.

Words are very important to individuals with Venus in Aquarius. Aquarius is in many ways the most abstract energy, operating entirely on the mental and social plane. With Venus in Aquarius, you will tend to express affection through your words and ideas, and in particular by sharing ideas and ideals for the future that include your partner as an integral part of the group.

Water Validation Checklists

If you have a Water Validation Checklist, you need to experience emotional, energetic and spiritual connections in your relationships in order to feel validated. Relationships are about nurturing and protecting, and showing how much we care about each other. You have a Water Validation Checklist if your Venus is in Cancer, Scorpio or Pisces.

Feels Validated When: You feel validated when other people share their feelings with you. You look for emotional bonds in your relationships. The more connected you feel to your partners, the more loved and validated you feel. For you, love and validation are all about expressing your deepest feelings. When other people create emotional bonds with you, you no longer feel alone. You are able to share your hopes, your fears, and your needs, and you recognize that other people share them with you. Ultimately, you feel validated when you know on a core emotional and spiritual level, that you are not alone in the world. You care about other people, and other people care about and want to protect and nurture you in return.

Feels Rejected When: When you're not able to experience an emotional connection with your partner, you feel rejected and abandoned. It's tremendously important to you that your partners be emotionally available. Although it's nice to have your partners tell you that they love and appreciate you, words are not enough. In order for you to truly feel validated, you have to experience an emotional connection that reinforces the words. When your partners put up walls and sever the emotional connections, you feel rejected (and in a very big way, too). You also feel rejected when your partners do not acknowledge or fully appreciate your feelings.

Instinctive Reaction When Rejected: When you feel rejected, your instinctive reaction is to recreate the emotional and energetic bonds you share with your partner by any means possible. You may (consciously or unconsciously) resort to emotional manipulation by becoming either too nurturing or too needy and dependent. When you feel too hurt and betrayed to take any direct action, you may retreat inside yourself to try to heal your wounds. You may also adjust your own boundaries—making them weaker where your partners are stronger—in an attempt to maintain the level of connection you used to share.

Wants to be Recognized by Others: You want to be recognized by others for your compassion, your spirit and your ability to love.

Expresses Affection: You show that you care about others by sharing your feelings with them. Your affection has a distinct nurturing quality to it. You want to heal, to protect, and to support the people you care about. You want to alleviate any pain or emotional discomfort in others, and help them to feel safe and protected—which to you, means loved.

Venus in Cancer

DIGNITY/DEBILITY: Venus has dignity by Face for the first 10 degrees of Cancer, and by Term from 20–27 of Cancer.

CORE NEEDS: To form emotional connections with a partner that mutually nurture and support.

CORE LESSONS: To develop good energetic boundaries and learn tough love. Too much nurturing can lead to codependency and enabling behavior.

Feels Loved When:	Sharing emotional connections with a partner; nurturing and being nurtured.
Feels Rejected When:	Denied emotional connections or faced with strong energetic boundaries; feelings are ignored.
Instinctive Reaction When Rejected:	Increase efforts to form emotional energetic bonds with partner; emotional manipulation by either becoming too nurturing (mothering/smothering) or too needy and dependent.
Expresses Affection:	Connect emotionally; nurture, pamper, support and empathize. Share feelings and emotional/spiritual connections.

If you have Venus in Cancer, supportive, nurturing emotional connections are what are important to you in relationships. Your definition of "love" most likely includes powerful emotional connections of great depth and epic proportions. When you're experiencing emotional connections with other people, especially when you are able to nurture them, or are being nurtured, you also feel loved, appreciated and validated.

Ultimately, your lessons will be about boundaries. With Venus in Cancer, when you care about someone, you also feel a very strong need to protect, shelter and nurture that person. Venus in Cancer carries an element of mothering, and it's very important to keep this aspect in perspective. One of the hardest lessons for Venus in Cancer individuals is learning tough love. Too much nurturing (either giving or receiving) can lead to codependency and enabling. Ultimately, you have to learn when and how to stop taking care of your partners. You have to let your partners take care of their own needs—and you have to take responsibility for meeting your own. You have to learn how to be nurturing and supportive, how to create and maintain emotional connections without taking on too much responsibility for someone else's life.

The bottom line, however, is that if you have Venus in Cancer, you feel loved and appreciated when you're experiencing emotional bonds, and when you're nurturing or being nurtured. When you're denied emotional connections, when you're shut off, confronted with strong boundaries, or when you're not able to take care of someone in the ways that you want to, you'll feel rejected. You'll *also* feel rejected when other people don't fully appreciate and acknowledge your feelings.

When you feel rejected, your instinctive reaction is to "reach out and touch someone." You will try to recreate the emotional and energetic bonds with your partner in any way you can. Some of the less elegant ways you may choose involve emotional manipulation—either becoming *too* nurturing (where mothering becomes smothering) or by becoming needy and dependent (in other words, using guilt).

If you have Venus in Cancer, you express affection through sharing your emotions and feelings with others. You show people that you care about them by trying to make them feel safe, protected, and nurtured.

Venus in Scorpio

Dignity/Debility: Venus is in Detriment in Scorpio; Venus has Term from 14–21 Scorpio and Face from 20–30 Scorpio.

Core Needs: To experience a deep, powerful, transformational emotional connection with their partners.

Core Lessons: To lighten up, and to learn to trust.

Feels Loved When: Experiencing deep, passionate emotional connections with a partner; bearing their soul and sharing their deepest, darkest secrets; being their partner's confidant.

Feels Rejected When: Denied deep emotional connections; trust or confidence is betrayed; partner won't open up old wounds; partner enforces boundaries.

Instinctive Reaction When Rejected: Retreat into self and nurse anger and pain; search for other ways to manipulate partner into emotional connections; plotting revenge.

Expresses Affection: Opening up to partner and sharing deep, personal and private thoughts and feelings. Experiencing emotional and physical intimacy.

Venus in Scorpio doesn't care to waste much time with pleasant, superficial relationships. Unless souls are being bared and wild and passionate emotions are being shared, it's just not a real relationship. Trust is very important as well: If you have Venus in Scorpio, you will feel the most valued when you are sharing your darkest secrets and fears with a partner, or when you are being your partner's confidant. You may also put a significant emphasis on the sexual aspects of a romantic relationship, although it's important to realize that sex is simply a tool to experience a greater sense of emotional intimacy and transformation.

If you have Venus in Scorpio, you feel the most loved and validated when you share a powerful emotional and spiritual connection with a partner. It takes time to build up a sufficient level of trust to share your secrets, and to create these types of connections, so you may tend to have relatively few intimate relationships (romantic or otherwise) at any given time. When you do create a connection with someone, it's a very significant commitment—on some level, you expect to be connected to your partners for a very long time. Even if you lose touch with someone, the fact that you're keeping their secrets and they're keeping yours will keep you connected on a spiritual level.

Once you've formed an emotional connection with someone, any disruptions to that connection will make you feel rejected and betrayed. Once you've let your emotional guard down, you don't expect your partner to put theirs up again.

When rejected, you will tend to retreat into yourself and to nurse the anger and pain; you will search for other ways to manipulate your partners into the emotional connections; you will wonder what it is that you did wrong and question your self-worth. Mostly, you'll plot revenge.

While relationships are healing and transformational to you, it's important that you recognize that not every relationship has to be a gut-wrenching, soul-bearing tempest. True intimacy takes time to develop, and requires a great deal of trust. You may have a habit of sharing too much too soon, because when it comes to emotional connections, you may take an all-or-nothing approach. It's *also* important that you recognize that it's possible to have an intimate relationship without sex. While sex can certainly be the shortest route to an intense and transformational connection with another person, it's not always the most elegant choice. Trust is once again the real issue.

Venus in Pisces

DIGNITY/DEBILITY:	Venus is Exalted in Pisces, and also dignified by Term for the first 8 degrees of Pisces.
CORE NEEDS:	To experience relationships as a spiritual merging and a soul union; to reconnect with the source through relationships.
CORE LESSONS:	To maintain good energetic and emotional boundaries in relationships; to learn to discriminate and protect oneself from other people's negativity.
FEELS LOVED WHEN:	Experiencing emotional connections with partner; connecting on a higher, spiritual level.
FEELS REJECTED WHEN:	Denied emotional connections; partner focuses too much on the physical aspects of the relationship and ignores the spiritual and emotional aspects.
INSTINCTIVE REACTION WHEN REJECTED:	Attempt to reconnect energetically with partner; try to adapt self to become more of what they perceive partner needs or wants; take on role of martyr and continue to pursue relationship and rejection.

EXPRESSES AFFECTION: Shared emotional connections and empathy; gifts and thoughts that will have a private, personal meaning to partner; healing and transmuting partner's pain and negativity.

Venus in Pisces needs to experience relationships as a spiritual merging and a soul union. Venus in Pisces seeks to reconnect with the source through relationships. If you have Venus in Pisces, you recognize the true core essence, the highest potential for light and love in everyone, and respond to this with genuine love and compassion. By connecting on this level, you hope to recapture some of the experience of being freed from the physical form and truly experiencing our absolute unity with all of creation. Relationships are all about the emotional, spiritual and energetic connections for you.

What you will have to learn, however, is how to maintain good energetic boundaries in relationships, and to protect yourself from other people's negativity. One of the functions of Pisces is to absorb negative emotions and transmute them, so you're always going to be healing in your relationships. It's just important that you become aware of this, and learn how to release the negative emotions that you're absorbing from your partners.

Although Venus in Pisces becomes far more spiritually aware, Venus in Pisces also loses its ability to discriminate. This generally means that you form connections with a very eclectic group of people in the course of your lifetime. However, it also means that you may tend to enter into relationships with people based on your perceptions of their highest self, but without looking too closely at where they are in their physical development and how connected they may be to their highest self at the time. You must remember that although Venus in Pisces heals through relationship, and has a wealth of compassion, this does not mean that you must sacrifice yourself in any way for a relationship, romantic or otherwise.

With Venus in Pisces, you feel the most valued and appreciated when you are able to experience emotional and spiritual connections with your partner. Keeping these lines of communication clear is exceptionally important to you. Pisces energy has the most difficulty recognizing and respecting boundaries. The fewer boundaries you perceive between you and your partners, the stronger the emotional and spiritual connection you will share, and the more loved and appreciated you will feel.

Of course, boundaries are very important, both for you and for your partners. Even so, when you encounter boundaries, you will feel rejected and unappreciated. Each one of us needs some personal space and privacy, but when your partners need to pull away and take some private time, you will feel abandoned. It's important to recognize that with Venus in

Pisces, your feelings of rejection and abandonment are likely to be very vague—very few of us are consciously aware of the kinds of energetic and emotional connections we create with other people, so it's unlikely that you would notice when the nature of those connections has changed. You may also feel rejected when your partners seem to put more emphasis on the physical aspect of the relationship and don't pay enough attention to the spiritual elements. This comes from your tendency to relate to people as if they were embodying their highest selves. When you're forced to accept the physical reality of your partners and relate to them on this level, you may feel less loved and appreciated.

When you do feel rejected, your instinctive reaction is to recreate the emotional and energetic connections. If your partner has made his or her boundaries stronger, you're likely to make yours even weaker to try to compensate. You will adapt and change in an effort to become more of what you think your partners need. The weaker you allow your own boundaries to become, the more likely you will suffer in the relationship.

With Venus in Pisces, you express affection through shared emotional connections and empathy. You appreciate gifts and thoughts that convey a private, personal meaning. You also express affection by healing and transmuting the negative energy of others, although you're probably not aware of this on a conscious level.

❖6❖
CAN WE MEET OUR NEEDS?

So we now understand that our core relationship needs have to do with feeling safe and feeling validated (loved, valued, appreciated, etc.). We also understand that the Moon relates to our Safety Needs (and Safety Checklist) and Venus relates to our Validation Needs (and Validation Checklist). Understanding the sign and condition of the Moon and Venus helps us to identify exactly what we need in every one of our relationships—they show how we want to feel safe and how we want to validated. But we're not quite done. Just because we understand what our core needs are, doesn't mean that we'll have an easy time *meeting* those needs.

Do we know what it means to feel truly safe or truly validated? Can we reasonably expect to meet the requirements on our checklists? In this chapter, we will explore the most significant challenges we may face when it comes to meeting our needs.

FEELING SAFE AND FEELING VALIDATED (PICK ONE)

The first question we need to ask with regards to meeting our relationship needs is: Can we feel safe and validated at the same time? This is not always easy. Our Safety Checklist and our Validation Checklist are completely independent of each other. They may not have any items in common. What's more, meeting the requirements of one checklist may directly trigger the other checklist. The things that make us feel validated may make us feel threatened. And the things that make us feel safe may also be the things that make us feel invalidated and unappreciated.

Let's use our relationship with emotions as an example. If we're threatened by emotional connections, if we don't like to open up and share our feelings with others, this would all be part of our Safety Checklist. If, on the other hand, our Validation Checklist tells us that in order to feel validated and appreciated, we have to share an emotional connection, we have a challenge to address. When we feel validated and experience emotional bonds, we won't feel safe. And when we feel safe because our partners are keeping an adequate emotional distance, we won't feel validated because we don't have an emotional connection.

Difficulties feeling safe and validated at the same time are the root of a great many challenging relationship patterns. By considering our reactions in terms of our Safety Needs and our Validation Needs, we can begin to understand *why* we may have had difficulties in our relationships. If we want to create a long-term romantic relationship, we need to be able to maintain at least the minimum balance in our Safety and Validation Accounts at all times—and we may have to adjust one or both of our checklists to do this. It's often easier to make adjustments to our *Safety* Checklists, because we naturally equate *safe* with *familiar*. Over time, we can adjust our Safety Checklists so that when we receive a deposit in our Validation Account it no longer makes a withdrawal from our Safety Account.

The question of whether or not we can feel both safe and validated is easily answered in astrology: Simply consider the relationship between the Moon and Venus. If the Moon and Venus are in compatible signs, then the things that make us feel safe (Moon) are also likely to make us validated (Venus). If the Safety Checklist Language and the Validation Checklist Language conflict because of the sign relationship between the Moon and Venus, it can indicate difficulties meeting our relationship needs. When the Moon and Venus are actually in aspect to each other, the Safety Checklist and the Validation Checklist have a direct connection. When the aspect is harmonious (conjunction, sextile, trine) this makes it easier to feel safe and validated together. When the aspect is stressful (opposition, square, quincunx) it creates definite challenges and can interfere with our ability to feel simultaneously safe and validated.

Identical Moon and Venus

If your Moon and Venus are in the same sign, then you speak the same language for your Safety Needs and your Validation Needs. In essence, if something makes you feel validated, it will also make you feel safe. If the Moon and Venus are actually conjunct each other (at the same degree) then the two checklists will be combined into one master list. The only way you will feel safe is if you feel validated, and the only way you will feel validated is if you feel safe.

Compatible Moon and Venus Signs

The next level of compatibility would be if the Moon and Venus are in the same element, especially if they are trine each other (120° aspect). This means that they effectively speak the same elemental language, and that it's likely that the two checklists have many items in common. In other words, it will be very easy to feel both safe and validated at the same time. If the Moon and Venus are in the same polarity (Fire and Air or Earth and Water), especially if they are sextile each other (60° aspect), the checklists will have less in common than if they were in the same element; however, the checklists won't have any conflicting items on them. It will be possible to meet the requirements of one checklist without triggering the other checklist in any way, and the two checklists often compliment each other. Table 1 illustrates the compatible Moon and Venus signs.

Table 1: Compatible Moon and Venus Signs

MOON SIGN	VENUS SIGN
Aries (Fire)	Leo or Sagittarius (Fire) Gemini or Aquarius (Air)
Taurus (Earth)	Virgo or Capricorn (Fire) Cancer or Pisces (Water)
Gemini (Air)	Libra or Aquarius (Air) Aries or Leo (Fire)
Cancer (Water)	Scorpio or Pisces (Water) Taurus or Virgo (Earth)
Leo (Fire)	Aries or Sagittarius (Fire) Gemini or Libra (Air)
Virgo (Earth)	Taurus or Capricorn (Earth) Cancer or Scorpio (Water)
Libra (Air)	Gemini or Aquarius (Air) Leo or Sagittarius (Fire)
Scorpio (Water)	Cancer or Pisces (Water) Virgo or Capricorn (Earth)
Sagittarius (Fire)	Aries or Leo (Fire) Libra or Aquarius (Air)
Capricorn (Earth)	Taurus or Virgo (Earth) Scorpio or Pisces (Water)
Aquarius (Air)	Gemini or Libra (Air) Aries or Sagittarius (Fire)
Pisces (Water)	Cancer or Scorpio (Water) Taurus or Capricorn (Earth)

Balancing Acts

When the Moon and Venus are in opposing signs (Table 2), it's still possible to feel safe and validated at the same time—however, it will require a certain amount of balancing between the two checklists. Each sign axis represents a core lesson, and the signs on either end of the axis approach this lesson from opposite points of view. Potentially, the two checklists could trigger each other—something that is more likely if the Moon and Venus actually oppose each other (180° aspect). It may help to remember that there is a point of balance where the two checklists can intersect, and where you can feel both safe and validated at the same time.

Table 2: Opposing Moon and Venus Signs

MOON SIGN	VENUS SIGN
Aries (Fire)	Libra (Air)
Taurus (Earth)	Scorpio (Water)
Gemini (Air)	Sagittarius (Fire)
Cancer (Water)	Capricorn (Earth)
Leo (Fire)	Aquarius (Air)
Virgo (Earth)	Pisces (Water)
Libra (Air)	Aries (Fire)
Scorpio (Water)	Taurus (Earth)
Sagittarius (Fire)	Gemini (Air)
Capricorn (Earth)	Cancer (Water)
Aquarius (Air)	Leo (Fire)
Pisces (Water)	Virgo (Earth)

Conflicts of Interest

If the Moon and Venus are in the same *modality* (Cardinal, Fixed or Mutable) but different elements, then the two checklists will have little in common. When the Moon and Venus are actually square each other (close to a 90° angle), it's almost certain that specific items on the checklists will conflict. Both checklists share a common focus, but they approach it at cross-purposes with each other. Creating a situation where we can feel both safe and validated will take effort. We will have to construct new checklists that support each other, rather than conflict with each other. Table 3 illustrates the conflicting Moon and Venus Signs.

TABLE 3: CONFLICTING MOON AND VENUS SIGNS

MOON SIGN	VENUS SIGN
Aries (Cardinal)	Cancer or Capricorn (Cardinal)
Taurus (Fixed)	Leo or Aquarius (Fixed)
Gemini (Mutable)	Virgo or Pisces (Mutable)
Cancer (Cardinal)	Aries or Libra (Cardinal)
Leo (Fixed)	Taurus or Scorpio (Fixed)
Virgo (Mutable)	Gemini or Sagittarius (Mutable)
Libra (Cardinal)	Cancer or Capricorn (Cardinal)
Scorpio (Fixed)	Leo or Aquarius (Fixed)
Sagittarius (Mutable)	Virgo or Pisces (Mutable)
Capricorn (Cardinal)	Aries or Libra (Cardinal)
Aquarius (Fixed)	Taurus or Scorpio (Fixed)
Pisces (Mutable)	Gemini or Sagittarius (Mutable)

No Common Ground

In the previous examples, even when the Moon and Venus had difficulty agreeing, they always shared some common ground that could be used to create a resolution to any conflicts. Sometimes, however, the Moon and Venus simply have nothing at all in common. On the one hand, unless the Moon and Venus are quincunx each other, this means the two checklists won't actually conflict with each other. On the other hand, it also means that our Safety and Validation Needs are so fundamentally different that it can be challenging to have both needs met at the same time. The problem is that we will tend to pick one set of needs in any given relationship—either our Safety

Needs or our Validation Needs—and those will be the only needs will be met on a regular basis. This is most often the case when the Moon and Venus are quincunx each other (150° aspect). Eventually, the needs that aren't being met will demand our attention—and since it's not likely that they can be met within the context of the relationship, we may have to end the relationship. The more aware we are of how we feel safe and how we feel validated, the easier it is to meet those needs. If we're aware of the challenge and of our patterns, we can concentrate on finding ways that *both* needs can be met in the relationship. We don't have to feel safe and validated at the same time, but we *do* have to maintain a healthy balance in both accounts. Table 4 illustrates the Moon and Venus signs with no common ground.

Table 4: Moon and Venus Signs with No Common Ground

MOON SIGN	VENUS SIGN
Aries	Virgo or Scorpio
Taurus	Libra or Sagittarius
Gemini	Scorpio or Capricorn
Cancer	Sagittarius or Aquarius
Leo	Capricorn or Pisces
Virgo	Aries or Aquarius
Libra	Taurus or Pisces
Scorpio	Aries or Gemini
Sagittarius	Taurus or Cancer
Capricorn	Gemini or Leo
Aquarius	Cancer or Virgo
Pisces	Leo or Libra

Saturn Aspects: Checklists From Hell

Saturn is the planet of limitations, boundaries and restrictions. Saturn teaches responsibility and hard work. Saturn is our internal authority figure. It's always keeping watch over us and it's almost never satisfied with the job that we're doing. Saturn also functions as our "inner parent."

Most of us are familiar with the term "inner child," which describes our core innocence. The inner child is the part of us that needs the greatest amount of love and attention. In addition to the inner child, we also each have an internal authority figure—the "inner parent." The inner parent is the part of us that provides structure, limits and discipline for the inner child. We need a sense of boundaries and rules and structure in our lives. We need to have an understanding of what kinds of behavior are acceptable as individuals and as members of a larger community. We need to understand what it means to be responsible for ourselves. This is the function of the inner parent. Of course, sometimes our inner parent is Bill Cosby, and sometimes it's Joan Crawford.

Mostly, our inner parent is made up of things that adults told us when we were children, and things that we decided on our own based on our experiences as children. While these instructions and beliefs served us at one point in our lives, they may not be helping us now. We each have hundreds of scripts running through our heads that shape how we relate to ourselves and to others. We didn't write most of these scripts, and many of them we don't even want. The voice that reads these scripts is our inner parent. Our inner parent is also responsible for *creating* many of these scripts in the first place. The only way that we can change them, however is to identify them first.

When our inner parent gets carried away, we can end up with Checklists From Hell. The conditions on the checklist are so severe that we can't ever meet them, and because we can't meet the conditions on our checklists, we also can't meet our needs. Believe it or not, our inner parent (and our ego) created these checklists in an effort to *protect* us. Our egos are afraid that even if we met the conditions on our checklists, it wouldn't be enough. The pain of realizing that our needs might never be met is simply too great, so the ego gives us an excuse. By creating checklists with impossible conditions, we are at least left with some hope. We can still cling to the belief that if we ever met the conditions on our checklists, our needs would be met. Of course, the conditions on our checklists are specifically selected so that we can never meet them and test this belief. The risk is simply too great.

Our inner parents are only trying to protect us, and up until now, they've done a reasonably good job of it. It's up to us to take over at some point, however, and start making our own choices. That means looking at what's on our checklists and deciding what we want to keep, and what we want to discard.

Moon-Saturn Aspects

Moon-Saturn aspects often create challenges with the Safety Checklist. The influence of Saturn means that safety is particularly important to individuals with these aspects. Unfortunately,

Saturn's influence often equates safety with rules, boundaries and structures. In moderate doses, rules, boundaries and structures do, in fact, help us to feel safer. When taken to the extreme, however, they make it difficult or impossible to experience the kinds of emotional connections and intimacy that are essential to our sense of safety. Boundaries only make us feel safe when they keep *most* people out; when they keep *everyone* out, they become prison walls.

Moon-Saturn aspects relate to the "Fortress of Solitude™" patterns described in Chapter 5 of *The Relationship Handbook.* Different aspects relate to different types of Fortresses (Survivalist Fortress, "I'm Always Out" Fortress or Home Care Fortress).

Only the "hard" Moon-Saturn aspects create potentially challenging patterns. Moon trine Saturn and Moon sextile Saturn generally indicate healthy boundaries, which support meeting one's Safety Needs.

Moon conjunct Saturn

When the Moon is conjunct Saturn, the tendency is to live in a "Survivalist Fortress." The individual's boundaries are so strong, and they are so well protected that they tend to isolate from other people and find it very difficult to create healthy, lasting, intimate emotional connections with anyone. Because conjunctions lack any sense of perspective, these individuals may not recognize that they have significant safety issues. The walls they live behind have been with them their entire lives, and they may not even be able to imagine life without them.

This is not to say that they don't long for intimacy. On the contrary, they often long for the day when someone will find a way to get around their defenses and come visit them inside their fortress.

Moon square Saturn

Individuals with the Moon square Saturn have a more dynamic relationship with their Safety Checklists. These individuals are the most likely to live in an "I'm Always Out" Fortress. They are afraid that their Safety Needs will never be met to their satisfaction, and they're not willing to take a chance and find out if their fears are well founded. Squares are action aspects, and individuals with the Moon square Saturn are often driven to take care of everyone else. These individuals are frequently obsessed with protecting and supporting others. They do this so that they can distract themselves from the fact that their own Safety Needs are not being met. They rarely stop doing things for others because they're afraid that if they give other people a chance to be there for them, their greatest fear will be confirmed: that they are, in fact, isolated and alone and no one cares about them.

Moon opposite Saturn

Oppositions always play out in relationships. We "own" one planet and project the other planet on our partners. With the Moon opposite Saturn, the majority of the time, Saturn is the planet that will be projected on others. Individuals with the Moon opposite Saturn may have a history of letting other people define the boundaries in their lives. What this means is that most of the items on these individual's Safety Checklists were put there by other people—most often their parents. And to make matters even more challenging, the items that other people put on their Safety Checklist are usually the direct opposite of the items that would actually help them to feel safe.

The challenge for these individuals involves learning to accept responsibility for making their own choices, becoming responsible for meeting their own Safety Needs and learning what it means to feel truly safe. When they follow the standards of the "outer parent" Safety Checklist, they can only experience a pale reflection of true safety. They give up their own autonomy in exchange for the sense of safety that comes from being protected by external authority figures, and for not having to accept any personal responsibility for their choices. When they begin to question the items on their Safety Checklist and revise their checklists to reflect their own, personal standards of safety, they give up the sense of safety that comes from earning the approval of their parents, but gain the true sense of safety that comes from living a life of integrity and personal responsibility.

Moon opposite Saturn can play out in the widest range of ways, and can be associated with any of the three types of Fortress of Solitude™: the Survivalist Fortress, the "I'm Always Out" Fortress, or the Home Care Fortress.

Moon quincunx Saturn

The quincunx is by far the most challenging aspect to work with. Quincunxes occur between planets in signs that have no common ground by element, polarity or modality. Because the planets are across the chart from each other, they can see each other clearly. Quincunxes often feel like oppositions, in that we believe that there must be some way to balance the two planets. However, while oppositions do in fact have a point of balance and integration, quincunxes do not. With quincunxes, we usually believe that we must make a compromise; in order to express one planet, we must ignore (or attempt to ignore) the other planet.

In terms of meeting our needs, quincunxes from the outer planets are especially challenging because they can create patterns of learned helplessness that are extremely difficult (although by no means impossible) to erase. The reason quincunxes are associated with learned helplessness is that we can never quite work out how or why the ignored planet will manifest itself. We can see no logical pattern, no rhyme or reason, and so it's difficult to learn how to work around the challenges of this aspect. With squares or oppositions we see a direct and obvious connection between action and reaction. When Saturn is square the Moon, for example, we can easily learn where the boundaries are, and adjust our behavior so that we can avoid the more unpleasant experiences of Saturn. When Saturn is quincunx the Moon, however, Saturn's influence seems entirely random.

In its most extreme manifestation, the Moon quincunx Saturn is associated with the "Home Care Fortress" where the individual relies entirely on other people to meet his or her needs and takes little or no personal responsibility for anything. This pattern is the result of many years of attempting to balance Saturn and the Moon, and failing, usually painfully, time after time, for apparently random reasons. The underlying false belief is that the Universe is fundamentally hostile, and that we have little or no control over the events in our lives. Healing this pattern means addressing this false belief directly, a process that requires great care and attention.

Venus-Saturn Aspects

Venus-Saturn aspects can make it difficult for us to meet our Validation Needs. Saturn's influence places the items on our Validation Checklists just beyond our reach. We continuously strive to meet these goals, and yet as soon as we reach them, Saturn raises the bar once more. Venus-Saturn aspects relate to the patterns "Not _____ Enough," "Can't Take a Compliment," and "If You *Really* Loved Me…," described in detail in Chapter 5 of *The Relationship Handbook.* Any or all of these patterns can be associated with any of the Venus-Saturn aspects. The aspects differ in terms of how we create the beliefs that formed these patterns.

As with the Moon-Saturn aspects, only the "hard" Venus-Saturn aspects are associated with challenging patterns that can interfere with meeting our Validation Needs. Venus trine Saturn and Venus sextile Saturn tend to be supportive energies that contribute to healthy self-worth and self-esteem.

Venus conjunct Saturn

With Venus conjunct Saturn, the difficulties in feeling loved and validated come from within. At a very early age, these individuals internalized some experience and created the belief that they were not worthy of being loved. The way that this energy plays out depends entirely on the modality of the conjunction. If the Venus-Saturn conjunction is in a Cardinal sign, the focus is identity, and the core belief is "There's something wrong with me, and that's why I can't be loved." If the Venus-Saturn conjunction is in a Fixed sign, the focus is self-worth, and the

"Not ___ Enough" pattern will play a significant role: The core belief is that "I don't deserve to be loved" or "I haven't earned the right to be loved." If the Venus-Saturn conjunction is in a Mutable sign, the focus is on healing and adaptation, and the belief is "I need to change who I am so that other people will love me."

In every instance, the issue with the Venus-Saturn conjunction is that the individuals withhold love from themselves, and therefore they find it difficult to have their Validation Needs met. The solution is to practice self-love and self-validation. As they learn to receive more love from themselves, they will also receive more validation from others.

Venus square Saturn

Venus square Saturn is most often associated with the "If You *Really* Loved Me…" pattern, where the individual demands constant and continuous proof that their partners truly love and appreciate them. Again, the underlying insecurity depends on the modality of the square. Cardinal squares mean, "I don't believe I'm good enough to be loved." Fixed squares mean, "I'm not worthy of being loved," or, "I have to earn love." And Mutable squares mean, "I have to change or become someone else in order for you to love me." Because squares are a dynamic aspect, we tend to project these beliefs on our partners, challenging our partners until they finally fail to meet our Validation Needs, and prove that our underlying fears are, indeed, accurate.

It's important to recognize that individuals with Venus square Saturn will often experience these patterns as being entirely outside of themselves. If they have a Cardinal square, they will attract partners who may treat them as if they are not up to their standards, or not equal in the relationship. If they have a Fixed square, they will attract partners who will require that they earn their partner's love and attention. And if they have a Mutable square, they will attract partners who expect them to change in some fundamental way so that they can be loved.

Venus opposite Saturn

Individuals with Venus opposite Saturn often discover that the items and standards on their Validation Checklists are not their own. The items on their Validation Checklist are usually designed to please their parents, because as children, they did not feel loved and accepted unconditionally. Again, the root of the belief depends on the modality of the opposition. Cardinal oppositions believe "Mommy and daddy don't love me because I'm bad," and unconsciously strive to deny their true self and become someone else. Fixed oppositions believe "Mommy and daddy don't love me because I'm not ____ enough," and strive to earn their parents' love and respect through their accomplishments and achievements. And Mutable oppositions believe "Mommy and daddy will love me if I become what they want me to be," and strive to be adaptable and flexible enough to always maintain favor.

These core beliefs and early childhood experiences will play out in our adult relationships until we learn to integrate and heal them. The biggest challenge for individuals with Venus opposite Saturn is to realize that they have been living their lives and basing their self-worth and self-esteem on other people's standards and not their own. As soon as these individuals become aware of this and choose to restructure their Validation Checklists, they experience a monumental shift in their lives. When they reconnect with their own, personal standards of integrity, they experience an immediate deposit in their Validation Account.

Venus quincunx Saturn

Venus quincunx Saturn also indicates that our standards for validation are not our own. The difference between Venus opposite Saturn and Venus quincunx Saturn is that when Venus is opposite Saturn, we at least have the ability to live up to the standards we believe our parents expect of us. We may never actually get there, but we know on a core level that it is possible. With Venus quincunx Saturn, however, we don't believe we can ever live up to those standards because we're never quite clear about what they are or what's expected of us. The result is a sense of learned helplessness. We believe that it's not even worth the effort to try to gain the approval and love of our parents (or our partners in relationship).

With the quincunx, however, we're rarely even able to make the connection between our Validation Checklists and our experience of our relationship to our parents. Quincunxes are so difficult to resolve that we quickly create the belief that they are entirely beyond our control. It's just the way the world is. The key to healing Venus quincunx Saturn is the same as with Venus opposite Saturn: adjusting our Validation Checklists so that they reflect our own, personal standards of integrity. The challenge is that with Venus quincunx Saturn we often feel so disempowered that we aren't even aware that we have a choice.

Uranus Aspects: Expecting Rejection, Fearing Abandonment, and Assuming Unreliability

Uranus is the planet that deals with the unexpected—Uranus exists to make sure that there isn't too much structure in the world, and its primary purpose is to disrupt the boundaries and limitations of Saturn. Uranus is unpredictable, unexpected, a flash of lightening. When looking at relationship patterns, Uranus aspects relate to issues of rejection and abandonment.

Uranus energy is the most unpredictable and unreliable energy out there. We can't define it, we can't anticipate it, and it comes and goes in an instant, leaving chaos in its wake.

Everyone experiences rejection at some point in his or her life. We've all felt abandoned, and we've all been in situations where other people did not do what they said they would. These are not pleasant experiences, but most of us survive and move on. For some of us, however, these experiences are all too common, and qualify as specific relationship and life patterns. While our inner parents and egos will be involved in these patterns, they didn't specifically create them. Our egos are trying to protect us from forces beyond our control.

All of our issues relating to abandonment and rejection come from our earliest childhood experiences. As infants, we are entirely dependent on our parents for our survival. We need our parents to be there for us when we need them, and we expect that our parents will be able to anticipate our needs. Our earliest experiences form our core impressions of the world. If our needs aren't met as infants, we expect that our needs will *never* be met. If we felt rejected as infants, this is what we'll look for during the course of our lives. And of course, since we look for rejection and abandonment, we find it. If our needs were met some of the time but not all of the time, we may create a belief that the world is full of unreliable people. Since we've never had the experience of someone staying with us long enough to meet our needs completely, we expect everyone we depend on to abandon us eventually.

We can change each and every one of these beliefs and alter our programming, but we first have to identify our patterns.

Moon-Uranus Aspects

All Moon-Uranus aspects are related to a common pattern: "Safe Doesn't Feel Safe." Even though individual aspects may also manifest as other patterns and issues with rejection and abandonment, anytime an individual has a strong Moon-Uranus connection, it's important to consider that they may not know what actual safety feels like. On the most fundamental level, safe equals familiar. Any situation, no matter how fundamentally threatening or unsafe it is, can become associated with safety because it is familiar and we know from past experience that we can and will survive it.

The challenge with this pattern is that when these individuals experience true safety in relationship—for example, when they are in relationship with someone who is reliable, trustworthy, respects their boundaries and has no intention of rejecting or abandoning them, the relationship feels incredibly threatening because it's entirely unfamiliar territory. The first challenge when addressing any Moon-Uranus patterns is to create a new, healthy definition of what is actually safe.

Moon-Uranus aspects represent an experience of our fundamental emotional, safety and survival needs not being met as infants. As a result of this experience, we created an expectation that our needs would never be met.

Moon conjunct Uranus

Individuals with the Moon conjunct Uranus have a fundamental expectation that their safety and survival needs will not be met in any kind of consistent or reliable manner. Because conjunctions lack any kind of perspective, individuals with the Moon conjunct Uranus automatically internalize this energy and unconsciously believe that the fact that their needs are not being met is their own fault. The modality of the conjunction will determine the most likely rationale behind this false belief. If the conjunction is in a Cardinal sign, the belief is that their needs will not be met because there is something wrong with who they are as an individual. This energy frequently manifests as a deeply-rooted sense of shame. If the conjunction is in a Fixed sign, the "Not _____ Enough" pattern usually steps in, creating the belief that they don't deserve to have their needs met, or that they need to earn the right to have their needs met. Finally, if the conjunction is in a Mutable sign, the belief is that they must become someone or something else in order to have their needs met.

The real issue, of course, is not that they can't rely on other people, but that the individuals with Moon conjunct Uranus fear that they can't rely on *themselves*. Individuals with the Moon conjunct Uranus must learn how to trust themselves, and they begin to do this by becoming aware of all of the promises and commitments they make to themselves, and consciously choosing to honor each and every one of them. Often these individuals are shocked when they notice how many promises they make to themselves that they break or ignore. As they begin to live up to their commitments to themselves (and to others), they will begin to experience other people as being more reliable and trustworthy as well.

Ironically, individuals with the Moon conjunct Uranus are the least likely to realize that they do, in fact, have issues about rejection and abandonment. Because this energy is so internalized, they often avoid the pain of abandonment or rejection by being the ones who reject and abandon others. Therefore, the Moon conjunct Uranus is far more likely to be associated with the "Abandon Ship" pattern than with the "Everybody Leaves" pattern.

Moon sextile Uranus

The only Moon-Uranus aspect that does not automatically indicate safety issues is Moon sextile Uranus. Sextiles are passive aspects that must be activated consciously to have any effect. In general, sextiles represent opportunities. As such, Moon sextile Uranus represents an opportunity to respond to unexpected and unanticipated circumstances in ways that may maintain the balance in one's Safety Account.

Moon square Uranus

The Moon square Uranus tends to play out in relationships, and often relates to issues and patterns of betrayal. This is a different pattern then with the Moon opposite Uranus, which also plays out entirely in relationships. With the Moon opposite Uranus, the individual expects that their partners will be unreliable and untrustworthy from the start. With the Moon square Uranus, on the other hand, there is more opportunity for the rejection or betrayal to be a complete surprise. Each time these individuals create a new relationship (and this applies to every relationship, not just to romantic relationships), they are prepared to trust their partners; they expect that each new relationship will be different from every old relationship. Until they learn to address their own issues with rejection, betrayal and abandonment, however, they will experience these lessons through relationships, and they will continue to create situations where their partners in relationship can betray their trust once again.

Uncomfortable as squares can be, they are actually very useful and powerful aspects. Squares want to be resolved through direct, concrete, creative action. The lesson with the Moon square Uranus is often one that is meant to make us aware of the areas in our lives where we overlook details and avoid taking personal responsibility, thereby creating opportunities for us to experience betrayal and abandonment. The message and lesson of the Moon square Uranus is similar to that of an old Arabian proverb: "Trust in Allah, but tie your camel."

Moon trine Uranus

The main challenge for individuals with the Moon trine Uranus is that "Safe Doesn't Feel Safe." The flowing energy of the trine to Uranus means that these individuals are extremely familiar with the exciting, unpredictable, unusual and innovative energy of Uranus. While these individuals are often very adventurous, taking risks that would set off most other people's safety alarms, they are also apt to feel trapped and threatened when confronted with healthy boundaries or sustained emotional connections. These individuals are often the most capable when faced with a crisis. The challenge is that they are so capable in crisis situations because those are the times when they feel the most safe. Eventually, they will have to learn how to feel safe without a crisis—because until they learn this, they will unconsciously create crisis after crisis in their lives.

Moon opposite Uranus

Individuals with the Moon opposite Uranus specifically experience issues with rejection and abandonment in their one-to-one relationships. The root cause (and strategy for change) is the same as with the Moon conjunct Uranus. The difference is that while individuals with the Moon conjunct Uranus internalize the energy, individuals with the Moon opposite Uranus externalize the energy and project it entirely on their partners in relationship. The biggest challenge for these individuals is to realize that it's *never* about the other person. They are unable to trust or rely on other people because on a fundamental level, they betray their own trust in themselves by not honoring their commitments to themselves and by stepping out of integrity in their own lives. They simply project these issues on their partners in relationship.

Experiences of abandonment and rejection are far more obvious with the Moon opposite Uranus, and this aspect is strongly associated with the patterns, "Everybody Leaves," "Trust Me," and "Abandon Ship." (See Chapter 5 of *The Relationship Handbook*.)

Moon quincunx Uranus

The Moon quincunx Uranus is one of the most challenging energies to experience because it emphasizes the random, unpredictable energy of Uranus. With every other Moon-Uranus aspect, we can learn to anticipate when Uranus will strike and make choices that will (theoretically) protect us from the pain of rejection or abandonment. With the Moon quincunx Uranus, however, the energy of Uranus always takes us by surprise. With the Moon quincunx Uranus, the "Safe Doesn't Feel Safe" pattern will always be evident. The "Everybody Leaves" pattern is also frequently involved. Individuals with the Moon quincunx Uranus often spend most of their lives in low-grade fight-or-flight mode, and have the most difficulty in maintaining a healthy balance in their Safety Accounts. It is, of course, possible to overcome this pattern and learn to maintain a healthy balance in one's Safety Account, but the process is apt to be lengthy because of the learned helplessness that so often accompanies the quincunx aspect.

Venus-Uranus Aspects

Venus-Uranus aspects create challenges in meeting our Validation Needs. Because of the nature of Uranus, the issue is less that our Validation Needs can't be met and more that we don't expect that our Validation Needs will be met on a consistent or ongoing basis. These patterns create the greatest challenges in romantic relationships. Even though we need to feel validated in every relationship, the only relationships where we actually expect our Validation Needs to be met in a significant way are our romantic relationships.

Venus-Uranus aspects can manifest as any of the rejection and abandonment patterns in Chapter 5 of *The Relationship Handbook*. The difference between these patterns when Venus is involved as opposed to the Moon is that the Moon-Uranus patterns create challenges in every area of our lives because they interfere with our ability to feel safe, while the Venus-Uranus patterns are limited to our relationships. Venus-Uranus aspects can even create an experience of "Safe Doesn't Feel Safe," at least when it comes to Safety Needs in the context of relationships. The fear of being rejected or of not being validated can drain our Safety Accounts, making us feel unsafe. The experience of not feeling safe because we expect that our Validation Needs won't be met becomes familiar, and so when our Validation Needs are actually being met, it feels unfamiliar, and therefore makes us feel unsafe (which, in turn, makes it difficult to experience our Validation Needs being met).

With Venus-Uranus aspects, only the "hard" aspects indicate challenges feeling loved and validated in relationship.

Venus conjunct Uranus

Individuals with Venus conjunct Uranus internalize the issues of rejection and abandonment. On some level, they must address the false belief that something is wrong with them. When the conjunction is in a Cardinal sign, the belief is that who they are is fundamentally flawed in some way. When the conjunction is in a Fixed sign, the belief is that they are somehow not ____ enough and are not worthy of being validated or loved. When the conjunction is in a Mutable sign, the belief is that they must change or somehow hide their true nature in order to be able to receive love and validation. This aspect often manifests a form of the "Can't Take a Complement" pattern that is usually associated with Venus-Saturn aspects. Because these individuals believe on a fundamental level that they are unlovable, they will instinctively deflect, devalue or simply ignore any attempts to make significant or enduring deposits in their Validation Accounts.

The most important lesson for individuals with Venus conjunct Uranus is to learn to accept, love and express their authentic selves. Once they heal the underlying false belief and begin to love themselves, they will be able to receive love and validation from others as well.

Venus sextile Uranus

As with the Moon sextile Uranus, Venus sextile Uranus is a passive aspect that indicates the opportunity to respond to the unusual and the unexpected. Venus sextile Uranus can indicate an adventurous streak that occasionally manifests in relationships (although not necessarily or exclusively in the bedroom).

Venus square Uranus

As with the Moon square Uranus, Venus square Uranus is most often associated with issues of trust and betrayal in our relationships. When Venus square Uranus plays out in romantic relationships, it is frequently associated with issues of infidelity and unfaithfulness. Either we will attract partners who eventually cheat on us, or we will be the ones who are unfaithful in the relationship. Venus square Uranus is often tied to the question of monogamy vs. fidelity. Individuals with Venus square Uranus may need a certain amount of variety in their romantic relationships. This need, however, is often difficult to accept or discuss because our model for romantic relationships assumes monogamy, and our society and culture in general, even today, tends to be very repressed sexually. The lesson of Venus square Uranus is often to be willing to build a new model for romantic relationships—one that may break with the traditional social conventions, but one that will allow the freedom to maintain *fidelity* in the relationship while meeting our Validation Needs fully and honestly.

Venus trine Uranus

When Venus is trine Uranus, the unpredictable, adventurous streak seen with Venus sextile Uranus is always visible. This energy can certainly result in intense, unconventional, and especially brief romantic relationships. The reason that this aspect is not linked to a challenging pattern is that individuals with Venus trine Uranus actually enjoy these types of encounters. Above all, they need variety and freedom in order to meet their Validation Needs. Because this energy works for them (even though it may not work at all for their partners!) it does not usually present a challenge.

Venus opposite Uranus

Individuals with Venus opposite Uranus often experience difficulties in their romantic relationships because they attract partners who are fundamentally incapable of meeting their Validation Needs on a continuous, reliable basis. The most dramatic example of this is women who fall in love with married men. Less extreme examples can be found in patterns of attracting partners who are untrustworthy, unreliable, and generally unavailable. Really, the only attraction to these partners is that the time actually spent together is usually electric. The underlying fear, of course, is that we will never be loved the way we want to because (Cardinal) there is something wrong with who we are, (Fixed) we're not worthy or not _____ enough, or (Mutable) we have to change our nature in order to be loved. The core issue (and strategy for change) is the same as with Venus conjunct Uranus, except with Venus opposite Uranus, we externalize it and project it on our partners. Once we believe that we deserve to be loved, we will begin to attract partners who are capable of loving us.

Venus quincunx Uranus

With Venus quincunx Uranus, the interruptions in receiving love and validation seem to come out of nowhere. It's very easy to attribute these interruptions to fate, timing and circumstances otherwise entirely outside of our control—or of the control of our soon-to-be-former romantic partner (see the "Brief Encounters" pattern in Chapter 5 of *The Relationship Handbook*). The reality, of course, is that we are responsible for creating and attracting these interruptions. This is a very big concept to accept, however. It's much easier to believe that the Universe simply conspires to interfere with our ability to feel loved and validated than it is to accept that our belief that the Universe interferes with our ability to feel loved and validated is what creates those experiences in the first place.

Neptune Aspects: Bad Boundaries and Hopeless Romantics

All Neptune aspects indicate issues with poor boundaries. Neptune energy dissolves all structure and makes discrimination quite difficult. Neptune is, of course, associated with fantasy, glamour, illusion, as well as with escapism and disillusionment.

"Boundaries" is a term that I've used a number of times, and now it's time to define it. Boundaries are lines, either literal or metaphorical, that define space. We each need a certain amount of personal space. When we have a good sense of boundaries, we have a healthy awareness of our space—how much we need, how much we fill, and when it begins to overlap and interact with other people's space. In different relationships, we will share different amounts of space with our partners. We create connections and bridges between our physical bodies, our emotional bodies, and our spiritual bodies. It's important for each of us to become more aware of our personal space, and how we share space and energy with others.

Inevitably, we will experience boundary violations—we will step inside someone else's space where we weren't specifically invited and where we're not particularly welcome. Often, other people will make us aware that we have crossed a boundary with them, and we will simply step back. We may not have recognized that we crossed a line, but now that we're aware of that line, we can contain ourselves so that we don't cross that line again.

We're constantly negotiating our boundaries in all of our relationships. We adjust how strong of an emotional connection we want to experience with others. We choose how much of our personal and private life we want to share. And, of course, we only allow a select few individuals to become physically intimate with us.

Generally when I talk about "bad boundaries," I'm referring to the energetic boundaries. If we have bad boundaries, we may not be aware that we're exceeding our own space and invading someone else's space. We may also find it difficult to define our own boundaries so that we can protect our own emotional, mental, spiritual and physical bodies from unwelcome contact. We may not be consciously aware of when other people have crossed our boundaries and invaded our space. Of course, bad boundaries operate on many levels.

Boundaries are entirely a product of our human experience in the third dimension. The truth is that we are all connected to every other person on the planet and to every single part of all of creation. We are part of all that is; all separation and all boundaries are illusions. Our egos, however, *need* boundaries, and our boundaries are how we define and maintain our sense of individuality. Relationships are about forming connections, but they're also about maintaining a clear awareness of where one person ends and the other person begins.

Moon-Neptune Aspects

Moon-Neptune aspects relate to poor energetic and emotional boundaries. Because of these poor energetic boundaries, individuals with Moon-Neptune aspects are often extremely sensitive, although they may not recognize this consciously. Moon-Neptune aspects are often related to "psychic" abilities, which are nothing more than increased sensitivity to the subtler forms of emotional and mental energy. Individuals with Moon-Neptune aspects are also likely to have allergies, because allergies result from an inability to keep toxins and irritants out of our bodies, and ultimately are a result of poor boundaries. In the most extreme cases, repeated boundary violations can result in severe, chronic auto-immune disorders where the body perceives that it is always under attack and the immune system begins to fight off everything, including the healthy, natural cells in the body.

Moon-Neptune aspects are almost always associated with the "Safe Doesn't Feel Safe" pattern. Healthy emotional and energetic boundaries are usually entirely unfamiliar to individuals with Moon-Neptune aspects, and therefore feel threatening.

Moon conjunct Neptune

Individuals with the Moon conjunct Neptune have the most difficulty with boundaries because they will tend to internalize and identify with the energy of Neptune. On the one hand, they have an instinctive and intuitive appreciation for the truth that there is no separation and that everyone and everything is an integral part of All That Is. On the other hand, while having our human experience, we need to pretend that we are separate individuals, maintaining our own boundaries and respecting the boundaries of others. It's not that individuals with the Moon conjunct Neptune don't respect boundaries, it's that they're almost entirely unaware of them.

Individuals with the Moon conjunct Neptune are perhaps the most susceptible to the adverse health effects of poor boundaries. They are apt to suffer from a variety of allergies, and their immune systems may be chronically overworked, making them more prone to colds, flu and infections. It is essential that these individuals learn to become aware of how their bodies are responding to their environments. This is the only way that they can begin to notice their energetic boundaries: Every time they experience a boundary violation, they will have some kind of a physical reaction to it. As they become more aware of where their boundaries actually are and begin to strengthen them, they will notice dramatic improvements in their physical health and well-being. Even so, it is essential that these individuals make an extra effort to supplement, nourish and strengthen their immune system.

Moon sextile Neptune

The Moon sextile Neptune is the least challenging Moon-Neptune aspect, and the only one that does not specifically indicate ongoing issues with poor boundaries. The Moon sextile Neptune indicates an opportunity to become sensitive to the subtle energies, but it does not represent a continuous flow of energy. We must consider other aspects to the Moon, however, before dismissing the Moon sextile Neptune out of hand. If the Moon receives stressful aspects from Mars, Saturn, Uranus, Chiron or Pluto, it is entirely possible that the Moon sextile Neptune may become the escape route of choice for the individual: a way to avoid the painful energies of the other aspects. If this is the case, the Moon sextile Neptune can present challenges—especially "Safe Doesn't Feel Safe"—because healthy boundaries mean facing the pain of the hard aspects to the Moon.

Moon square Neptune

Individuals with the Moon square Neptune are especially aware of boundary violations, at least when it comes to other people violating their boundaries. Initially, they may be frustrated that they seem to attract so many people into their lives who invade their space, forge intimacy immediately, and otherwise extend themselves where they are not wanted nor invited. The challenge is to recognize that these individuals are only able to violate our boundaries because we allow them to do so. Individuals with the Moon square Neptune often need to learn how to assert their boundaries in order to maintain a healthy balance in their Safety Account. Although less common, these individuals may also need to explore where they themselves are violating other people's boundaries and become more skillful at noticing and respecting these boundaries with others.

Moon trine Neptune

The Moon trine Neptune is another particularly challenging aspect. Because trines represent a constant, continuous, uninterrupted flow of energy, individuals with the Moon trine Neptune are perhaps the most sensitive of all. This heightened sensitivity can lead to emotional information overload, a condition that ultimately drains the Safety Account. At the same time, this energy is so familiar that "Safe Doesn't Feel Safe," and healthy, authentic and appropriate boundaries may feel incredibly threatening. Not only do individuals with the Moon trine Neptune need to be careful of other people violating their boundaries and invading their space, but they must become acutely aware of their own energy, so that they can learn to respect other people's boundaries. Individuals with the Moon trine Neptune are perhaps the least aware of boundary violations, and the most prone to unknowingly invading other people's space energetically and emotionally.

The Moon trine Neptune is also a very challenging aspect because it represents an easy and automatic escape route whenever these individuals feel the least bit unsafe or uncomfortable. These individuals are far more likely to look to fantasy, alcohol or drugs in unhealthy ways in order to avoid or escape the pain and discomfort of their experience of reality. It is not ethical or even remotely accurate to assume that an individual with the Moon trine Neptune has some kind of substance abuse problem. However, every individual with the Moon trine Neptune will have some kind of escape—some Neptune-oriented behavior that takes them out of their life when things become too unsafe or too uncomfortable. It could be television, movies, dance, art, music, video games, science fiction or fantasy, and it does not necessarily represent a problem. Everyone needs an escape once in a while. With the Moon trine Neptune, however, there is an increased danger that the escape behavior could become an addiction, and individuals with the Moon trine Neptune simply need to be aware of this fact.

Moon opposite Neptune

Individuals with the Moon opposite Neptune are the most prone to the "I Am You and You Are Me and He is She and We Are All Together" pattern where they seek to merge completely with their partners in relationship and even feel incomplete without a partner. These individuals may have reasonably healthy energetic and emotional boundaries in their daily life, and in social situations; however, when it comes to one-to-one relationships, especially romantic relationships, they have no boundaries whatsoever. The challenge is that once they enter into a one-to-one relationship, the vast majority of the balance in their Safety Accounts depends on maintaining the intense, merged, emotional and energetic connections with their partner.

Any interruptions or fluctuations in this connection will immediately make them feel critically unsafe, and can result in unskillful, codependent, or otherwise regrettable behavior.

Individuals with the Moon opposite Neptune must learn how to maintain an awareness of their own individual identity while in relationship, and more importantly, must learn that they are always responsible for meeting their own Safety Needs on their own.

Moon quincunx Neptune

Individuals with the Moon quincunx Neptune are the least aware of their lack of boundaries. They often feel that they are able to maintain healthy boundaries in their relationships, and they are the least likely to find healthy boundaries threatening. It's only when we include allergies, illness and immune system deficiencies in the definition of poor boundaries that the patterns become evident. Quincunxes always seem to come out of left field, and we have the greatest difficulty in understanding the cause-and-effect relationship to these aspects.

Individuals with the Moon quincunx Neptune do experience regular boundary violations in their relationships. When the level of boundary violations reaches a critical mass, they will often experience some kind of health crisis—allergies, illness, or worse. The result of this health crisis is that the individuals have to isolate themselves, effectively removing themselves from the boundary violations. The challenge in healing this pattern is that it seems entirely far-fetched to make the connection between emotional and energetic connections in relationships and periodic immune system malfunctions. It takes time for energetic issues to manifest in the physical, so there is always a delay between experiencing the boundary violation and manifesting the physical symptom.

Often, the only thing these individuals can do is to assume that they are suffering boundary violations on an ongoing basis and create a space and time each and every day when they can be alone, so that they can recover from these boundary violations. By taking a few minutes each day for meditation, or even just for personal time, they can reduce the need for their bodies to create a health crisis that forces them to retreat to a safe space.

Venus-Neptune Aspects

Venus-Neptune aspects primarily play out in the context of romantic relationships. The general theme has to do with the difference between fantasy and reality. With Venus-Neptune aspects, the items on our Validation Checklist are often imbalanced and unreasonable. We expect our partners to live up to our fantasies and when they fall short of our ideals, we feel disillusioned, disappointed, and invalidated. Venus-Neptune aspects are almost always looking for the "Happily Ever After" without realizing that there is no such thing. We are perfectly capable of creating and experiencing the kind of romantic relationship we have always dreamed of, but it is a continuous process of creation. Happily Ever After takes a lot of work, and this truth often comes as a nasty shock to individuals with Venus-Neptune aspects. The gift, however, is that because these individuals have such a clear vision of their ideal romantic relationship, once they are willing to work at it, they are usually able to manifest it in their lives.

With Venus-Neptune aspects, only the "hard" aspects create specific challenges. Individuals with Venus and Neptune in more harmonious aspect may in fact be "Hopeless Romantics," but for the most part, they will enjoy this energy. Even when they are single and longing for their perfect romantic partner, they are often sustained by the dream and remain steadfastly optimistic about what tomorrow may bring.

Venus conjunct Neptune

Individuals with Venus conjunct Neptune are usually very aware—not to mention proud of the fact—that they are "Hopeless Romantics." While their personal idea of romance may not specifically correspond with the traditional Hollywood romances, they long for a partner with whom they can share their vision for the perfect romantic experience. The most significant challenge with this aspect is that, as already noted, not everyone shares the same definition of romance. It is particularly important that individuals with Venus conjunct Neptune find romantic partners who speak the same Validation language as they do. Individuals with Venus conjunct Neptune have a particularly difficult time learning other Validation languages because Neptune's influence makes it difficult to notice that not everyone shares their views on love and romance.

Venus sextile Neptune

Venus sextile Neptune is by far the mildest of the Venus-Neptune aspects. Whether they admit to it or not, individuals with Venus sextile Neptune are inevitably closet romantics at heart. What they consider to be romantic will depend entirely on the contents of their Validation Checklist, of course—candlelight, flowers and soft music may, in fact, leave them cold. Rest assured, however, that within each individual with Venus sextile Neptune resides a true romantic, waiting for the opportunity to shine.

Venus square Neptune

Individuals with Venus square Neptune often experience this aspect in patterns of deception or betrayal in their romantic relationships. These betrayals are different than the betrayals that come from Uranus aspects. With Uranus aspects, we are surprised by the true nature of our partners.

With Venus square Neptune, we see, but refuse to accept the truth of who our partners are, and instead remained attached to the fantasy for as long as possible.

These individuals are also prone to the "Someday My Prince(ss) Will Come" pattern, and with Venus square Neptune this pattern creates significant challenges. The square between Venus and Neptune is a call to take constructive action and actively build the kind of romantic relationship that we dream about. This process, however, requires that we first accept responsibility for having created our past, less successful romantic relationships. We must also be willing to explore our Validation Checklists and our Marriage Blueprints (covered in Chapter 6 of *The Relationship Handbook*, and Chapter 9 of this handbook) to make sure that our expectations are reasonable, our boundaries are healthy, and our dreams are attainable.

Venus trine Neptune

Individuals with Venus trine Neptune frequently believe that their ideal romantic partner is out there, waiting for them, and that they are destined to meet, fall in love and ride off into the sunset just like in the movies. These individuals also experience the "Some Day My Prince(ss) Will Come" pattern. However, this does not always represent a problem for them. Many individuals with Venus trine Neptune are so happy with the dream of their perfect romance that when they do attract a romantic partner and fall in love, that partner automatically becomes their ideal mate. The pink fog of Venus trine Neptune smooths over any imperfections that might interfere with the blissful enjoyment of their romantic dream.

Other individuals with Venus trine Neptune aren't quite as fortunate. They may find it far more difficult to attract a suitable partner. One reason for this is that trines are inherently lazy, and Venus trine Neptune firmly believes that romance just happens, and shouldn't take any effort on our part. Sometimes, individuals with Venus trine Neptune have to be willing to do the work—both internally and externally—in order to clear the path so that they can create and experience their ideal romantic relationship.

Venus opposite Neptune

Individuals with Venus opposite Neptune have the greatest difficulty reconciling the fantasy of their romantic partners with the reality of them. Since oppositions always play out in one-to-one relationships, every time individuals with Venus opposite Neptune enter into a relationship, they project Neptune on their partner. These individuals often fall in love at the drop of a hat, swooning over the perfect dream they see in their new paramour. How well they handle the disappointment when the reality begins to shine through depends entirely on how much they are able to love themselves. The ideal that these individuals see in their partners is nothing more than a projection of their own Divine Selves.

The less accepting these individuals are of their own value, worth and beauty, the more likely they are to look for a partner to "complete them." And the more they need a partner to complete them, the more painful the experience will be when they discover that their perfect prince or princess is, in fact, just another frog. On the other hand, the more accepting these individuals are of their own divine nature, the more they are able to meet their own Validation Needs, and the easier the transition will be from the fantasy to the reality of the relationship.

Venus quincunx Neptune

Individuals with Venus quincunx Neptune also tend to idealize their romantic partners. The difference is that they are frequently drawn to partners who do not in any way return their interest. In its mildest manifestation this is the aspect of unrequited love. In more extreme cases, it is the aspect of the restraining order. When these individuals do find romantic partners, their partners often fall short of their ideal and fail to meet their Validation Needs in a lasting or satisfying manner. The core belief with Venus quincunx Neptune is that we can never get what we truly want; our reality can never match up with our dreams.

The real issue with Venus quincunx Neptune often has to do with the nature of our dreams—because the things that we believe that we want may not, in fact, be in alignment with the things that truly matter to us in terms of meeting our Validation Needs. One way that this aspect can manifest is that we internalize the dominant societal standards of beauty, even though we may not particularly agree with them. We feel obligated to pursue romantic partners that embody this standard of beauty. Often, we become obsessed with these standards of beauty because we believe that we, ourselves, do not measure up to them. The lesson and the challenge is to overcome our social conditioning and embrace our true values. When we learn to appreciate true beauty in others, we discover it in ourselves. When we adjust our expectations and the items on our Validation Checklist, we find it remarkably easy to feel validated on a personal level. The compromise is that we simply have to give up our need to be validated by society.

Pluto Aspects: Power, Control, Manipulation and Abuse

Pluto is the most destructive force in the universe—a force that completely obliterates all that is not true and eternal. Since our egos are neither true nor eternal, existing as they do to help us maintain the illusion of separation from all of creation while we have our human experiences, our egos find Pluto energy very threatening. When we encounter Pluto issues, we first confront our fear of being destroyed by forces that we cannot control, and then we confront our ego's desperate need to try to exercise control to prevent the inevitable.

All fear comes from the ego, and ultimately all fear is directly related to the ego's fear of being destroyed. The more we identify with the ego, the more fear we will experience—specifically, the more afraid we will be of death.

Death is inevitable. It is part of the cycle of life, and our higher selves understand that death is always followed by a birth or rebirth. Death is nothing more than a transition. Remember, we are eternal, multi-dimensional beings, aspects of the Creator and integral parts of All That Is. The ego doesn't understand this, however, and since the ego is not eternal, when it dies, it's apt to stay dead.

Death is unavoidable and entirely beyond our control. This doesn't stop the ego from trying to control it, of course, and this is where we encounter issues of power, control, manipulation and abuse. Our egos can devote a great deal of energy attempting to hold off the inevitable. The bigger the opponent, the more power, influence and control we need in order to believe that we can survive. The more we fear, the more we feel the need to control.

In every case, when we're confronted with the fear of death, all we can do is surrender. Death is inevitable, and nothing we can do will change that fact. Rather than devoting all of our energy and focus trying to maintain an illusion of control, we can simply let go and channel that energy towards more positive and productive avenues. We simply need to remember the truth that nothing that is real can die. The only things that can die are our illusions.

While it's all well and good to know that all that's being destroyed are our illusions, it often takes a lifetime to gain this level of perspective on Pluto aspects. Meanwhile, most of our experiences of Pluto energy tend to be very unpleasant.

Pluto and Abuse

Before considering the possible manifestations of Pluto aspecting the Moon or Venus, I want to take a moment and remind you of some extremely important considerations.

First of all, astrology does not and cannot predict behavior. We cannot look at an aspect or configuration in a person's chart and know how they experienced the energy, or how it played out in their lives. Astrology operates on the symbolic level: We can understand the energy, the spiritual urge, and even the flavor of an experience, but we cannot know the details of what actually happened just by looking at the chart.

Just because a person has a Moon-Pluto aspect or a Venus-Pluto aspect it does not mean that he or she suffered any kind of abuse as a child, sexual, emotional, physical or otherwise. *It is entirely unethical and completely irresponsible to bring up the subject of abuse with a client. The client must be the one who initiates the discussion and sets the boundaries for what, how, and how much they care to discuss.*

Again, not every individual with a Moon-Pluto or Venus-Pluto aspect experienced abuse as a child. That being said, every client I have ever had who revealed to me that they had, in fact, suffered some kind of abuse as a child, has had one of these aspects. When looking at the possibility of abuse in the chart, it's also important to only consider aspects that are *applying*. Separating aspects represent events that have already occurred—pre-natal experiences, if you will. Applying aspects, however, represent events and energies that are about to happen.

I had a client who insisted that he had almost no memories of his childhood. That, of course, is a warning bell in and of itself. Anytime we "forget" large parts of our lives, it's usually because we're repressing painful or traumatic experiences. He had a prominent and very tight Moon-Pluto aspect in his chart, which also involved his 10th house. I had an extremely strong suspicion that the reason that he had no memories of his childhood was that he had been severely emotionally abused by his mother (10th house).

Of course, I don't know this for certain because I dropped the subject, and I wouldn't dream of confronting him with my theories. I also did not suggest that he attempt to recover his repressed memories. He did not come to me asking for help with this issue—it simply came up when talking about his parents. More importantly, I am not a psychiatrist or a psychologist, and it would have been unethical for me to probe any deeper, even if he seemed receptive to it. Had he expressed any concern at his lack of memory of his childhood, I would have referred him to a licensed, trained therapist, qualified to assist him.

I know that many astrologers are, in fact, also licensed therapists who would be qualified to explore any repressed memories or childhood traumas. Even so, I still urge caution. Even if there was abuse, it's not possible to determine the exact nature of the abuse from the chart because *astrology does not predict behavior.*

Moon-Pluto Aspects

Individuals with the Moon in any aspect to Pluto are always aware of the dynamic of power and control in any situation. Understanding who has the power, and endeavoring to own as much power as possible is an instinctive survival mechanism. For individuals with a Moon-Pluto aspect, safety is fundamentally associated with power, although power itself may not be safe to them.

Moon conjunct Pluto

Individuals with the Moon conjunct Pluto tap into the tremendous power of Pluto on a very personal level. These individuals are extremely powerful, although it is far more accurate to say that these individuals are vessels and conduits for power and change. The challenges of this aspect come from a fear that the power will inevitably destroy us, or that we will not be able to channel or direct the power consciously. The more we attempt to deny or repress the power, however, the more it controls us. The most common pattern associated with this aspect is "You Wouldn't Like Me When I'm Angry," detailed in Chapter 5 of *The Relationship Handbook.* The only strategy for dealing with Pluto energy is complete and utter surrender. As soon as we give up our attempts to control or change the energy of Pluto, we allow Pluto to express through us, helping us to reconnect with our true, authentic selves, who are, in fact, infinitely powerful.

Ultimately, the fear is that if we ever truly acknowledged or expressed our needs, the vast intensity of our needs would destroy us—and probably take a good part of the neighborhood with us, to boot. As a result, this aspect also carries the "Safe Doesn't Feel Safe" pattern, and one of the lessons is to create a new, healthy definition of safety.

Moon sextile Pluto

The Moon sextile Pluto is the only Moon-Pluto aspect that does not automatically represent issues with power, control, manipulation or abuse. Individuals with the Moon sextile Pluto have the opportunity to tap into vast resources of power; however, if they do not choose to do so, all they are left with is the potential. These individuals are usually able to maintain a reasonable balance in their Safety Accounts in times of intense crisis or transformation because they can tap into the power and energy of Pluto at will.

Moon square Pluto

Individuals with the Moon square Pluto are perhaps the most sensitive to being controlled or manipulated by other people. The fear of being manipulated or controlled, of course, usually results in manipulative and controlling behavior. Safety for individuals with the Moon square Pluto involves believing that they are in complete control of any given situation and are strong enough and powerful enough to defend themselves against any attempts to change, manipulate, or control them. This constant state of alert, of course, is entirely an ego-based solution, and therefore the actual result is that these individuals never quite feel safe because they are always worried that they may lose power or control of the situation. When associated with abuse, the Moon square Pluto relates to acts of violence and physical abuse as well as emotional abuse.

Moon trine Pluto

In many cases, individuals with the Moon trine Pluto are very comfortable with power and influence, and feel that change, transformation, and intensity are fundamentally important to both their emotional connections and to their general sense of safety. These individuals may be a bit *too* intense for some of their partners, particularly partners who have their own issues with Pluto. For the most part, however, they will attract partners who are specifically drawn to their power and consciously seek the transformational energy of Pluto.

The Moon trine Pluto can also be associated with abuse, and relates to beliefs and behavior patterns where we only have two options: to be abused, or to be the abuser.

When associated with abuse, the Moon trine Pluto symbolizes ongoing abuse because there is nothing to interrupt or interfere with the flow of energy between the Moon and Pluto. Moon-Pluto abuse is not necessarily or even primarily sexual. The abuse is more likely physical, emotional, or psychological in nature. Often the abuse is ongoing because the non-abusing parent (or parents, if the abuse is perpetrated by another person) turns a blind eye to the situation, denies it completely or otherwise is complicit in the abuse by refusing to acknowledge or stop it.

Remember: *trines are not nice!*

Moon opposite Pluto

Individuals with the Moon opposite Pluto usually project their issues with power and control onto other individuals and experience them through their one-to-one relationships. This pattern can create significant barriers to emotional intimacy, because the fear is that if we get too close to our partners in relationship, we will be consumed, destroyed or otherwise transformed against our will. This belief is usually well supported because these individuals rarely have a comfortable middle ground in terms of emotional and energetic connections. Either they keep their distance, or they merge too quickly and too powerfully.

These individuals may also be acutely aware of the dynamic of power in each of their relationships, pressing their advantage when they feel that they have the power, and pulling away when they feel that the power resides with their partners.

Moon quincunx Pluto

The quincunx aspect once again creates some of the most significant challenges. Individuals with the Moon quincunx Pluto often believe that their survival is at the mercy and whim of powerful forces entirely beyond their control. These forces will often masquerade as the government, the economy, the corporation, or the administration. Sometimes they can simply manifest as the firm conviction that the Universe just has it in for them, personally. The experience is one of learned helplessness and minimal safety, and the belief is that we will never have absolute power or control over our own life. The lesson is to learn to accept that our experience of reality, no matter how real it seems, is in fact entirely our own creation. Our thoughts and beliefs create our reality. All we need to do to reclaim our power and take control of our own destiny is to be willing to believe that we can, in fact, do this. Once we accept that the only power the outside forces have over us is the power that we give them, we can reclaim this power for ourselves.

Venus-Pluto Aspects

The issues with power and control that come from Venus-Pluto aspects tend to show up the most noticeably in romantic relationships, although the dynamic itself frequently originates from our relationships with our parents. Individuals with Venus-Pluto aspects often have an abundance of beauty, money, or both. Whether this is a blessing or a curse depends on the nature of the Venus-Pluto aspect. When Venus-Pluto aspects are associated with abuse, the abuse is usually sexual.

Venus conjunct Pluto

Individuals with Venus conjunct Pluto are often powerfully charismatic. Whether or not they meet the conventional standards of physical beauty, they possess something compelling that commands attention and recognition. In some, it is monumental sex appeal; in others, it is that elusive "star quality." In a culture that seems to believe that being famous is one of the highest achievements one can attain, it's often difficult to imagine how having Venus conjunct Pluto could be a challenge. For many individuals, however, it is.

While Venus conjunct Pluto can mean that other people will be drawn to us and will make frequent and significant deposits in our Validation Accounts, these deposits are often related to only one aspect of who we are. Individuals with Venus conjunct Pluto—especially when on the Ascendant or in the 1st house—are often blessed with exceptional physical beauty. While these individuals live their lives being validated for their beauty, they often begin to fear that they are only appreciated for their appearance. It becomes increasingly difficult to know if people love them for who they truly are, or only love them because of their looks. As Venus conjunct Pluto can also relate to considerable financial resources, very wealthy individuals also suffer from this pattern. The Venus conjunct Pluto energy is what draws others to them, but it's difficult to know if their partners in relationship are ever able to see past the money or the beauty to know and validate the real person within.

Venus sextile Pluto

Individuals with Venus sextile Pluto have the best of both worlds. Because sextiles represent opportunities, these individuals have the ability to tap into the powerful energy of Pluto when they choose to, and let it lie dormant when it doesn't serve them.

Venus square Pluto

Individuals with Venus square Pluto have the greatest struggle with why other people are attracted to them. They long to be noticed and appreciated for their authentic selves, and often fear that other people love them only for their external selves—because of their beauty, their wealth, or both. The irony is that once these individuals are willing to accept that their power is a fact of life for them, they can choose to build on it, directing this energy in creative, constructive and supportive ways. Their beauty and/or wealth may capture the attention of the world, but once the world is paying attention, these individuals can demonstrate that they are much more than just a pretty face or a blank check.

Venus trine Pluto

Individuals with Venus trine Pluto, perhaps even more than individuals with Venus conjunct Pluto, are faced with the challenges of remarkable physical beauty and powerful sex appeal. This energy can be extremely difficult to experience, and particularly while growing up, can be especially threatening. Many individuals with Venus trine Pluto unconsciously choose to hide their sex appeal and protect themselves from unwanted advances, often by gaining weight. In a society where "thin" is almost synonymous with "sexy," "fat" is the best defense against unwanted advances.

Individuals with Venus trine Pluto will frequently use sex as a weapon, manipulating other people so that they can maintain the power and control in the relationship. This behavior is often unconscious, and almost always used defensively. It is a survival skill learned through childhood and adolescence to help deflect the unwanted attention of others.

When associated with abuse, Venus trine Pluto is usually related to sexual abuse. As with the Moon trine Pluto, Venus trine Pluto indicates that the abuse was ongoing, and that there was no interference, no protection, and no way to stop it.

Venus opposite Pluto

Individuals with Venus opposite Pluto have the most direct and conscious experience of the dynamic of power and control in their relationships. Until they learn how to integrate this energy, every one-to-one relationship is apt to be a continuous power struggle for these individuals. In every relationship, one person will be destroyed or otherwise transformed by the energy of Pluto, and the battle is over which person it will be. This aspect is frequently associated with the "My Way or the Highway" pattern from Chapter 5 of *The Relationship Handbook.* Individuals with Venus opposite Pluto often feel the need to control exactly how other people can meet their Validation Needs. This, of course, makes it difficult for these individuals to feel truly loved and validated in their relationships. As always where Pluto is concerned, the only solution is to surrender completely and know that all that Pluto ever destroys are our illusions.

Venus quincunx Pluto

The core belief of Venus quincunx Pluto is often that we must change, compromise or otherwise become something else in order to feel loved and validated. The struggle is often between our own, authentic standards of beauty and value and our internalized perceptions of what society accepts as beautiful or valuable. These individuals must learn how to discover their authentic selves, and learn to love themselves unconditionally for who they truly are, even as they resist the pressure from society that tells them that they must become something else in order to be happy and successful.

Chiron Aspects

Chiron is an asteroid that was discovered in 1977 that generally receives some special attention from astrologers—even astrologers who routinely ignore the other asteroids. One of the key things that makes Chiron exceptional is that rather than being a part of the asteroid belt between Mars and Jupiter (where the rest of the asteroids reside), Chiron's orbit takes it from inside the orbit of Saturn to outside the orbit of Uranus. Chiron is thought to be the key that allows us to bridge the gap between the inner planets and the outer planets: the go-between that will help us to move onto the next stage of human evolution as we learn to integrate and personalize the energy of the outer planets.

The myth and archetype of Chiron is that of the wounded healer. Chiron was a centaur, renowned as one of the finest physicians in the world. He was accidentally hit by one of Hercules' poisoned arrows, and suffered a wound that he was not capable of healing. Because he was immortal, he lived in agony, able to heal others, but never able to heal his own wound. Elsewhere, Prometheus was being punished for bringing fire to humans, sentenced by Zeus to be chained to a rock and to have his liver eaten each day until some immortal agreed to give up his or her immortality and take his place. Chiron agreed to do so, freeing Prometheus. Zeus took pity on Chiron, and freed him from his pain, transforming him into the constellation of Sagittarius.

Whenever we look at Chiron, the key issues relate to our core spiritual wound and our attempts to heal that wound. Through facing our Chiron wounds, we are able to connect with our true spirituality, transcend the pain and discover how we are able to heal others. Chiron also relates not only to our own wounds but also to how we in turn wound others.

While I certainly agree that Chiron is a very important planet to observe and that it is strongly connected to our spiritual growth, I'm not yet convinced how Chiron aspects actually manifest in the chart with respect to relationships.

In transit, even though Chiron is often associated with healing crises both on the physical and the spiritual levels, Chiron seems to act to the outer planets in the same way that Mercury does to the inner planets: It carries the light of the outer planets and determines when and where that light will enter our physical bodies. In and of itself, I'm inclined to consider Chiron to be a rather neutral energy.

Working from the core myth and archetypes of Chiron, Chiron aspects would tend to relate to issues of our core wounds and the ways that we both are forced to confront these wounds, and the ways that we wound others. I'm inclined to dismiss trines and sextiles to Chiron but I do feel that it's important to notice conjunctions and hard aspects between Chiron and the Moon or Venus. I tend to view these as indications that until the individual has truly acknowledged and worked through his or her Chiron wound, their relationships will trigger that wound, and they in turn are likely to inflict that wound on their partners. The nature of the wound is determined by Chiron's position by sign and house in the natal chart.

Any Chiron aspect to the Moon or Venus is significant when there is also an aspect between one of the other outer planets to the Moon or Venus. Because Chiron carries the light of the outer planets, this kind of double aspect indicates that the core issues related to the outer planet aspects will be even more significant and prominent for the individual.

❖7❖
Relationship Wants: The Descendant and The Vertex

We've pretty much covered what we *need* in relationships through looking at the Moon and Venus in the chart. Now we need to address what it is that we *want* in relationships. What are we attracted to? What are the qualities that we seek out in others?

Well, on the most basic level, we want the things that we don't have (or that we don't think that we have). Much of our drive towards relationships is a desire to complete ourselves, to find someone who will help to balance and fulfill our sense of identity. Remember though, that relationships are about mirroring and projecting, and the qualities that we most admire or dislike in others are in fact parts of ourselves that we haven't accepted and integrated yet.

The 7th house and the Descendant are the sections of the chart that are reserved for our one-to-one relationships. The Descendant is the point opposite the Ascendant. In many ways, it's the back door to our chart. We focus so much of our energy through the mask of our Ascendant, as this is how we generally venture out into the world and interact with others, that we often pay little attention to our Descendant, even though this is where we receive visitors. The Ascendant is how we go out into the world of relationships, but the Descendant is where we attract others; the sign of the Descendant shows the qualities that we find the most attractive in our relationship partners.

Understanding the Angles

The angles of the chart are very different from the planets in the chart. First of all, the planets are physical bodies, while the angles are simply sensitive points in the chart. This is an exceptionally important distinction. The planets, as physical bodies, have "lives" of their own, as it were; they are actors, and as such, they *act*—the planets do things; they represent urges and needs; they make things happen in our lives. The Angles, on the other hand, are entirely passive; they don't make anything happen.

The best way of looking at the angles is to consider that they're doors that connect us with the outside world. The only way for us to connect with the rest of the world, to express our needs and feelings and to connect with others, is through one of the doors in our chart. The four main doors are the Ascendant (our "front door" where we go out into the world, and where people we don't know well come to visit us); the Descendant (our "back door" used by friends and relationships and those closer to us); the Midheaven (the door to the roof where we are the most visible to the world in general); and the *Immum Coeli* (the secret door to our private family room in the basement, accessible to only our closest family members).

These doors each have their own "filters" associated with them, that both govern what we expect to find when we open the door and that affect how we appear to others when they relate to us through that door. A person with Gemini rising expects that every time he or she opens their front door that they will find something new and interesting that they will want to explore. A person with Cancer rising, on the other hand, hopes that when they open their front door they'll find someone waiting for them with a bowl of chicken soup and a teddy bear.

One thing that we must realize when we work with the angles is that we're *always* working with two points at the same time. It's not possible to look at the Ascendant without also considering the Descendant. Planets that conjunct the Ascendant also oppose the Descendant. Planets trine the Ascendant are sextile the Descendant at the same time.

Since the Angles don't shape the energy of the signs in the way that the physical bodies do, when considering the angles, we're looking at a *sign axis* rather than an individual sign. The angles always involve an opposition aspect and a need to find balance between the two opposing signs. The Ascendant/Descendant axis is the axis of one-to-one relationships. The Ascendant is our front door: it's how we go out into the world as individuals. More to the point, it's how we actively relate to others in relationships. The Descendant is our back door: it's where we receive individuals who know us well; it's how we expect to receive others in relationship and how we expect others to relate to us.

The biggest challenge when it comes to the Ascendant/Descendant axis is that we have the most difficulty gaining a sense of true perspective with these angles. We're so close to the Ascendant (and to the 1st house) that we're not really able to view it for what it is: a filter; a set of expectations and preconceptions that conditions and shapes how we express ourselves in the world. On the other hand, we're able to see the Descendant and the 7th house so clearly, and we're so used to experiencing these energies through our relationships, that we tend to assume that they're not really a part of ourselves. We believe that they belong to others and that we don't really have any influence over them.

Many of our relationship lessons have to do with becoming aware of our conditioning and our expectations in our relationships—with how we relate to others and how we expect them to relate to us. When we recognize that we do indeed have complete control over these aspects of our lives, we can begin to identify and change our relationship patterns.

The Aries-Libra Axis

The Aries-Libra axis, like the Ascendant/Descendant axis, is the axis of one-to-one relationships. The core lesson of the Aries-Libra axis is to learn how to balance our need for individual expression with our need to relate to other individuals.

Aries Ascendant/Libra Descendant

Individuals with Aries rising approach the world in a focused, self-centered, direct, and active manner. They tend to be rather action-oriented, and often appear to be somewhat overbearing and impulsive to others. They perceive the world to be a place where they must make their own path, and go into relationships with a significant amount of self-confidence and self-assurance. These individuals have Libra on the Descendant, and will tend to be attracted to partners who are more focused on relationship, and on maintaining balance and harmony. What the Aries rising individual needs to learn through their relationships is how to compromise somewhat, and to take their partner (and other individuals) into account before making decisions and acting on them. The more focused on the self-centered Aries energy the individual is, the more likely they will be to attract Libra energy partners who will tend to deny their own individuality in relationships and automatically capitulate to the Aries person's desires. These relationships will ultimately be frustrating and unsatisfying. As the Aries rising person learns how to take others more into account, he or she will start to attract Libra relationships with individuals who understand how to maintain their individuality while still finding a balanced relationship.

Libra Ascendant/Aries Descendant

Individuals with Libra on the Ascendant approach the world looking for balance and harmony, diplomacy and justice. These individuals are extremely concerned about how their actions impact and affect others. They perceive the world to be a fundamentally beautiful and peaceful place, but they are also exceedingly aware of how precarious that balance is, and that they must be willing to accept responsibility for their actions. These individuals have Aries on the Descendant, and will tend to attract partners who are more focused on themselves, and who are able to take direct and impulsive action without worrying about the repercussions of their actions. The Libra rising individual will learn how to express their individual identity fully in relationships through their connections with Aries type individuals. The hardest lesson for Libra to accept is that in order to experience true balance, they must not only acknowledge the needs and desires of others, but they must also express and pursue their own needs and desires and individuality at the same time. The more afraid the Libra rising individual is of expressing their identity, the more demanding, overbearing and controlling their Aries relationships will be. When they get tired of having their partner make all of the decisions in the relationship and learn how to stand up for their own needs, they will begin to attract more self-aware Aries relationships with individuals who are both very sure of their own identity and also willing to accept and support their partner's needs at the same time.

The Taurus-Scorpio Axis

The Taurus-Scorpio axis relates to the natural cycles of growth and destruction, death and rebirth. The core lesson of this axis is to learn to accept the cycles of nature, to know when to build and support things, and to accept when it's time to tear them down and let them die to make way for new growth.

Taurus Ascendant/Scorpio Descendant

Individuals with Taurus on the Ascendant approach the world looking for stability and comfort, and steady growth in all things. These individuals are very concerned with maintaining the status quo, and appear very resistant to significant changes in their lives. They have a great deal of patience and stamina and perceive the world as a place where things will grow and mature given enough time and care. These individuals have Scorpio on the Descendant and will tend to attract partners who are more concerned with change, with tearing down the physical structures and boundaries, and with connecting with the core, turbulent emotional center of everything they encounter. The Taurus rising person will learn how to accept the necessity of change and transformation through their relationships with Scorpio individuals. The more resistant to change and addicted to the physical the Taurus Ascendant individual is, the more they will attract partners who embody the inevitable and uncontrollable destructive forces associated with Scorpio. Through their relationships, they will be forced to give up their attachment to the physical, as emotional crises force them to accept fundamental changes in their lives.

Scorpio Ascendant/Taurus Descendant

Individuals with Scorpio on the Ascendant approach the world with a very focused and passionate point of view. They will not be satisfied until they have discovered what lies beneath the surface—until they have discovered the hidden, unconscious, powerful, and transformational emotional core that we all ultimately share. These individuals go out into the world looking to connect with others on a very deep, personal, private level, and expect to encounter and experience the change and fundamental instability that comes with operating on such a strongly emotional foundation. These individuals have Taurus on the Descendant and will tend to attract partners who are far more stable, grounded, and oriented towards the physical plane. The Scorpio rising person will learn how to accept the necessity of stability and growth through their relationships with Taurus individuals. The more ungrounded the Scorpio rising person is, the more resistant and stubborn their Taurus partners will tend to be. The Taurus partners will refuse to buy into the Scorpio maelstrom, which will tend to frustrate the Scorpio rising individual who needs to form emotional connections in relationships. Ultimately, as the Scorpio individual learns how to slow down and accept that sometimes stability is necessary, they will be able to connect with their Taurus partners on an emotional level and find that their Taurus partners are more willing to contain and support the emotional energy of Scorpio.

THE GEMINI-SAGITTARIUS AXIS

The Gemini-Sagittarius axis is the axis of the mind. Gemini relates to the lower mind—the part of us that is focused on details and on logic (the left brain), while Sagittarius relates to the higher mind—the part of us that looks for unifying concepts and philosophies and operates in a more abstract realm (the right brain). The core lesson of this axis is to learn to balance and integrate the lower and higher minds.

Gemini Ascendant/Sagittarius Descendant

Individuals with Gemini on the Ascendant approach the world with a great deal of curiosity and fascination. They expect that the world will be a wondrous place for them to explore and enjoy, and they generally have a very innocent and playful attitude. These individuals are drawn to the details and are particularly fascinated with exploring the nature of duality and making connections between opposing concepts. These individuals have Sagittarius on the

Descendant and will tend to attract partners who take a broader view of the world and are more concerned with discovering the unifying Truth of all things, rather than with spending time on more mundane concepts. The Gemini rising person will learn how to unite their experiences and perceptions and put them in a larger context through their relationships with Sagittarius individuals. More importantly, perhaps, the Sagittarius relationships will help teach the Gemini rising individuals how to focus and expand their naturally limited attention spans.

Sagittarius Ascendant/Gemini Descendant

Individuals with Sagittarius on the Ascendant approach the world in search of the Truth. They have a single-minded and very focused point of view, a core philosophy that guides them. They expect that everything that they encounter and experience will fit neatly into this belief system, and that they will enjoy absolute freedom and autonomy as they set out on their quest. These individuals have Gemini on the Descendant, and will tend to attract partners who are more concerned with day-to-day experiences and with exploring the details of the world than they are with discovering a unifying philosophy. The Sagittarius rising individual may have a tendency to focus too much on the abstract; they certainly have a higher mind understanding of the world, but they must learn how to integrate some of the Gemini focus on individual details to discover how to communicate this Truth and how to find practical applications for it in daily life. They will learn these skills through their relationships with Gemini individuals.

THE CANCER-CAPRCORN AXIS

The Cancer-Capricorn axis is the axis of group responsibility. The core lessons of this axis relate to learning how to meet our needs on an individual basis and how to help others to meet their needs. This axis also relates to the issues of personal responsibility and group responsibility.

Cancer Ascendant/Capricorn Descendant

Individuals with Cancer on the Ascendant perceive the world to be a place where their core survival needs may not be met. They take a fundamentally emotional view of their interactions with others and therefore tend to be very sensitive both on an emotional and on a spiritual level. Cancer energy wants to nurture and to be nurtured; however, the dynamic of the Cancer Ascendant/Capricorn Descendant can play out in two apparently different ways. Cancer energy is always worried about meeting its emotional needs. The two extreme ways that this energy can express are as an individual who is completely dependent on others and unable to take care of him or herself at all; or as an individual who is completely obsessed with nurturing and caring for others and making sure that their needs are met, while at the same time, never letting others take care of them. With Capricorn on the Descendant, these individuals will be attracted to partners who embody the responsible, structured, mature energy of Capricorn. On the one hand, they could attract a partner who will embody the protector/caretaker role and who will be more than happy to assume all responsibility for the relationship. On the other hand, they could attract a partner who has such strong boundaries and is so self-reliant that they are unable to accept help, love, or emotional connections. In either case, the Capricorn relationships will teach the Cancer rising person about energetic and emotional boundaries, and about taking personal responsibility for themselves (and about not taking on inappropriate responsibilities for others).

Capricorn Ascendant/Cancer Descendant

Individuals with Capricorn on the Ascendant perceive the world as a structured, ordered place where established rules, traditions, and social structures must be accepted and supported. These individuals are very concerned about doing their part and about taking personal responsibility, as well as taking responsibility for contributing back to society. They tend to take a very grounded, practical view of the world, and appear focused on obtaining a certain level of achievement and social status. These individuals have Cancer on the Descendant, and will be attracted to partners who are more open to the emotional and nurturing aspects of life. Here again, there are two different ways that this dynamic can play out, depending on which aspects of the Capricorn/Cancer axis the Capricorn rising individual is working on integrating. One option is that they may find that they attract partners who seem unable to take care of themselves. While playing the role of the protector and provider is at least initially appealing to the Capricorn rising individual, ultimately, he or she will have to learn that each one of us must take personal responsibility for our lives. Alternatively, they may attract partners who are openly and actively nurturing, and who will force them to learn to open up emotionally and to allow others to support them from time to time. This is one of the big lessons for Capricorn: that being truly responsible means being willing to accept help from others.

THE LEO-AQUARIUS AXIS

The Leo-Aquarius axis is the axis of unconditional love. The core lessons of this axis relate to learning how to balance the individual love from the heart (Leo) and the compassionate and universal love from the head (Aquarius).

Leo Ascendant/Aquarius Descendant

Individuals with Leo on the Ascendant perceive the world as a warm, expansive, and above all, fun place. These individuals want to shine; they want to share their unique gifts with others, and, of course, they want to be recognized for their gifts and their contributions. They are particularly concerned with expressing their true selves in one-to-one relationships, and very much enjoy giving of themselves to others. These individuals have Aquarius on the Descendant, and will be attracted to partners who are more objective, and, quite frankly, not especially comfortable with being the center of attention. On a very fundamental level, Leo is the most comfortable when it is the center of attention. Since Aquarius energy is entirely focused on the group dynamic and tends to shy away from individual recognition, what draws Leo rising individuals to their Aquarius partners is the fact that the Aquarius partners make an excellent audience and will rarely ask to share the spotlight. Of course, not every Aquarius partner will be so accommodating, and ultimately, that's not the real attraction. Aquarius partners will help the Leo rising individuals to become aware of appropriate boundaries. Essentially, Aquarius partners can teach the Leo rising individuals when it's time to get off the stage and give someone else a chance—an awareness that is especially important to the integration of Leo energy.

Aquarius Ascendant/Leo Descendant

Individuals with Aquarius on the Ascendant perceive the world as a logical, ordered place with occasionally rigid social structures. Within these structures, however, these individuals understand that they can enjoy total freedom of expression. More importantly, though, individuals with Aquarius rising are very aware of their individual contributions to society. They expect the rules to apply to everyone equally and fairly. These individuals have Leo on the Descendant, and will be attracted to partners who are primarily interested in the integrity of the group because they love an audience—they need other people to appreciate and validate them for how wonderful, loving, special and gifted they are as individuals. These Leo partners serve to teach the Aquarius Rising individuals how to find true balance in their relationship as individuals to society. The shift is from the belief that everyone is equal to the belief that everyone is equally special, and therefore deserves a certain amount of individual attention and validation for their unique gifts. The Aquarius rising individuals will tend to attract partners who demand to be noticed and appreciated, until eventually they themselves learn that they deserve some attention, too.

The Virgo-Pisces Axis

The Virgo-Pisces axis is the axis of matter and spirit. The core lessons of this axis relate to learning how to balance the needs of the physical with the needs of the spiritual—how to bring spirit into matter and matter into spirit and ultimately discover that the two in fact are one and the same and can not be separated.

Virgo Ascendant/Pisces Descendant

Individuals with Virgo on the Ascendant are often very detail-oriented in their approach to the world. They care about the little things, and look for ways to be of service through helping to improve and perfect the physical. When they enter into relationship, they are meticulous, and often overly analytical They notice every last detail of their partners, and pride themselves on being able to discriminate between individuals who will enrich their lives and individuals who will not. These individuals have Pisces on their Descendant. If the Descendant is our back door where people come to relate to us, Pisces on the Descendant is an eight-foot-tall, three-foot-deep reinforced steel door with a state-of-the art security system. Nothing short of a nuclear missile can get through this door without the proper access codes. Unfortunately, this door is standing alone in a field, and there are no walls around it. Individuals with Pisces on the Descendant are frequently unaware of the fact that they have exceptionally poor boundaries in relationship. In fact, not only do they have exceptionally poor boundaries, but they also will tend to be attracted to people who have exceptionally poor boundaries, too. Virgo rising individuals find the spiritual, compassionate energy of Pisces both powerfully attractive and exceptionally frustrating. Ultimately, it is entirely possible to be meticulous in the physical and enjoy powerful spiritual connections. However, until the Virgo rising individuals learn to embrace their own spiritual nature, they will tend to attract partners who enjoy tremendous spiritual energy and have little or no ability to navigate the physical realities of life.

Pisces Ascendant/Virgo Descendant

Individuals with Pisces rising are always aware of the spiritual truth of the world. They know on a fundamental level that all separation is illusion and that the truth is that we are all connected and integral parts of All That Is. These individuals are often very sensitive to other people's energy, and are usually very aware of other people's emotional states. This, of course, is simply a nice way of saying that individuals with Pisces rising have especially poor boundaries in their relationships. These individuals have Virgo on the Descendant, and will tend to attract partners who are grounded, practical, and often entirely focused on the material plane. It's very easy for Pisces rising individuals to let their Virgo partners assume responsibility for the tedious physical tasks. This will not work out well in the long run, however, because as long as the Virgo partners are taking on full responsibility for the physical, they will cut themselves off from the spiritual, and the Pisces rising individuals need spiritual connections with their partners. The lesson, of course, is for the Pisces rising individuals to recognize that they can, in fact, maintain a connection to the spiritual truth of the Universe, and still learn to pay enough attention to the physical details to live comfortably in the world.

The Vertex

The Descendant represents the qualities that we're attracted to in others on a conscious level; we also have unconscious desires, however, and we can learn more about these by looking at another angle in the chart: the Vertex.

The Vertex is the point of intersection of the Prime Vertical and the Ecliptic in the West. Fortunately, unless you're studying for the NCGR Level II exam, the only thing you need to know about finding the Vertex is that Solar Fire™ calculates it just fine.

The Vertex is a rather interesting point in the chart. For the most part, it seems to function as a kind of an unconscious Descendant—it certainly indicates very strong attractions in relationships, and these relationships usually feel rather "karmic" or "fated." The Vertex is not a point to be trifled with, however. I know of one astrologer (although I can't remember his name) who believes that the Vertex acts as a sort of release valve in the chart—when our emotional pressure builds up and we can't contain it anymore, the Vertex is the point where we tend to explode. Considering that I've seen the Vertex be extremely central in too many event charts involving fires, explosions and rather extraordinary disasters, this is certainly food for thought.

The primary difference between how we interpret the signs of the Descendant and the Vertex is to remember that the Vertex represents unconscious and subconscious desires, while the Descendant represents more above-board and straightforward desires.

The Vertex, being an angle, does have a complimentary angle in the chart: the Anti-Vertex. Although the Anti-Vertex would theoretically operate as a kind of an unconscious Ascendant, I don't know any astrologers who work with this point in the chart. We need to be aware of it, however, because the Vertex, like the Descendant, is really about the balance of two opposing signs. We're far less conscious of how we work with our Anti-Vertex, however, than we are with how we work with our Ascendants. This makes it more challenging to discover and work with the balance point of the Vertex/Anti-Vertex angle.

Vertex in Aries

Individuals with the Vertex in Aries will be unconsciously attracted to partners who are impulsive, passionate, forthright, and self-motivated. Aries individuals do not lose themselves in other people, and they rarely seem to compromise their desires or ideals. In relationships Aries energy can often take control (Aries is a natural leader, because Aries does not like to follow others).

Vertex in Taurus

Individuals with the Vertex in Taurus are unconsciously attracted to partners who embody the grounded, practical, stable, physical and sensual energy of Taurus. Taurus individuals don't like surprises; rather, they want their lives to proceed in a predictable, regular fashion and to demonstrate slow and steady growth. Taurus individuals tend to be very creative, and are primarily drawn to the kinds of artistic expressions that don't involve the use of tools or instruments—gardening, pottery, crafts, singing—these are all very Taurus-like ways of expressing creativity and beauty. Taurus individuals are also extremely physical and sensual; they express affection through physical closeness, touching and holding, and through gifts and other tangible examples of their love.

Vertex in Gemini

Individuals with the Vertex in Gemini are unconsciously attracted to the social, playful, flexible, curious, and quick energy of Gemini. Gemini is a Mutable Air sign, and by far the fastest moving, most adaptable, and most socially oriented energy in the zodiac. These individuals are likely to be drawn to people who have quick minds and sharp wits, and who are always open to trying new experiences and to meeting new people.

Vertex in Cancer

Cancer is a Cardinal Water sign and is motivated to express identity through reaching out and forming deep and nurturing emotional connections with other individuals. Individuals with the Vertex in Cancer are unconsciously attracted to this energy, and will seek out deep and nurturing emotional bonds in their relationships, whether they are aware of this tendency or not. One of the lessons with Cancer energy is to find the balance between self-reliance and being open to receiving the love and support of others. Cancer energy can sometimes become overly needy and clinging, fearing that it will not be able to survive without the emotional support of others. Cancer energy can also express in the opposite extreme, as someone who is constantly nurturing and protecting others, who is always giving, but who never allows others to give in return (for fear that others wouldn't return their love). When Cancer energy operates on an unconscious level through the Vertex, it can manifest as a mothering type energy in relationships, either in the role of caretaker or of the person being cared for. Mothering can quickly become smothering, particularly when we are not consciously aware of this dynamic in relationships.

Vertex in Leo

Individuals with the Vertex in Leo are unconsciously attracted to partners who are warm, open, and generous, but who also demand a great deal of attention and recognition. Leo individuals tend to be very energetic and creative, and intensely charismatic, but they also seek almost constant reassurance and validation from others.

Vertex in Virgo

Individuals with the Vertex in Virgo are attracted to partners who embody the precise, analytical, practical, service-oriented energy of Virgo. Virgo individuals are always concerned with the details, with making sure that all of the little things have been taken care of. This is simply an extension of Virgo's fundamental need as a Mutable Earth sign to heal, complete, and perfect the physical and material world. Virgo individuals tend to live very much in their heads. Virgo is ruled by Mercury, the planet of thought, language and communication, and Virgo individuals tend to try and apply logic, reason, and analysis to everything, including their relationships. Virgo energy is rather ambivalent about emotional connections. On the one hand, as an Earth sign, Virgo is generally comfortable with experiencing emotional connections; on the other hand, however, being as mentally-oriented as it is, Virgo is just as comfortable keeping things on the more mental/social realm usually associated with the Air signs.

Vertex in Libra

Individuals with the Vertex in Libra are unconsciously drawn to individuals who are very relationship-oriented and who seem to desire a balanced, harmonious, calm, and diplomatic relationship. Libra energy is all about finding balance in one-to-one relationships. Being a Cardinal sign, Libra seeks an expression of identity, and being an Air sign, Libra is concerned with the mental and social realm. This means that individuals who embody Libra energy tend to be very uncomfortable with deeper emotions and primarily concerned with making sure that everything appears to be calm, beautiful, and balanced on the surface.

Vertex in Scorpio

Individuals with the Vertex in Scorpio are unconsciously attracted to partners who embody the intense, transformational, deep and penetrating energy of Scorpio, the Fixed Water sign. Scorpio energy is focused on exploring the unconscious, the dark, unseen parts of our psyche. Scorpio seeks to merge with another individual on a soul level, experiencing an intense and total emotional connection on all levels, such that at least for a moment, all sense of individual identity is lost.

Vertex in Sagittarius

Individuals with the Vertex in Sagittarius are unconsciously attracted to partners who are fun-loving and freedom-loving; who go after the things that they want, defend the things that they believe in, and live by a code of honesty and truth above all else. Sagittarius energy is about the quest for Truth and the search to understand our relationship as individuals to the rest of the universe. Sagittarius individuals tend to be very outgoing and enthusiastic (after all, Sagittarius is ruled by Jupiter, the planet of expansion and growth). They also require absolute trust and honesty in all of their relationships. As a Fire sign, Sagittarius enjoys intense emotional experiences, primarily joy and anger; however, Sagittarius is a Mutable Fire sign, and therefore is exceptionally changeable and will not tend to sustain emotions for long periods of time.

Vertex in Capricorn

Individuals with the Vertex in Capricorn are unconsciously attracted to partners who embody the practical, ambitious, structured, mature, and responsible energy of Capricorn. Capricorn individuals are oriented towards the physical plane, but their primary motivation (as Capricorn is a Cardinal Earth sign) is to create a physical and tangible expression of their unique individual identities. Capricorn individuals are ruled by Saturn, and tend to be very concerned with boundaries, structures, rules and regulations. They are very motivated to accomplish and achieve their goals; however, they are also very focused on making sure that they follow the accepted procedure and stay within the appropriate boundaries while they work towards their goals. Capricorn individuals are generally very responsible and mature, and they tend to want to take control of a given situation. One of the unconscious desires of the Vertex in Capricorn is often to find a partner who will be the adult in the relationship—a partner who will take care of us, who will be responsible, will provide for us, and who will in many ways, be a parent to us, setting boundaries and limitations for our behavior and maintaining the structure and integrity of the relationship.

Vertex in Aquarius

Individuals with the Vertex in Aquarius are unconsciously attracted to partners who have a very strong sense of group identity, and who value their ideals and personal freedom above all else. Aquarius individuals have clearly-defined personal goals and objectives, and are able to adhere independently to their ideals.

Vertex in Pisces

Individuals with the Vertex in Pisces are unconsciously attracted to partners who embody the spiritual, compassionate, sensitive energy of Pisces. Pisces individuals are notorious for having poor energetic boundaries. However, these individuals are also especially loving, supportive, and healing.

What Else Do We Want? What Else Do We Lack?

When we begin to compare charts in Chapter 11, we'll be looking at how the two charts interact on an elemental level. It's always a good idea, though to have a good overview and context for the individual charts first, not only because it helps us to put the whole relationship question into the proper perspective, but also because it can point out other energies that an individual may tend to attract into their lives.

Any time we encounter a person with a strong imbalance of elements or modalities, we're looking at a potential relationship pattern. A person with very little Air in his or her chart may find that they are drawn to partners who have a very strong emphasis in Air—again, the reason being that when we perceive a lack in ourselves, we'll try and fill it any way we can. The essential thing to remember here is that we *all* have *all 12 signs in our charts!* If we have no planets in a given sign or element, that doesn't mean that we can't experience or express that energy. What it means is that we don't tend to encounter that energy in ourselves on a regular basis, and so we will find that energy very attractive in others. We always place a higher value on the things that we believe we lack, and we admire, desire, or envy these things in others.

Planets in the 7th and 8th Houses

It's important to consider planets in the 7th and 8th houses of the natal chart because these are the houses that "belong" to other people. The 7th house is the guest room, and the 8th house is where our guests keep all of their stuff. We're likely to project any planets we have in the 7th and 8th houses onto others, and to experience them primarily through one-to-one relationships.

Depending on the planets involved, a strong 7th and 8th house emphasis in a person's chart can sometimes indicate a pattern of giving away one's power to others in relationships. This is particularly important to consider with the Sun, Moon and/or Mars in the 7th house.

Individuals with Saturn in the 7th house may have a tendency to project their Saturn issues on their partners. Instead of taking personal responsibility for their actions, they project Saturn (and their sense of responsibilities and boundaries) on their partners and expect their partners in relationship to set the boundaries and bear the burden of responsibility. As a result, they will tend to attract partners who embody the authoritative/restrictive/limiting energy of Saturn.

8
Putting It Together Part 1: Relationship Needs and Wants

Let's take some time to apply what we've covered so far. Throughout this handbook, we'll be looking at the relationship patterns of three famous couples, and we'll be following a standard template that will help us to create a synthesized understanding of their individual charts, as well as how they are likely to interact with and relate to each other.

In this chapter, we'll continue our exploration of our first celebrity couple, Elizabeth Taylor and Richard Burton. We covered the overview of Taylor's chart in Chapter 3, so we'll pick up where we left off and look at her relationship needs.

Elizabeh Taylor (Continued)

Part 5: Relationship Needs

Taylor's Safety Needs are ruled by her Moon in Scorpio and her Validation Needs are ruled by her Venus in Aries.

Safety Needs

Taylor's Moon is in Scorpio (in Fall and Peregrine). Her Scorpio Moon needs deep, transformational emotional connections, but at the same time is terribly threatened by these experiences. She's likely to be extremely sensitive emotionally thanks to her Moon in a partile square to Jupiter (and a particularly nasty one, at that, since not only are her Moon and Jupiter square each other (at the same degree), they're also contra-parallel each other, which reinforces the difficult energies of this aspect). Her Moon is applying Trine to Pluto, so her emotional needs are apt to be very intense, and potentially quite destructive. In short, the powerful, deep emotional and spiritual connections that she needs in order to feel safe are the things that also make her feel the most threatened.

Validation Needs

Taylor's Venus is in Aries (in Detriment and Peregrine). In relationships, what makes her feel the most validated is when she can do whatever she wants to do whenever she wants to do it, without having to worry about whether or not her partner feels the same way.

Part 6: Can Needs Be Met?
Feeling Safe and Feeling Validated (Moon and Venus Connection)

Taylor's Moon and Venus are quincunx each other. This presents one of the most difficult challenges in terms of feeling safe and validated at the same time. The choice here is to either feel safe or loved. Because the Moon and Venus have nothing in common by element or modality, it's very difficult to meet both sets of needs simultaneously. Because her Moon and Venus are quincunx each other, anytime she makes a deposit in her Safety Account, it eventually makes a withdrawal from her Validation Account, and any deposit in her Validation Account will result in a withdrawal from her Safety Account. The challenge is that there never seems to be a direct, logical connection between the deposits in one account and the withdrawals from the other, because quincunxes always seem to come out of left field.

General Safety Issues

The first issue as far as Taylor's Safety Needs go is that she may not know what it means to truly feel safe. The Moon in Scorpio always has some core safety issues, because the emotional connections the Moon in Scorpio needs to experience are fundamentally threatening (at least to our egos) because they require us to surrender our sense of individuality. In order for her to experience these connections, she will need to build up a very strong basis of trust. Trust, however, is a key issue, as we will see, because of strong Uranus aspects to both her Moon and Venus.

Another red flag when it comes to feeling safe is the fact that her Moon is opposite Chiron. I don't yet have enough of a handle on Chiron to provide detailed and specific interpretations. However, there is no question in my mind that Chiron should never be ignored. Unsatisfying as it is, whenever Chiron is involved, it always seems to indicate some kind of core wound. Could Chiron be linked to Taylor's chronic health issues? Perhaps. I truly believe that there is much more to Chiron than just a "wound." However, all I currently have to offer is the standard Chiron keyword interpretation.

Uranus Aspects: Issues with Rejection, Abandonment and Unreliability

With her Moon quincunx Uranus, trust is a key issue for Taylor, as this aspect indicates likely issues with rejection and abandonment. The quincunx aspect is particularly difficult, because it often seems to come out of nowhere. With more direct aspects where the two planets have something in common by either element or modality (squares and oppositions, for example), we can at least identify the situations when we can expect the unexpected disruptions of Uranus; eventually, we can see at least some kind of cause and effect relationship. With the quincunx, however, the disruptions seem entirely random. This can create a state of learned helplessness. In the most extreme cases, we may give up on the idea of ever feeling safe because we can't even carve out a small area of our lives that operates predictably.

Also, we see issues with rejection and abandonment because Uranus is conjunct Venus (with a six *minute* orb). The pattern here is most likely one in which *she* does the rejecting and abandoning (before her partners have a chance to reject or abandon her). Because Venus is trine Jupiter (while her Moon is square Jupiter), she's more likely to give precedence to her romantic and Validation Needs than she is to her emotional and Safety Needs, always hoping that she'll find a relationship that will work for her, and always encountering the same safety concerns when she's in relationship. Not only does she have an easier time meeting her Validation Needs, but she also can maintain the illusion that she is in control—she's the one that is making the decisions, and she's the one ending the relationships, not the other way around.

Both the Moon and Venus are ruled by her Mars in Pisces, part of a Pisces Stellium. The emphasis of Pisces energy in her chart, combined with her mutable Ascendant/Descendant indicate very poor emotional and energetic boundaries when it comes to relationships.

Pluto Aspects: Power Control, Manipulation and Abuse

Taylor's Moon is applying trine to Pluto (5 degrees), and her Venus is applying square to Pluto (3 degrees). The Moon trine Pluto indicates safety issues related to power and control, although it's difficult to pinpoint what those issues are. We can probably guess that she either feels safe when she is the one in control of the situation, or when she is clearly at the mercy of someone else. The trine between the Moon and Pluto means the power and intensity is always present.

The square between Venus and Pluto indicates more active issues with power and control. Knowing Taylor as we do, we can look at this aspect as the belief that beauty is power. While her beauty made her a star, adored by millions, it also may have created some negative beliefs. She may always wonder if people love and appreciate her for who she truly is, or if they are only validating her because of her physical beauty. This could make it very difficult for her to truly feel loved—she may tend to question the motives behind the emotion.

Part 7: Relationship Wants
Conscious Desires: Descendant in Gemini

On a conscious level, Taylor is attracted to fun, light-hearted, charming and social partners, who are apt to avoid any kind of deep emotional experiences. These partners are most likely to meet her Validation Needs—her Venus/Uranus in Aries will find these partners very suitable. Eventually, though, her emotional needs will demand to be met, and the Descendant in Gemini partners will run for the hills, terrified of her Moon in Scorpio emotional needs.

Unconscious Desires: Vertex in Cancer

On an unconscious level, with her Vertex in Cancer, she will be attracted to partners who are very emotional, and possibly rather needy at the same time. Cancer energy, remember, has to do with both nurturing and with being nurtured, and she'll be drawn to partners who have these needs, in no small part because of her own emotional needs. Her Vertex in Cancer relationships are apt to be rather stormy because of her core emotional issues. While on the one hand she needs the powerful emotional exchanges, on the other hand she finds these very threatening. When the relationship moves beyond the "You take care of me and I'll take care of you" realm, she will need some space—Venus in Aries doesn't like to be tied down, and the Moon in Scorpio simply has to put up walls every once in a while. This isn't likely to sit too well with her Vertex in Cancer partners, because Cancer's emotional needs are constant—when the emotional connections are taken away, Cancer will actively pursue them to try to reactivate them. In short, while her Vertex in Cancer partners will meet her Safety Needs (at least at first), they're unlikely to be able to meet her Validation Needs.

RICHARD BURTON

Next, let's look at one of the more important romantic partners in Elizabeth Taylor's life (important enough to her that she married and divorced him twice!), Richard Burton. Richard Burton's natal chart is pictured in Figure 10.

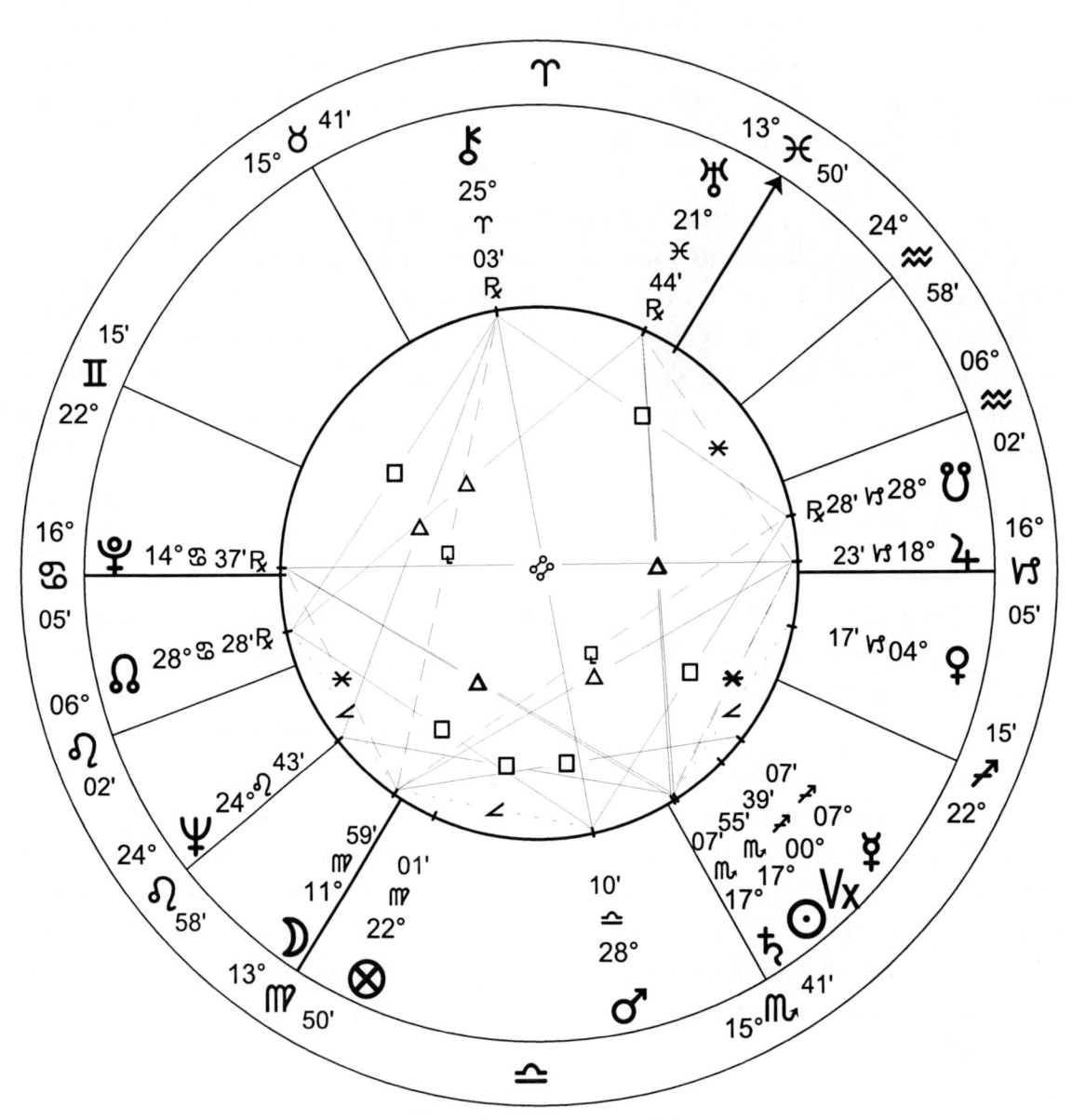

Richard Burton
November 10, 1925, 7:58 P.M.
Pontrhydfendigaid, Wales
52°N17′ 003°W51′

Figure 10: Richard Burton's Natal Chart

Part 1: Elements and Modalities

Element/Modality	Personal Planets	Personal Points	Outer Planets
Fire	☿	Vx	♇ ♆
Earth	☽ ♀ ♃	☋ ⊗	
Air	♂		
Water	☉ ♄	As Mc ☊	♅ ♇
Cardinal	♀ ♂ ♃	As ☊ ☋	♇ ♆
Fixed	☉ ♄		♆
Mutable	☽ ☿	Mc ⊗ Vx	♅

Part 2: Temperament

Hemisphere	Planets	Quadrant	Planets
Northern (House 1–6)	☉ ☽ ☿ ♀ ♂ ♄ ♆	I (House 1–3)	☽ ♆
Southern (House 7–12)	♃ ♇ ♅ ♇	II (House 4–6)	☉ ☿ ♀ ♂ ♄
Eastern (House 10–12, 1–3)	☽ ♇ ♅ ♆ ♇	III (House 7–9)	♃
Western (House 4–9)	☉ ☿ ♀ ♂ ♃ ♄	IV (House 10–12)	♇ ♅ ♇

Elementally, Richard Burton has an emphasis on the receptive elements of Earth (3 planets) and Water (2 planets). He has one planet in Fire and one in Air. He has a good balance of the modalities with a slight emphasis on Cardinal (identity) energy. Ironically for an actor, he has a more introverted temperament, with all of his personal planets in the Northern hemisphere except for Jupiter, setting in the 7th house.

There's not too much useful information here, so we'll move on.

Part 3: Essential Dignities

Pt	Ruler	Exalt	Trip	Term	Face	Detri	Fall	Score
☽	☿	☿	☽ +	♀	♀	♃	♀	+3
☉	♂	--	♂	♀	☉ +	♀	☽	+1
☿	♃	☊	♃	♃	☿ +	☿ −	☋	−4
♀	♄	♂	☽	♀ +	♃	☽	♃	+2
♂	♀	♄	☿	♂ +	♃ m	♂ −	☉	−3
♃	♄	♂	☽	♃ +	♂ m	☽	♃ −	−2
♄	♂	--	♂	♀	☉	♀	☽	−5 p
♅	♃	♀	♂	♂	♂	☿	☿	--
♆	☉	--	♃	♃	♂	♄	--	--
♇	☽	♃	♂	☿	☿	♂	♄	--
⚷	♂	☉	♃	♂	♀	♀	♂	--
☊	☽	♃	♂	♄	☽	♄	♃	--
☋	♃	♂	☽	♄	☉	☿	♂	--
As	☽	♃	♂	☿	☿	♄	♂	--
Mc	♃	♀	♃	♃	♃	☿	☿	--
Vx	♃	☋	♃	♃	☿	♀	☊	--
⊗	☿	☿	☽	♄	☿	♃	♀	--

Part 4: Dispositor Tree Diagram

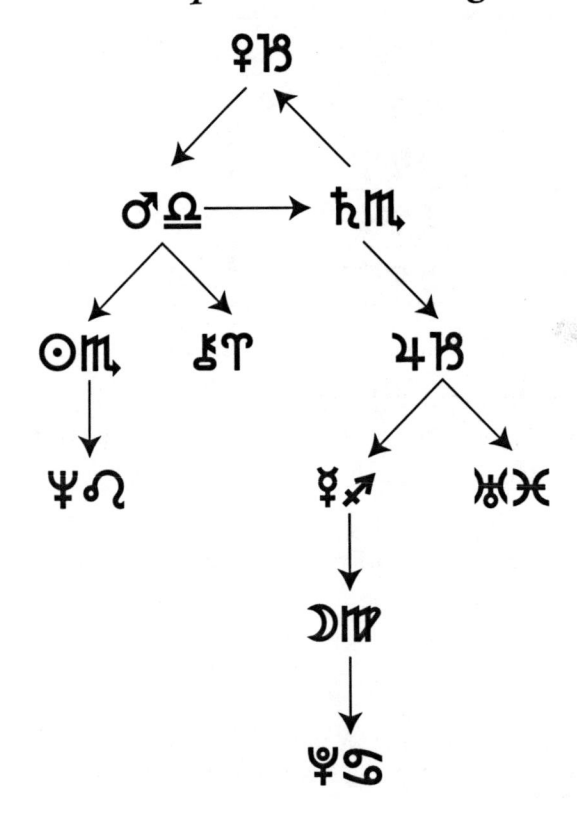

With Burton's chart, we're looking at a ruling committee of three planets: Venus in Capricorn, Mars in Libra, and Saturn in Scorpio. Of these three planets, only Venus has any clear-cut dignity (Term, and out-of-sect Triplicity—Venus is the Triplicity ruler of Earth in a day chart). Mars also has dignity by Term, but loses points because it's in Detriment. Saturn in Scorpio is in the worst relative shape: it's Peregrine (without essential dignity) *and* it's combust (conjunct the Sun). Although definitely a member of the ruling committee, Saturn will have the least say in the proceedings—not only is it hidden (because of being combust), but Mars rules Saturn both by Rulership and Triplicity. In many ways, Saturn is apt to be the "yes man" of Mars. While Mars has to listen to Venus, Mars can exert its influence over Saturn, which in turn will exert *its* influence over Venus. Since Venus only has dignity by Term, Venus is not able to exert too much control and influence over the committee. The planet that is the most likely to get its way is Mars. We shouldn't dismiss Saturn entirely, however, because Saturn does exert a certain amount of influence over Mars. Saturn is Exalted in Libra, and this gives the Mars in Libra a distinct Saturn quality. Mars in Libra needs to feel that it's acting in a responsible, structured manner.

It's interesting to note that this ruling committee is likely to be particularly concerned with relationships. Venus, of course is the planet that rules relationships; Mars in Libra will want to take action in ways that maintain balance and harmony in relationships; and Saturn in Scorpio is concerned with maintaining good boundaries to support responsible and enduring emotional and spiritual connections.

Part 5: Relationship Needs

Burton's core relationship needs involve structure, physical contact, and dedication to the integrity of the relationship. Both his Moon and Venus are in Earth signs, and the tangible elements of his relationships will be the most important to him.

Safety Needs

With his Moon in Virgo, Burton is the most comfortable when he is able to work to improve the boundaries and integrity of his relationships. He enjoys being of service and helping his partners to meet their physical needs.

Validation Needs

With his Venus in Capricorn, Burton feels validated and loved when he believes that his partner is as dedicated to supporting and maintaining the structure of the relationship as he is. There is a very strong element of protection with both his Safety and Validation Needs. He is likely to feel safe and loved when he is able to protect, support and provide for his partners in relationships.

Part 6: Can Needs Be Met?
Feeling Safe and Feeling Validated (Moon and Venus Connection)

Since both his Moon and Venus are in Earth signs, it is very easy for Burton to feel safe and loved at the same time.

General Safety Concerns

Burton has no hard aspects to his Moon, so it is relatively easy for him to meet his Safety Needs.

General Validation Concerns

Burton does have a semi-square between Venus and Saturn, which may indicate challenges in meeting his Validation Needs. He may have unrealistic expectations of what has to happen in order for him to feel loved and validated—and he may also feel the need to make equally grand and extravagant gestures in an effort to show his partners that he cares for them.

Part 7: Relationship Wants
Conscious Desires: Descendant in Capricorn

On a conscious level, Burton is attracted to Capricorn energy—mature, structured, responsible, settled partners. With Jupiter in Capricorn on the 7th house cusp, he may look for partners who are strong, ambitious, and successful in their own right. He may, however, be more concerned with the physical and material wealth of his partners, and overlook their spiritual accomplishments. Since Burton's Moon and Venus are both in Earth signs, Descendant in Capricorn partners are likely to do an excellent job of meeting both his Safety and Validation Needs.

It's important to note that Burton's relationships are apt to be especially powerful: he has Pluto on his Ascendant, opposing Jupiter on his Descendant. He will experience the energy of this Jupiter-Pluto opposition through his relationships. They will be intense, transformational, larger-than-life, and often explosive.

Unconscious Desires: Vertex in Sagittarius

On an unconscious level, however, Burton will be attracted to more free-spirited, passionate individuals, because his Vertex is in Sagittarius. What appeals the most to him about the

Sagittarius individuals is apt to be their focus and dedication to discovering their own, personal truth. However, these individuals will still need to be structured and disciplined: Burton's Vertex in Sagittarius is ruled by his Jupiter in Capricorn. Anyone *too* free-spirited won't make the cut.

Appealing though his Vertex in Sagittarius partners may be, they are not likely to meet either his Safety or his Validation Needs.

❖9❖
Relationship Houses

Consider which houses have to do with relationships. The 7th house immediately comes to mind, of course. This is both the house of marriage and committed relationships, and the house the represents the generic "other person" in any relationship. The 5th house of love affairs and the 11th house of friendships may also come to mind. You may also think of the 8th house, although chances are, you're thinking of it for the wrong reasons (sex doesn't belong in the 8th house).

The fact is, however, that because our lives are about relationships, *every* house in the chart is about relationships. The 1st house is our relationship to ourselves (one we so often overlook). The 2nd house is our relationship to money and our resources. The 3rd house is our relationship to our siblings and our neighbors. The 4th house is our relationship to our family in general, and our fathers in particular. The 5th house contains love affairs, sexual relationships, and our relationships with our children. The 6th house is our relationship with our co-workers, our employees and service providers, as well as with our pets. The 7th house, as we already know, is the default house of one-to-one relationships, and specifically relates to contractual relationships such as marriage; the 7th house also governs our relationships with our open enemies. The 8th house is our relationship with other people's resources. The 9th house is our relationship to organized religion and philosophical ideals. The 10th house contains our professional relationships, and our relationships to the public, as well as our relationship to our mothers. The 11th house is our relationship with our friends and peers. And the 12th house is our relationship with our hidden enemies, and also in many ways, our relationship to our spirituality.

Before we move on, however, let's return to the 8th house. Modern astrology believes that sex belongs in the 8th house. Modern astrology believes this because modern astrology believes that Scorpio and the 8th house are the same thing, which is entirely unfounded. The modern association between the 8th house of death and sex is entirely Freudian in nature, and in fact, only dates back to 1917. Alan Leo made the first ever recorded reference that connected the 8th house and sex, and it was a grand total of one sentence. Yes, the 8th house does involve close, intense emotional connections between two individuals, and yes, these connections can be sexual. However, the kind of sex that belongs in the 8th house usually requires an extensive leather wardrobe to go with it. The ancients understood that sex is *fun*, which is why it belongs in the 5th house.

In terms of our relationships, the relationship houses and the rulers of these houses influence our Relationship Blueprints. While astrology can help us to see the shape and color of our Relationship Blueprints, in order to make use of our Relationship Blueprints we have to explore them in far greater detail than that. Astrology can only provide a limited amount of information about our Relationship Blueprints.

Astrology does provide some very useful information in terms of our romantic relationships—specifically, showing how easily our romantic relationships can change form, from friendships to love affairs to marriage. We will explore this first. Astrology can also provide some insight into the contents of our Marriage Blueprint by exploring our experience of our parent's relationship. Finally, we'll look at how to use astrology to explore the dynamics of other categories of relationships. These last examples work in theory, but in practice they rarely provide useful information.

Friends, Lovers or Spouses?

Since we consider *all* relationships when we identify relationship patterns, it's important to recognize that there are different *kinds* of relationships. Even when it comes to romantic (or potentially romantic) relationships, we have different categories—and each relationship category belongs in its own house in the chart.

When most of us think of "relationship houses" we automatically think of the 7th house. The 7th house is, after all, the house of one-to-one relationships. In interrogatory astrology (Horary and Electional astrology) the 7th house represents the generic "other person." However, it's important to understand exactly what constitutes a 7th house relationship.

The 7th house is the house of any *contractual* relationship. It's the house of the marriage partner, as well as the house of the business partner. When we enter into any kind of legal agreement with another person (including buying or selling something), it's a 7th house relationship. Now, when it comes to romantic relationships, the 7th house is a bit more flexible. A romantic relationship becomes a 7th house relationship when the individuals in the relationship believe that the relationship is serious enough to belong in the 7th house. According to Dr. J. Lee Lehman. Ph.D., as soon as a couple starts to live together, it's a 7th house relationship, whether they're legally married or not.

The 5th house, on the other hand, is the house of love affairs. This is the house of casual dating and casual sex—and even not-so-casual dating and sex. Sometimes whether a romance is a 5th house or a 7th house relationship is a matter of perspective.

Finally, we have 11th house relationships, which are platonic friendships. These are the relationships we have with our peers—the people with whom we choose to spend time (fully clothed).

So why is it important to understand the different houses and the different types of relationships? Because it's important to consider how easy it is for an individual to move their relationships from one house to the next. Can we stay friends with our former lovers? How successful are we likely to be in taking our casual romantic relationships to the next level of commitment? Would we ever consider dating (or marrying) one of our friends?

To answer these questions, we look at the rulers of each of the houses.

First, we evaluate each of the house rulers individually. How strong is each planet? How well placed? Is there one ruler that is significantly stronger than the others? This could indicate a preference for the kinds of relationships associated with that house. For example, if the 5th house is ruled by the Moon in Cancer (Rulership), and the 7th house is ruled by Mercury in Pisces (Detriment, Fall and Peregrine), it's very possible that the individual will be more comfortable with his or her 5th house relationships; when relationships move into the 7th house, they may become more challenging.

Next, we evaluate the relationships between the three planets to see if there are any easy, flowing connections between the three types of relationships. Consider any aspects between the rulers, any emplacements (i.e., the ruler of the 5th in the 7th house), and any receptions between the rulers. In general, any connection between two houses indicates an ability to move relationships between those houses. The only exception is when the rulers of two houses are in hard aspect to each other—particularly when they are square or quincunx each other.

If there are no connections between the houses, it means that once a relationship starts in a given house, it stays there. Friends will stay friends, and lovers will stay lovers, and neither one is likely to become a spouse.

This is particularly important information when counseling clients on their romantic relationships. If a client wants to get married (7th house relationship) but has no easy way to move from the 5th house to the 7th house, then they must change their approach to dating. If they want a 7th house partner, they have to be very clear about this, and under no circumstances can they let the relationship slide into the 5th house. In practice, this means no sex until it's very clear and mutually agreed upon that the relationship is serious and monogamous.

Evaluating the Parents in the Natal Chart: Uncovering the Marriage Blueprint

While astrology can provide some insights into our experience of our parent's relationship (which forms the basis for our Marriage Blueprint), this is one of the areas where astrology's use is strictly limited. Evaluating the parents in the natal chart can sometimes reveal a key or important theme in the Marriage Blueprint, but the most effective tool is to ask the client about their perception and experience of their parent's relationship.

When looking at the parents in the natal chart, the ruler of the 4th house represents the father, and the ruler of the 10th house represents the mother. This is one of the many areas where classical and modern astrology differ, and it's also one of the many areas where modern astrology is flat out misguided. The only reason that modern astrology associates the mother with the 4th house is that modern astrologers, particularly those who have been exposed to the "Astrological Alphabet" assume that there is some fundamental connection between Cancer and the 4th house, and, by extension, the Moon. Since the Moon and Cancer are associated with all things feminine and maternal, modern astrology decided that the *mother*, and not the father belongs in the 4th house.

I have looked at hundreds of charts and had my interpretations validated by hundreds of clients, and in every case, the dynamic and experience of one's parents clearly supports the ruler of the 4th house representing the *father*, and not the mother. You, of course, are welcome to test this out for yourself, and I encourage you to do so.

When considering the parents and their relationship in the natal chart, it's essential that we remember that the only thing we can see in the natal chart is the *individual's personal experience of their parents and their parent's relationship*. These experiences and perceptions are the basis for a great number of beliefs that influence a great number of relationships. However, these experiences and perceptions may have absolutely no truth for anyone else. It doesn't matter if our parents experienced their relationship as loving and supportive; what matters is whether *we* perceived it that way. Our perceptions and experiences are what make up our relationship blueprints.

Naturally, the main thing to consider when looking at the parent's relationship in the natal chart is the relationship between the ruler of the 4th (father) and the ruler of the 10th (mother).

If these planets are in harmonious aspect to each other, it's likely that the individual will have experienced his or her parent's relationship as loving, successful and supportive. If, on the other hand, the rulers are in hard aspect to each other, it's far more likely that the individual experienced his or her parent's relationship as difficult.

When considering the relationship between the parents, we can occasionally go even deeper. Often times, there are important clues that reveal the dynamic of power in the relationship. Consider where the rulers are by house. If the ruler of the 10th (mother) is in the 4th house (father), then the father is inevitably the one who set the rules and had the power in the relationship. Consider any receptions between the rulers. If the ruler of the 10th (mother) rules the ruler of the 4th (father), then the mother was the one who ran things and the father always deferred to her.

It's also helpful to consider both the essential and the accidental dignity of the parental rulers. Dignified planets tend to be more forceful and direct; Peregrine or debilitated planets, on the other hand can indicate a lack of support or lack of control. In particular, consider whether one (or both) of the parental rulers are conjunct (or to a lesser degree, in aspect to) Chiron, Uranus, Neptune, Pluto or conjunct the Sun. When the ruler of one of the parents is conjunct Chiron, it often indicates some kind of core wound with that parent; I've frequently seen this indicate a parent in poor health or with some other chronic disability. When the ruler is conjunct Uranus, the parent is often absent or otherwise perceived as being unreliable. Neptune aspects can also indicate an absent parent, although frequently the absence is caused by drugs, alcohol, or being at sea in the Navy or the Marines. Pluto in aspect to or conjunct the ruler of a parent brings up issues of power and control, and occasionally abuse. Finally, if the ruler of one of the parents is within 8 degrees of the Sun, the planet is combust and totally hidden by the Sun: This is another indication of an absent or unavailable parent.

Relationships to Authority

When we consider our relationships to authority figures and our "Authority Blueprint" we *also* look at our parents. This time, however, we look at our relationship as individuals to each of our parents, instead of considering our experience of our parents' relationship to each other.

Our parents are our first experience of authority. They set the rules and the boundaries for us. They helped define our sense of how the world works, and how we as individuals will relate to society. Again, however, when exploring the Authority Blueprint, the most effective approach is to simply ask the client about his or her relationship with his or her parents.

What we want to consider here is the relationship between the ruler of the 1st house (which represents the individual) and the rulers of the 4th house (male authority figures) and the

10th house (female authority figures). Begin by considering the condition of each ruling planet on its own. How strong is it? How skillful is the planet when it comes to fulfilling its function? What kind of authority figure is that planet likely to be?

For example, the Moon in Cancer would be a very caring, compassionate authority figure. The Moon in Capricorn, on the other hand, would be far more concerned with rules and regulations, procedure and traditions, and would probably be more focused on bureaucracy than on helping support individuals. Jupiter in Sagittarius would be outgoing, generous, social and fun-loving. Jupiter in Gemini would probably tend to micro-manage.

Now, aren't the qualities of the male and female authority figures also going to be the qualities of how we experienced our parents? Of course they are. That's why we tend to project our unresolved issues with our parents onto other authority figures in our lives. Even if you didn't go into the family business, you're *still* working for your parents! We will experience our relationships to our supervisors and superiors in the workplace in the same way we experienced our relationships to our parents.

Once we've got an idea of how we're likely to experience the authority figures in our lives, we then look at the relationship between ourselves (1st house ruler) and the authority figure to explore the dynamic of our relationship to authority. Just because it seems that we've described a supportive and attractive authority figure, doesn't mean that we will enjoy the experience.

Looking back at our earlier example, the Moon in Cancer authority figure (the caring and compassionate one) seems to be more attractive than the Moon in Capricorn bureaucrat. But much depends on our own point of view. We may experience the Moon in Cancer authority figure as smothering and manipulative; we may value our privacy and need good emotional and energetic boundaries in the workplace. We will not get that with the Moon in Cancer authority figure. The Moon in Cancer authority figure will *care* about us—they'll want to know about our personal lives, and they will need to create emotional connections with us. If we are represented by Saturn in Libra, for example, we're apt to have some serious problems maintaining appropriate boundaries in our relationships to these authority figures.

Do we have a better chance of getting along with male authority figures or female authority figures? Consider the difference between the relationship between the ruler of the 1st and the ruler of the 10th (female authority figures) and the ruler of the 1st and the ruler of the 4th (male authority figures). When counseling clients about their careers or challenges in their work environment, it's essential to consider their Authority Blueprints.

The most obvious limit to this approach is the fact that frequently, the 1st and 4th or the 1st and 10th will be ruled by the same planet. While this certainly indicates a powerful identification with that parent, it doesn't shed much light on how the individual experienced his or her relationship with that parent. Certainly, we can get some information by evaluating the essential and accidental dignity of the ruling planet, but really, the most effective approach is to ask the client.

Other Relationship Houses

It's possible to gain some insight into other types of relationships by considering how we (the ruler of the 1st) relate to the ruler of other houses. To consider relationships with siblings and neighbors, consider the relationship between the ruler of the 1st and the ruler of the 3rd. Since our Sibling Blueprint, which originates here, mainly influences our relationships with our co-workers, we would begin here when looking at workplace relationships, and then look at the relationship between the ruler of the 1st and the ruler of the 6th (the primary house of workplace relationships). To explore our relationships with our children, we would look at the relationship between the ruler of the 1st and the ruler of the 5th. Finally, in theory, we should also consider the relationship between the ruler of the 1st and the ruler of the 7th, because the 7th house represents the generic "other person" in relationship.

I invite you to experiment with these approaches. Occasionally, they may reveal some fascinating information or raise some interesting questions. However, my personal feeling is that this is another case of astrology not being the most effective or efficient tool for the job. The most efficient tool is to ask the client directly.

10

Putting It Together Part 2: Finding the Relationship in the Natal Chart

So let's look at the Marriage Blueprint and the question of Friends, Lovers or Spouses in action. First, we'll continue our interpretation of Couple Number 1, Elizabeth Taylor and Richard Burton, and then we'll introduce Couple Number 2.

Elizabeth Taylor (Continued)

Part 8: Parents & Marriage Blueprint

As far as her Marriage Blueprint goes, Taylor's father is represented by Mars in Pisces, dignified by Triplicity, but also combust—he was lucky, but also not entirely present, perhaps (combust planets are hidden by the Sun and are not visible). Her mother, on the other hand, is represented by Venus in Aries, almost exactly conjunct Uranus, and semi-square Mars. She would have experienced her mother as impulsive and self-involved, and frequently at odds with her father. Her father would have gone along with whatever her mother wanted, and probably pretty much tried to stay the heck out of her mother's way. Even so, Mars in Pisces rules Venus in Aries, so no matter what her mother did, her father was still very much in charge. Even though he operated behind the scenes, he still set the boundaries and limits in the relationship. Whether this is an accurate description of her parent's relationship is not important; what it does describe, however, is how she most likely perceived and experienced her parent's relationship, and this is what constitutes the basis of her Marriage Blueprint.

Working from this Marriage Blueprint, Taylor wouldn't see any problem with acting out and keeping the focus of the relationship primarily on her own needs and desires—that's what her mother seemed to do. Taylor expects her partners to be there for her when she wants them and to leave her alone when she doesn't, and basically to read her mind as to what mood she happens to be in at any given time. More importantly, Taylor may carry the belief that she can't survive without a man in her life. Just as her mother needed her father to set the limits and be the power behind the throne, Taylor may have an unconscious belief that she can't survive on her own and that she needs a man to support, protect and defend her. Whether this is how she consciously approaches her relationships is more or less conjecture. What's important is to recognize that this is the point of origin for her expectations about how romantic relationships are supposed to play out.

Part 9: Friends, Lovers or Spouses?

Taylor's 5th house of love affairs is ruled by Mars in Pisces in the 3rd house. Her 7th house of marriage is ruled by Mercury in Pisces in the 3rd house. Her 11th house of friends is ruled by Venus in Aries in the 4th house.

From a relative strength standpoint, Mars, ruling the 5th house of love affairs, is the happiest and strongest of the planets in question. From this, we might consider that her casual relationships are likely to be the most enjoyable. Mars, the ruler of the 5th is widely conjunct Mercury in Pisces, ruling the 7th house, so it's very easy—and in fact, probably *too* easy—for her love affairs to move into the more serious 7th house marriage relationships. Mercury in Pisces, however, is in very poor condition—in Detriment *and* in Fall, and Peregrine to boot. Her instinctive approach to her 7th house relationships may be unsuccessful; in order to maintain and sustain these relationships, she may need to adjust her expectations.

While the connections between the 5th house and the 7th house are very easy, no such connections exist between the 5th house and the 11th house, or the 7th house and the 11th house. Venus, the ruler of the 11th house is semi-square Mars, the ruler of the 5th house. It's unlikely that anyone would move from the "friend" category to the "lover" category, and equally as unlikely that an ex-lover would find a home in the 11th house of friends. It's marginally easier for her to maintain a friendship with ex-husbands, however. While there is no direct aspect between Venus and Mercury, they are (widely) contra-antiscia to each other, which would indicate a mildly stressful connection.

Richard Burton (Continued)

Part 8: Parents & Marriage Blueprint

Burton's father is represented by Mercury in Sagittarius in the 5th house, and his mother is represented by Jupiter in Capricorn in the 7th house. Jupiter in Capricorn rules Mercury in Sagittarius, so essentially, in Burton's Marriage Blueprint, the wife calls all of the shots. He would have experienced his mother as the one who set the rules and maintained the boundaries, although neither parent is particularly strong. His Jupiter in Capricorn has dignity by Term (an interest in the matter) but is debilitated because it's in Fall (physical circumstances beyond its control). The youngest of 12 children, this Jupiter in Capricorn is, perhaps an accurate description of his experience of a very overworked mother.

Part 9: Friends, Lovers or Spouses?

Burton's 5th house of love affairs is ruled by Mars in Libra in the 4th house; his 7th house of marriage is ruled by Saturn in Scorpio in the 5th house; and his 11th house of friendships is ruled by Venus in Capricorn in the 6th house. Now, where have we seen these three planets before? Oh, that's right—they're the three planets that make up the ruling committee of his entire chart! Saturn, the ruler of the 7th house of marriage is in the 5th house of love affairs—this is the most direct connection between the houses. However, the dispositor relationship between the three houses means that he will have an easy time moving his relationships from house to house.

Now it's time to introduce Couple Number 2: Jennifer Aniston and Brad Pitt.

Jennifer Aniston

Jennifer Aniston's natal chart is shown in Figure 11.

Jennifer Aniston
February 11, 1969, 10:22 P.M.
Sherman Oaks, California
34°N09′04″ 118°W26′54″

Figure 11: Jennifer Aniston's Natal Chart

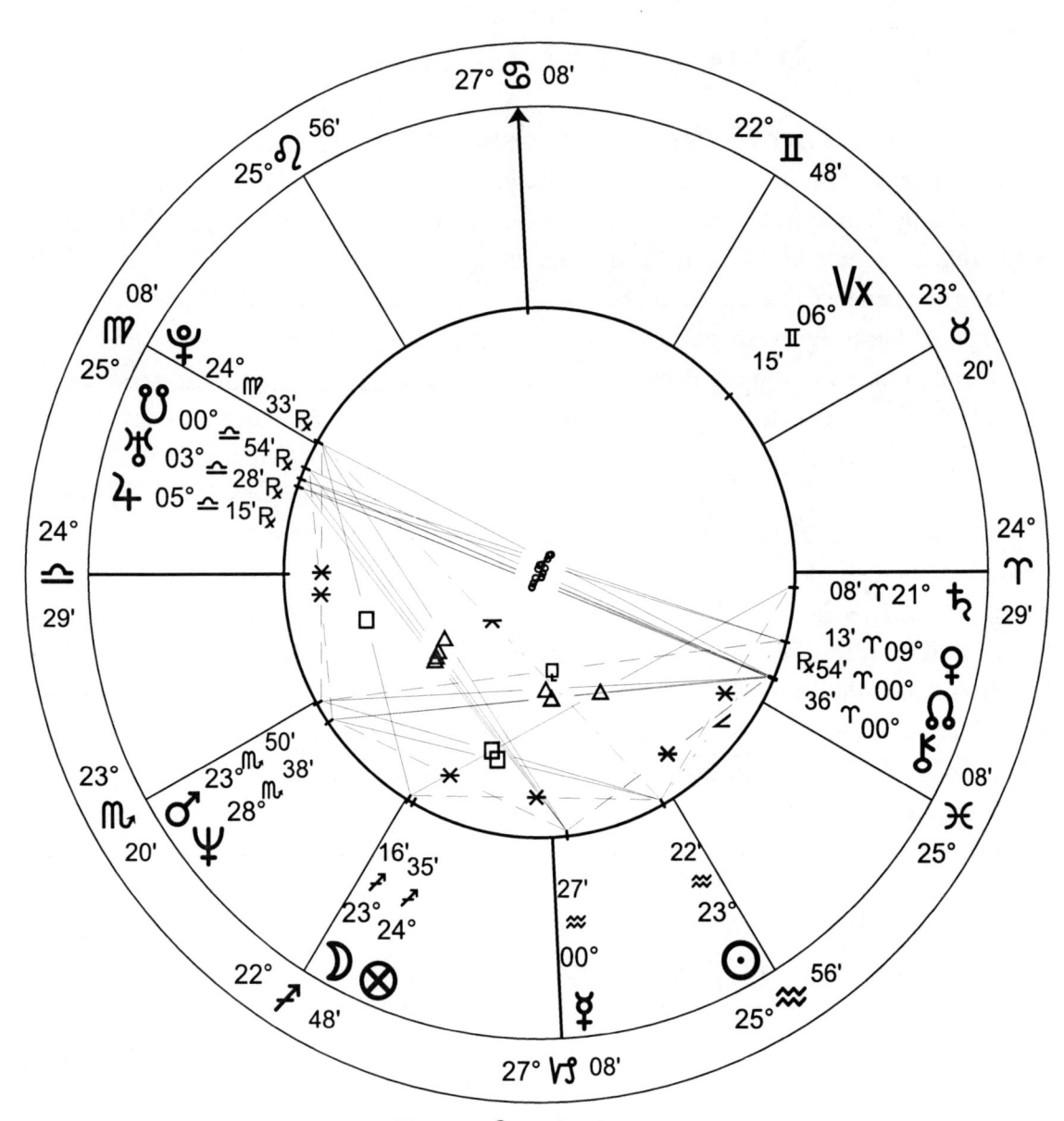

Part 1: Elements and Modalities

Element/Modality	Personal Planets	Personal Points	Outer Planets
Fire	☽ ♀ ♄	⊗ ☊	⚷
Earth			♇
Air	☉ ☿ ♃	As ☋ Vx	♅
Water	♂	Mc	♆
Cardinal	♀ ♃ ♄	As Mc ☊ ☋	⚷ ♅
Fixed	☉ ☿ ♂		♆
Mutable	☽	⊗ Vx	♇

Part 2: Temperament

Hemisphere	Planets	Quadrant	Planets
Northern (House 1–6)	☉ ☽ ☿ ♀ ♂ ♄ ⚷ ♆	I (House 1–3)	☽ ♂ ♆
Southern (House 7–12)	♃ ♅ ♇	II (House 4–6)	☉ ☿ ♀ ♄ ⚷
Eastern (House 10–12, 1–3)	☽ ♂ ♃ ♅ ♆ ♇	III (House 7–9)	
Western (House 4–9)	☉ ☿ ♀ ♄ ⚷	IV (House 10–12)	♃ ♅ ♇

Jennifer Aniston has an emphasis in Fire and Air in her chart. She will tend to be very active and very social. She has absolutely no Earth in her chart, but this most likely means that she has spent much of her life trying to be practical, stable and grounded in an effort to compensate for this self-perceived lack of stability. Earth, however, tends to be too slow and plodding for her temperament. With so much Fire and Air, Aniston will be the happiest when she can move quickly, acting and thinking without worrying about the more mundane issues. Now, while Aniston may only have one personal planet in Water (Mars in Scorpio), that planet (as we are about to see) is pretty darned influential in her chart. She's not likely to feel that she lacks emotions; however, she may be the most comfortable with joy and anger, the two emotions most commonly associated with the element of Fire.

She has a strong emphasis on both Cardinal and Fixed energy, which indicates that her two core issues are identity and self-worth. She will be more inclined to start and sustain projects than she will be to complete them, and the lack of Mutable energy in her chart could indicate that she needs to learn to be more flexible.

She is primarily introverted by temperament, with seven planets below the horizon, and she has a good balance of self-reliance and desire to relate to others.

Part 3: Essential Dignities

ESSENTIAL DIGNITIES (LEHMAN)								
Pt	Ruler	Exalt	Trip	Term	Face	Detri	Fall	Score
☽	♃	☋	♃	♄	♄	☿	☊	−5 p
☉	♄	--	☿	♃	☽	☉ -	--	−10 p
☿	♄	--	☿ +	♄	♀	☉	--	+3
♀	♂	☉	♃	♀ +	♂ m	♀ -	♄	-3
♂	♂ +	--	♂ +	☿	♀ m	♀	☽	+8
♃	♀	♄	☿	♄	☽	♂	☉	−5 p
♄	♂	☉	♃	♂	♀	♀	♄ -	−9 p
♅	♀	♄	☿	♄	☽	♂	☉	--
♆	♂	--	♂	♄	♀	♀	☽	--
♇	☿	☿	☽	♂	☿	♃	♀	--
⚷	♂	☉	♃	♃	♂	♀	♄	--
☊	♂	☉	♃	♃	♂	♀	♄	--
☋	♀	♄	☿	♄	☽	♂	☉	--
As	♀	♄	☿	♂	♃	♂	☉	--
Mc	☽	♃	♂	♄	☽	♄	♂	--
Vx	☿	☊	☿	☿	♃	♃	☋	--
⊗	♃	☋	♃	♄	♄	☿	☊	--

Part 4: Dispositor Tree Diagram

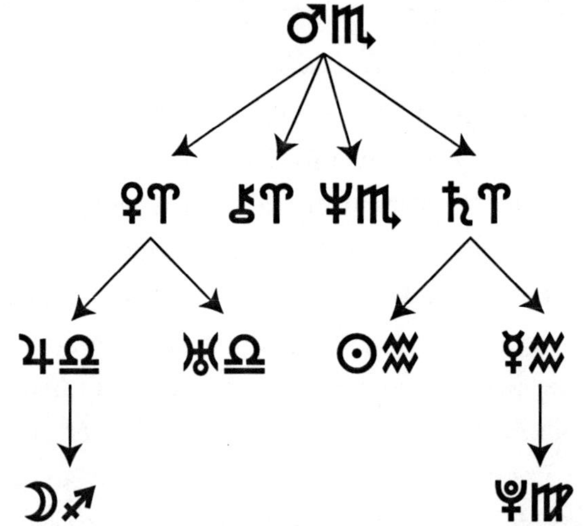

With a dispositor tree like this, Aniston is obviously much more than just a pretty face! Her entire chart is ruled by Mars in Scorpio. When she wants something, she is going to get it, and woe to anything that stands in her way! On the left flank, she has Venus in Aries ruling Jupiter and her Moon—she will never lose sight of who she is as an individual in her relationships (or anywhere else, for that matter). On the right flank, her Sun and Mercury report to Saturn in Aries. She's likely to have a very interesting take on authority figures and the "rules" of life. She's probably very aware of them, and absolutely can't stand them because they seem to limit the ways in which she can express herself and go after the things that she wants. She's not likely to confront authority (or the existing social structures) directly; however, she's also not likely to give up until she's found a way to circumvent or change the rules so that they no longer hinder her from reaching her goals.

Part 5: Relationship Needs
Safety Needs

Aniston's Moon is in Sagittarius indicating that she feels safest when she is able to express her true feelings—honesty is perhaps the single most important quality for the Moon in Sagittarius. She feels safe when she can explore her own Truth and pursue her own path of discovery. She needs trust and faith. She will be the most threatened by lies and betrayal, and she needs to have the freedom to follow her own instincts.

Validation Needs

Aniston's Venus in Aries indicates that she feels the most loved and validated when she is able to do her own thing in relationships. She needs to be independent; she needs to be an individual; and she needs to be able to act impulsively and express the truth of who she is. It's nice if her partner wants to participate, but it's not a requirement.

Part 6: Can Needs Be Met?
Feeling Safe and Feeling Validated (Moon and Venus Connection)

Although Aniston's Moon and Venus do not aspect each other, they are both in Fire signs, and therefore they share many qualities in common. When her Safety Needs are being met, it's very easy for her Validation Needs to be met as well, and vice versa.

Uranus Aspects: Issues with Rejection, Abandonment and Unreliability

Aniston's Venus is in a very wide opposition to Uranus, which may indicate issues with rejection and a slight fear of abandonment. Because her Venus is in Aries (and her Moon is in Sagittarius), she's most likely to be the one to end her relationships before she can be rejected or abandoned.

She will always choose to be true to herself. If she feels that she can't be herself in a relationship, she will abandon the relationship without a second thought.

Pluto Aspects: Power, Control, Manipulation and Abuse

Aniston's Moon is square Pluto, which may indicate that she is particularly sensitive to being controlled or manipulated. This aspect is likely to emphasize the Sagittarius need for personal freedom. She may feel particularly threatened when she feels that her friends (Pluto is in the 11th house) and peers are attempting to shape or define her beliefs or perceptions of herself.

Part 7: Relationship Wants
Conscious Desires: Descendant in Aries

On a conscious level, Aniston is attracted to the independent, direct, focused and active energy of Aries. What appeals the most to her in a partner is that her partner is absolutely and unquestionably an individual. She herself has a very strong personality, and needs to be in relationship with other individuals who are able to stand up to her, so that when they explore the balance of the relationship, they're each operating from a position of strength.

With Saturn in Aries conjunct her Descendant, Aniston is strongly attracted to the archetype of the rebel—someone who follows his own rules and lives by his own personal standards of integrity, even when those standards are not supported by the rest of society. Saturn in Aries is in Fall, and it represents the struggle between individuality and authority. Aniston is apt to project this energy on her partners, although ultimately, the lesson is for her to embrace and learn from this struggle within herself.

Unconscious Desires: Vertex in Gemini

On an unconscious level, Aniston is attracted to the playful and curious energy of Gemini. She admires partners who know how to have fun, and who can challenge and stimulate her intellectually and socially.

Both the Aries partners and the Gemini partners are likely to meet her core Safety and Validation Needs.

Part 8: Parents & Marriage Blueprint

Aniston's father is represented by Saturn in Aries in the 6th house; her mother is represented by the Moon in Sagittarius in the 3rd house. While neither her Moon nor Saturn are in very good shape, they are trine each other. Whatever her experience of her parents as individuals, her perception of their relationship is likely to be that it was easy, harmonious and enjoyable. It's likely that Aniston has a very healthy Marriage Blueprint.

Part 9: Friends, Lovers or Spouses?

Aniston's 5th house of love affairs is ruled by Saturn in Aries in the 6th house; her 7th house of marriage is ruled by Mars in Scorpio in the 2nd house; and her 11th house of friendships is ruled by her Sun in Aquarius in the 4th house. Aniston has a nice connection between her 5th and 11th houses. She may find it easy to stay friends with former lovers, or to begin casual relationships with friends. She may have more difficulty, however moving from the 5th house to the 7th house, or from the 7th house to the 11th house. Saturn in Aries, the ruler of her 5th house, is quincunx Mars in Scorpio, the ruler of her 7th house. At the same time, Mars rules Saturn, so we're looking at one strong, positive connection, and one strong challenging one. While she may have some success in taking her casual relationships to the next level of commitment, it won't be an easy path. What poses the greatest challenge for Aniston is the fact that the ruler of her 7th house of marriage is square the ruler of her 11th house of friendships. She's not likely to look for serious romantic partners from among her friends, and she's also not likely to want to stay friends with her former 7th house partners.

BRAD PITT

Brad Pitt's Natal Chart is shown in Figure 12.

Brad Pitt
December 18, 1963, 6:31 A.M.
Shawnee, Oklahoma
35°N19′38″ 096°W55′30″

Figure 12: Brad Pitt's Natal Chart

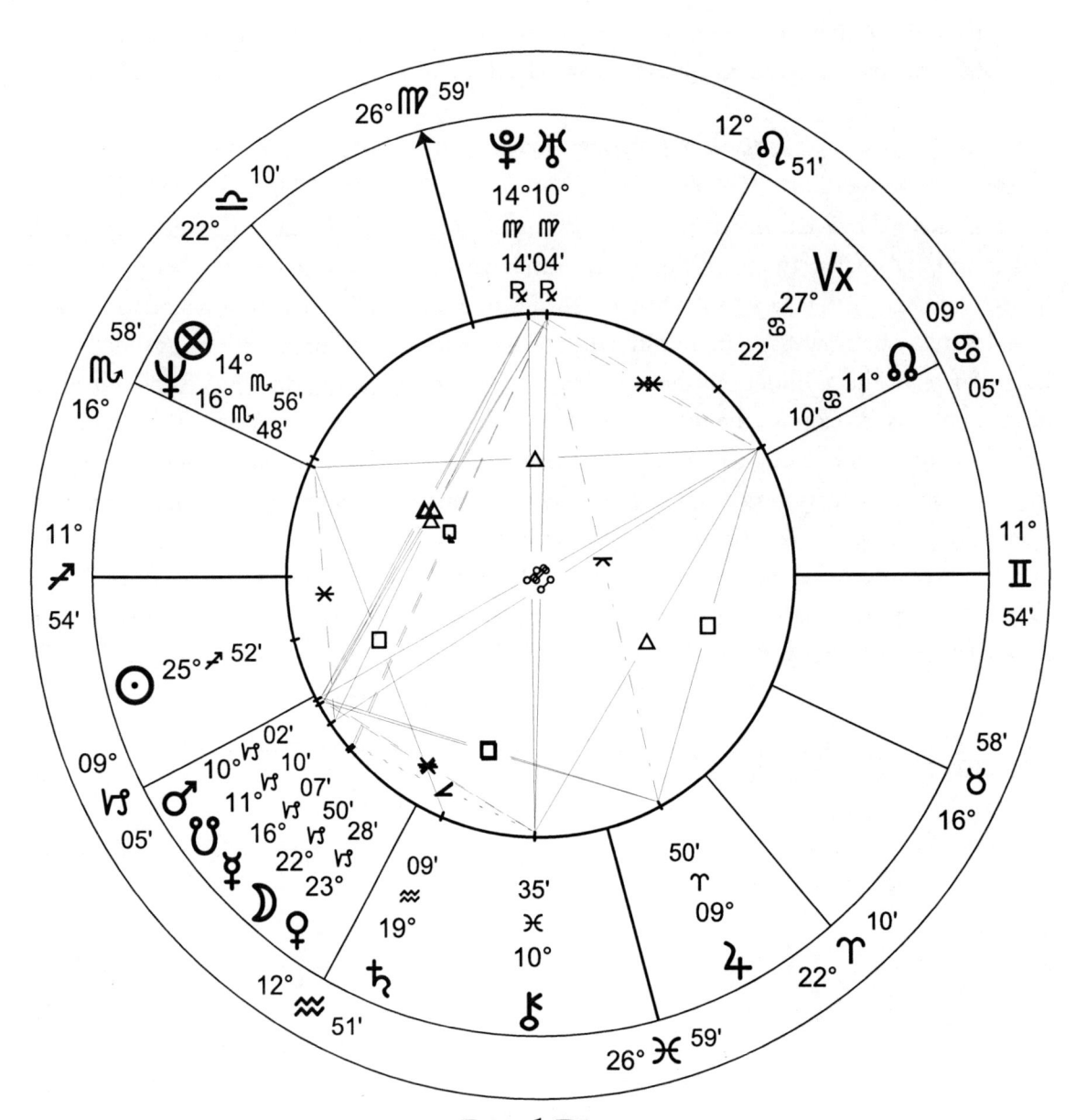

Part 1: Elements and Modalities

Element/Modality	Personal Planets	Personal Points	Outer Planets
Fire	☉ ♃	As	
Earth	☽ ☿ ♀ ♂	Mc ☋	♅ ♇
Air	♄		
Water		☊ ⊗ Vx	⚷ ♆
Cardinal	☽ ☿ ♀ ♂ ♃	☊ ☋ Vx	
Fixed	♄	⊗	♆
Mutable	☉	As Mc	⚷ ♅ ♇

Part 2: Temperament

Hemisphere	Planets	Quadrant	Planets
Northern (House 1–6)	☉ ☽ ☿ ♀ ♂ ♃ ♄ ⚷	I (House 1–3)	☉ ☽ ☿ ♀ ♂ ♄ ⚷
Southern (House 7–12)	♅ ♆ ♇	II (House 4–6)	♃
Eastern (House 10–12, 1–3)	☉ ☽ ☿ ♀ ♂ ♄ ⚷ ♆	III (House 7–9)	♅ ♇
Western (House 4–9)	♃ ♅ ♇	IV (House 10–12)	♆

Brad Pitt has a tremendous emphasis on Earth in his chart (thanks to his four planets in Capricorn). This, combined with five Cardinal planets indicates that he carries a very strong Cardinal Earth signature and is motivated to find tangible, lasting expressions of his individual identity, be grounded and practical, concerned with personal responsibility, and is likely to have very strong boundaries. His lack of planets in Water means that he may also be very adept at exploring and expressing his emotional and spiritual nature. In fact, he may put too much emphasis on his emotional and spiritual nature, because he believes that he has to make up for some inherent lack in himself. The same may apply to his social and intellectual pursuits, because the only planet he has in Air is Saturn in Aquarius.

The combination of the five Cardinal planets and the seven planets in the 1st quadrant mean that temperamentally he is extremely self-reliant. He is predominately introverted (seven planets in the Northern Hemisphere), and with seven planets in the Eastern hemisphere, he may prefer to discover his own path rather than accept help or advice from others.

Part 3: Essential Dignities

ESSENTIAL DIGNITIES (LEHMAN)								
Pt	Ruler	Exalt	Trip	Term	Face	Detri	Fall	Score
☽	♄	♂	☽ +	♂	☉	☽ -	♃	-2
☉	♃	☋	♃	♂	♄	☿	☊	-5 p
☿	♄	♂	☽	♃	♂	☽	♃	-5 p
♀	♄	♂	☽	♂	☉	☽	♃	-5 p
♂	♄	♂ +	☽	☿	♂ +	☽	♃	+5
♃	♂	☉	♃ +	♀	♂	♀	♄	+3
♄	♄ +	--	☿	♀	☿	☉	--	+5
♅	☿	☿	☽	♀	♀	♃	♀	--
♆	♂	--	♂	♀	☉	♀	☽	--
♇	☿	☿	☽	♃	♀	♃	♀	--
⚷	♃	♀	♂	♃	♃	☿	☿	--
☊	☽	♃	♂	♃	☿	♄	♂	--
☋	♄	♂	☽	☿	♂	☽	♃	--
As	♃	☋	♃	♀	☽	☿	☊	--
Mc	☿	☿	☽	♂	☿	♃	♀	--
Vx	☽	♃	♂	♄	☽	♄	♂	--
⊗	♂	--	♂	♀	☉	♀	☽	--

Part 4: Dispositor Tree Diagram

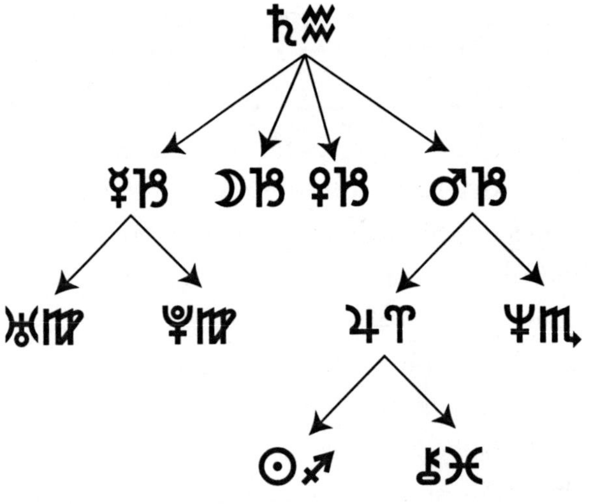

Saturn in Aquarius is the sole dispositor of Brad Pitt's chart. He will have an exceptionally well-developed sense of authority. He will view his entire life in terms of what is acceptable and what is responsible. Even though he has four planets in the more conservative Saturn-ruled sign of Capricorn, Saturn in Aquarius is ultimately a more progressive energy. Pitt is more than willing to break the rules and defy authority if the rules or structures no longer support the freedom, equality and independence of the group.

Part 5: Relationship Needs

Pitt's Moon and Venus are both in Capricorn. What makes him feel safe and validated are boundaries and structures.

Safety Needs

Pitt's Moon in Capricorn feels safest when he believes that he is responding and reacting in an appropriate and responsible manner. The Moon in Capricorn is in Detriment, so it operates on the mental/emotional plane, which usually translates to worry. It's very common for Moon in Capricorn individuals to worry about how to find an acceptable way to express their feelings. The Moon in Capricorn also feels safe when it can provide protection and material support to others.

Validation Needs

Pitt's Venus in Capricorn feels validated and loved when it experiences tangible representations of the relationship. Pitt takes his relationships very seriously, and demands the same level of personal responsibility and commitment from his partners that he brings to the relationship. Venus in Capricorn tends to express and interpret appreciation and affection through physical representations (such as gifts) or physical contact.

Part 6: Can Needs Be Met?
Feeling Safe and Feeling Validated (Moon and Venus Connection)

Pitt's Moon is conjunct his Venus in Capricorn. The things that make him feel safe are the same things that make him feel loved and validated: structure and boundaries. He has no aspects between his Moon or Venus to any outer planets. The only challenges he may face in terms of meeting his needs come from having such a strong Saturn ruling both his Safety and Validation checklists. His Moon in Capricorn has dignity by Triplicity, so it's lucky, but it's still in Detriment—he is likely to worry about finding the appropriate and acceptable ways to express his feelings and form emotional connections with others. His Venus in Capricorn is Peregrine, which means he may be more likely to fall into some of the traps of Venus in Capricorn such as keeping score in relationships.

Part 7: Relationship Wants
Conscious Desires: Descendant in Gemini

On a conscious level, Pitt is attracted to the intellectual, playful, and social energy of Gemini. While he may find this energy fascinating and entertaining and it certainly will help compliment the lack of Air in his chart, his Capricorn planets, and his Moon and Venus in particular, have an exceptionally low tolerance for Gemini energy—it's simply too frivolous and far too irresponsible. Gemini is quincunx Capricorn by sign, and the two signs have absolutely no common ground.

Unconscious Desires: Vertex in Cancer

On an unconscious level, however, Pitt is attracted to the emotional and nurturing energy of his Vertex in Cancer, and these relationships are likely to be a much better fit for him. Cancer energy is the compliment of Capricorn energy, and relationships with Cancer individuals are far more likely to meet his Safety and Validation Needs.

Part 8: Parents & Marriage Blueprint

Pitt's father is represented by Jupiter in Aries in the 4th house, and his mother is represented by Mercury in Capricorn in the 2nd house. There is no aspect between Jupiter and Mercury, although they are square by sign. Jupiter is reasonably strong, with dignity by Triplicity; Mercury is Peregrine. It's likely that Pitt's father was the most dominant figure in the relationship, and his mother would tend to defer to his father's wishes, even when she didn't particularly agree with them. Pitt's experience of their relationship seems somewhat neutral—his parents probably didn't seem to be deliriously happy with their relationship, but it was also probably not particularly contentious.

Part 9: Friends, Lovers or Spouses?

Pitt's 5th house of love affairs is ruled by Mars in Capricorn in the 2nd house; his 7th house of marriage is ruled by Mercury in Capricorn in the 2nd house; and his 11th house of friendships is ruled by Venus in Capricorn in the 2nd house. Since the rulers of all three of these houses are in the same sign, he has no difficulty at all in moving his relationships from one house to the next. As the rulers of all three relationship houses are in his 2nd house of personal resources, he's also likely to place a very high value on his relationships. Because Mars in Capricorn is by far the most dignified planet among the three rulers, Pitt may have the most success with his 5th house relationships.

☆11☆
Evaluating Compatibility

Finally, we arrive at the heart of what most people assume relationship astrology is about: evaluating compatibility. By now, we're acutely aware of how complex human relationships are. Moreover, we've also gained an appreciation for the ways in which astrology can help us to navigate and understand our relationships, and also the areas where astrology is of limited use.

Astrology does not and cannot predict behavior. It's futile enough to use astrology to attempt to predict how one individual will behave on his or her own. When we remember this, the idea that astrology could determine how two unique individuals—each with absolute free will—will interact with each other is, quite frankly, laughable.

Astrology does not, will not and cannot determine how "successful" a relationship between two individuals will be. (One reason for this is that there is no objective way to measure the "success" of a relationship in the first place.) Not only can astrology not predict how two individuals will experience their relationship with each other, astrology also can't predict how long any given relationship will last.

If all this is true, you're probably wondering why you've invested so much time in reading a book on relationship astrology!

It is, in fact, all true, at least for a given value of "true." Astrology does not provide answers about relationships. What astrology provides are the right questions to ask, and by asking and exploring these questions, astrology can help provide a useful map of a relationship that the individuals can then use to help them navigate the terrain. Astrology can help us to become *aware* of the structure and dynamic of our relationships, so that we can *own* our part in creating our relationships, and *choose* how we experience them.

In this chapter, we will explore and explode the myth of compatibility and learn how to use the various astrological tools of chart comparison to construct an accurate and useful map of any given relationship.

The Myth of Compatibility

The myth of compatibility is essentially that astrology can evaluate compatibility at all. I label this as a myth because while it is possible for astrology to map out some of the most likely dynamics between two individuals, the approach taken by every single book on relationship astrology that I've personally come across is entirely worthless.

The most common myth of compatibility is based on comparing Sun signs. This approach, still terribly popular today, follows along the lines of "If you're a Leo, you should be looking for Libra or Aries partners, and you should stay away from Scorpios and Aquarians." It is exactly as useful and as accurate as evaluating compatibility based on hair color. While the Sun sign does play an important role in compatibility (as we will shortly see), it is neither the most important nor the most significant element, and, as with everything else, it must be evaluated in the context of the larger understanding of the individual's relationship needs and patterns.

More advanced astrology books attempt to use synastry, the analysis and interpretation of the aspects between two individual's charts, to help the lovelorn to find their perfect romantic partners. Almost without fail, these books claim that one should look for a partner with as many harmonious aspects as possible from their chart to yours; it's implied that our ideal mates will have nothing but trines and sextiles between their chart and ours, and no hard aspects whatsoever. This approach is also entirely without merit.

While trines and sextiles between two individual's charts do indicate areas where the energy flows easily and effortlessly, this is does not necessarily mean that the two individuals will *enjoy* that experience. As always, everything has to be considered in the context of the individual and the individual natal charts. If the two individuals in question each have primarily hard aspects in their chart—squares and oppositions, for example—they will need these same kinds of aspects in their relationships. These individuals are used to action; trines are lazy. A relationship with nothing but flowing aspects would bore them to tears.

Another implied aspect of the myth of compatibility is that a relationship that consists of primarily easy and harmonious aspects between the two individual's charts will be much easier and therefore will last much longer than a relationship that presents more obvious challenges because of hard aspects between the charts. Once more, this is entirely unfounded. Astrology does not predict behavior, and it is absolutely impossible to determine how long a relationship will last. Relationships last as long as both individuals are learning their lessons from each other at the same pace. Even though astrology cannot predict how long a relationship will last, it is significant to note that most long-term relationships involve at least one hard aspect from one person's Saturn to one of the other person's personal planets. The "challenging" aspects seem to be the ones that give a relationship the staying power.

The real myth of compatibility is that somehow there is one perfect person with whom we are meant to build the kind of romantic relationship almost never experienced outside of the movies, and that we will know this person because their chart will somehow match up perfectly with our own. This is, perhaps, the most dangerous part of the myth of compatibility.

There is no such thing as the "perfect partner." Or rather, *every* partner in relationship with us is, by definition, perfect, at least when considered from a more Universal perspective. *Any* relationship can work, and whether or not the relationship succeeds has almost nothing to do with the level of "compatibility" that the two individuals may share. Relationships are about meeting our needs, and relationships where the partners meet each other's Safety and Validation Needs will tend to last.

We can find some very useful information when we compare the charts of two individuals in relationship; however, this information has to be considered in context. Comparing two charts will not tell us how "compatible" two individuals are. It will, however, help us to identify how likely it is for the individuals to meet each other's needs. Often, we can also identify the source and nature of the attraction, and identify the areas of the relationship that will require the most focus and attention.

COMPATIBILITY PART 1: ELEMENTAL COMPATIBILITY

Just as we put the natal chart in perspective before we tried to interpret the little details, we will do the same thing with the connections between the two charts. Stephen Arroyo has an absolutely fantastic approach to this that I always apply to my relationship charts, with a bit of expansion. Arroyo takes the signs of the Sun, Moon and Ascendant and compares them on an elemental basis between the two charts. What he evaluates here is how well the two individuals are likely to interact on an energetic level.

Arroyo feels that while it's not necessary to have specific connections between the same elements (i.e., Sun to Sun or Moon to Moon), it's important to have connections between these three elements in the charts. The extent that these connections exist is the extent that the two individuals are likely to energize and recharge each other.

The most positive and energizing connections occur when two points are in the same elements, but in different signs. The planets or angles don't have to trine each other; the point here is that the simple elemental connection is powerful and rejuvenating on its own, and indicates some very enjoyable common ground between the two individuals. Planets and angles in the same polarity (i.e., sextile or opposing each other by sign) are also nice, although not quite as energizing as the elemental connections.

When two points are in the same sign they neither recharge each other nor drain each other. It's generally a positive contact, but if there aren't any recharging elements present, it's important to note that the individuals will have to look outside of the relationship to energize themselves.

Squares between the signs are both exciting and draining energetically. If too many of these exist without some strong harmonious elemental bonds to balance things out, the two individuals may tend to burn each other out very quickly and find it difficult to spend large amounts of time together.

Although I give priority to the Sun/Moon/Ascendant, I also expand on Arroyo's ideas to include the other two key relationship points, Venus and the Vertex. I've found that the elemental energies of these points does tend to make a difference, and can help to compensate for a lack of connections between the Sun, Moon and Ascendant alone.

As shown in Table 5, the signs can be classified by polarity (masculine/positive or feminine/negative), modality (Cardinal, Fixed or Mutable), and by element (Fire, Earth, Air, Water).

Table 5: Classification of the Signs

SIGN	POLARITY	ELEMENT	MODALITY
Aries	Masculine	Fire	Cardinal
Taurus	Feminine	Earth	Fixed
Gemini	Masculine	Air	Mutable
Cancer	Feminine	Water	Cardinal
Leo	Masculine	Fire	Fixed
Virgo	Feminine	Earth	Mutable
Libra	Masculine	Air	Cardinal
Scorpio	Feminine	Water	Fixed
Sagittarius	Masculine	Fire	Mutable
Capricorn	Feminine	Earth	Cardinal
Aquarius	Masculine	Air	Fixed
Pisces	Feminine	Water	Mutable

In general, signs that are in the same element are the most compatible in the sense that they exchange energy and flow in the most easy and harmonious way, and, as Stephen Arroyo says, they tend to "recharge" each other. Signs in the same element are trine each other.

The next most comfortable relationship between signs is between signs that are in the same polarity, but different elements and modalities. The masculine/positive signs are the Fire and Air signs; the feminine/negative signs are the Earth and Water signs. These signs are sextile each other.

Signs in different elements that share the same modality and the same polarity are opposite each other. This is a balancing aspect, and can be either "easy" or "stressful" depending on the individuals. This relationship can involve a great deal of projection and transference—each person projects or transfers qualities and attributes that they haven't recognized and integrated in themselves onto their partner. There is a great deal of truth to the cliché "opposites attract" because each partner may feel that the other partner balances them out, or fills in the qualities that they lack in themselves.

Another combination of signs that can go either way is same sign combinations or conjunctions. Like the opposition, when two people come together with strong emphasis in the same signs (i.e., two people with strong Aries placements), there is certainly common ground; however, this combination can be ultimately draining since the two individuals each need the same energy to recharge, and they don't recharge each other. (Different signs in the same element do recharge each other.) With oppositions, the tendency is to be faced with the parts of ourselves that we don't own; with conjunctions, we are faced with ourselves. Again, how comfortable this aspect is has everything to do with how comfortable the two individuals are with themselves.

Signs that share the same modality but different polarities and elements are square each other, and this is considered to be a "hard" or "stressful" aspect. The energy does not flow easily or comfortably between these signs; however, this relationship is stimulating and generates action.

Finally, it's possible that two signs can have nothing in common either by element, polarity or modality. When the signs are next to each other on the wheel, they are semi-sextile each other, and, because one sign naturally evolves into the next, this is considered to be a weak but potentially positive placement.

When the signs are five signs apart, however, they are quincunx each other. These can be the most difficult pairings of all because there is (traditionally) no common ground between the planets.

Table 6 illustrates the compatibility relationships between the signs.

Table 6: Compatibility Relationships Between Signs

Sign	Most Compatible — Trine	Most Compatible — Sextile	Neutral — Oppose	Neutral — Conjunct	Friction — Square	Least Compatible — Semi-Sextile	Least Compatible — Quincunx
Aries	Leo, Sagittarius	Gemini, Aquarius	Libra	Aries	Cancer, Capricorn	Taurus, Pisces	Virgo, Scorpio
Taurus	Virgo, Capricorn	Cancer, Pisces	Scorpio	Taurus	Leo, Aquarius	Aries, Gemini	Libra, Sagittarius
Gemini	Libra, Aquarius	Aries, Leo	Sagittarius	Gemini	Virgo, Pisces	Taurus, Cancer	Scorpio, Capricorn
Cancer	Scorpio, Pisces	Taurus, Virgo	Capricorn	Cancer	Aries, Libra	Gemini, Leo	Sagittarius, Aquarius
Leo	Aries, Sagittarius	Gemini, Libra	Aquarius	Leo	Taurus, Scorpio	Cancer, Virgo	Capricorn, Pisces
Virgo	Taurus, Capricorn	Cancer, Scorpio	Pisces	Virgo	Gemini, Sagittarius	Leo, Libra	Aries, Aquarius
Libra	Gemini, Aquarius	Leo, Sagittarius	Aries	Libra	Cancer, Capricorn	Virgo, Scorpio	Taurus, Pisces
Scorpio	Cancer, Pisces	Virgo, Capricorn	Taurus	Scorpio	Leo, Aquarius	Libra, Sagittarius	Aries, Gemini
Sagittarius	Aries, Leo	Libra, Aquarius	Gemini	Sagittarius	Virgo, Pisces	Scorpio, Capricorn	Taurus, Cancer
Capricorn	Taurus, Virgo	Scorpio, Pisces	Cancer	Capricorn	Aries, Libra	Sagittarius, Aquarius	Gemini, Leo
Aquarius	Gemini, Libra	Aries, Sagittarius	Leo	Aquarius	Taurus, Scorpio	Capricorn, Pisces	Cancer, Virgo
Pisces	Cancer, Scorpio	Taurus, Capricorn	Virgo	Pisces	Gemini, Sagittarius	Aries, Aquarius	Leo, Libra

Compatibility Part 2: Safety and Validation Needs

Everything in relationship comes back to our relationship needs, safety and validation. After getting a feel for the overall energetic connections between the two individuals, we ask the single most important question (and not for the last time, either): How easily will these two individuals meet each other's Safety and Validation Needs?

Of course, this question can only be answered in the context of the individual natal charts. Whether or not our partners in relationship can meet our Safety or Validation Needs first depends on whether or not our Safety or Validation Needs can be met at all. Review each individual's natal chart, making note of any aspects from the outer planets to the Moon or Venus that may interfere with feeling safe or validated in general.

Consider which language each person speaks for safety and validation. If the individuals speak the same language (Moon or Venus in the same element), they have an excellent chance at meeting each other's Safety Needs. The connection does not have to be from Moon to Moon or Venus to Venus, either. If person A has a Water Safety Checklist and person B has a Water Validation Checklist then person B will naturally meet person A's Safety Needs, and person A will naturally meet person B's Validation Needs. It's helpful when the two individuals speak at least similar languages for safety and/or validation. Fire and Air can communicate, and Earth and Water can communicate.

If, on the other hand, there are no connections between the individual's Safety and Validation Languages, it presents a fundamental obstacle in the relationship. The two individuals will each have to learn how to speak their partner's languages in order to meet each other's needs. This is by no means an insurmountable obstacle. However, it won't happen automatically, and until the individuals become fluent in each other's language, they are likely to experience some challenges in the relationship.

Flowing aspects and compatible signs between one person's Sun, Moon, Mercury and/or Venus to the other person's Moon and/or Venus can help compensate for a lack of shared language. As long as the Moon or Venus is being energized, the Safety or Validation Needs are being met on some level.

COMPATIBILITY PART 3: COMMUNICATION STYLES

Communication is an essential part of successful relationships. Without communication, we can't help our partners know how to meet our Safety and our Validation Needs, which are the *real* cornerstone of successful relationships. Understanding our partner's Safety and Validation Languages is an important part of healthy relationships. But now that we've done this, it's also important to look at how easily two individuals are likely to communicate in general, and not only in terms of their Safety and Validation Needs. To answer this question, consider the relationship between Mercury in each person's chart. If the signs of each person's Mercury are compatible, especially if there is a conjunction, trine, sextile or even an opposition between the two planets, the individuals are likely to have a relatively easy time understanding each other. On a very fundamental level, they share a certain amount of common ground in terms of their own, personal experiences of reality.

On the other hand, if the two planets are square each other by sign or aspect, expect more friction and tension in terms of their communication. This, mind you, is not necessarily a bad thing. While squares are ultimately draining, in moderate doses, they are stimulating and energizing. If each person's Mercury is square the other's it's important to evaluate if this friction is apt to become a problem—particularly if it is likely to interfere with either person's ability to feel safe or validated. An individual with the Moon square Pluto, for example, may be very sensitive to any kind of conflict in a relationship, and may find the challenges communicating to be threatening. It's also helpful to look for any flowing aspects between Mercury and any other planet to see if there is an escape valve to relieve the pressure and give the individuals a break.

The only Mercury to Mercury aspects that automatically present challenges are when each person's Mercury is quincunx to the other's. When the two planets are in signs that quincunx (or even semi-sextile) each other, they have no common ground at all and may find it difficult to communicate. As long as the two planets are not in harmonic aspect to each other, however, it is possible to work around this, so long as each person's Mercury makes a more flowing aspect to one or more planets in the other person's chart. However, when one person's Mercury is actually quincunx the other person's Mercury, they often find it next to impossible to understand each other, and it requires a tremendous amount of effort and energy for them to see eye-to-eye with each other.

INTRODUCING THE SYNASTRY GRID

The synastry grid is a table that shows how each individual's planets aspect the other individual's planets (see Figure 13). One person's planets are listed across the top, and the other's planets are listed down the left side. Any aspects between two planets are listed in the corresponding grid boxes, along with the orb of the aspect and whether the aspect is applying (A) or separating (S).

All synastry aspects are not created equal, however. In Figure 13, the grid is divided into different squares, highlighting the specific areas of interest: Inter-Personal connections, Karmic connections and Generational connections.

Figure 13: Synastry Grid

	☽	☉	☿	♀	♂	♃	♄	♅	♆	♇	⚷	☊	☋	As	Mc	Vx	⊗
☽	✶ 3A27	☌ 4S43	☌ 4S33						☌ 5S23		△ 7A07			□ 4S32			
☉	☌ 2S28			⚺ 0S46		□ 2S44		⚺ 0S51		△ 2A18	☍ 1A12					△ 4A10	
☿	□ 0A09	□ 0A19							□ 0S32					☌ 0A20	✶ 1S07	⚻ 0S02	
♀	✶ 2A59	✶ 3A09							△ 2A19		⚻ 0S11			□ 1A43			
♂						△ 3A23	□ 2A08									⚺ 1A06	
♃	✶ 2S57			□ 1S15			□ 1S20		☍ 1A49	△ 0A43						☍ 3A42	
♄	☌ 1S40		⚺ 0A01		□ 1S56		⚺ 0S04		△ 3A05	☍ 1A59						△ 4A58	
♅	△ 6A17								△ 1A31	✶ 2A37	☌ 4S33	☍ 4S33				△ 0S21	
♆			☍ 6A51								⚺ 1A34						
♇	△ 0S50	△ 7A20	□ 2S32				□ 2S27			☌ 5S36							
⚷		∠ 2A47	☌ 7A55				☌ 8A00		□ 4A51			⚺ 1S14				□ 2A58	
☊							☍ 1S51		☌ 8A15			△ 2A11	✶ 2A11			☌ 6A23	△ 0S49
☋							☌ 1S51					✶ 2A11	△ 2A11			☍ 6A23	✶ 0S49
As	△ 0S39		□ 1A03	⚻ 0A28			□ 0A58		☌ 4A07	✶ 3A01						☌ 6A00	
Mc	△ 1A37	☌ 6S34	☌ 6S24			⚺ 1A21	∠ 1A28		△ 6A23								
Vx	□ 6A38		⚻ 1A30	□ 0A55			✶ 0A20	⚻ 1A25	□ 5A57			△ 4A21		☌ 6A48			△ 1A22
⊗								✶ 1A48	△ 2A54	☍ 4A16	☌ 4A16			✶ 0A04	☍ 7A16		

■ Inter-Personal Connections (Mutual) ■ Karmic Connections
■ Inter-Personal Connections (One-Way) ■ Generational Aspects

Figure 13: Synastry Grid

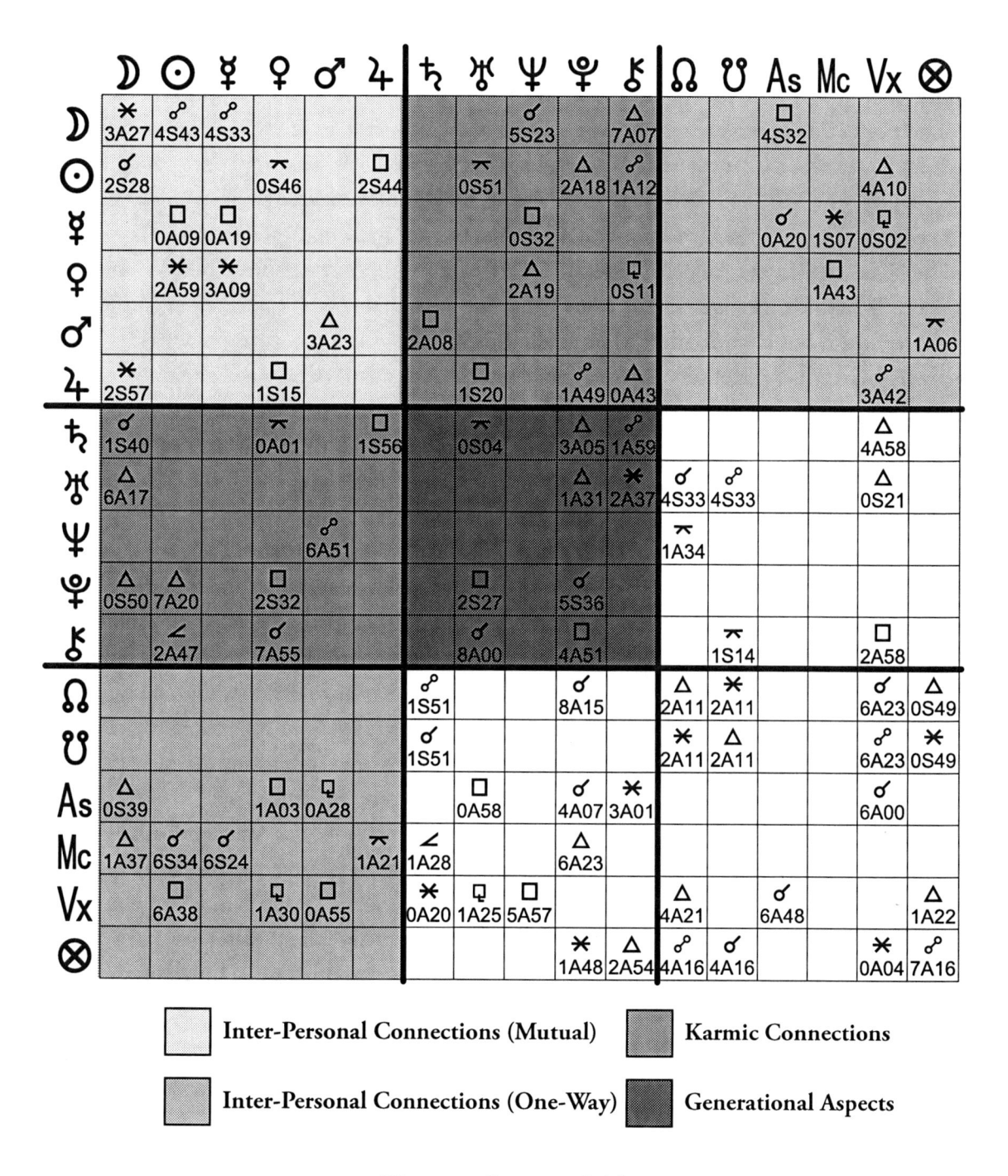

Inter-Personal Connections (Personal to Personal)

Aspects between the inner planets (Sun through Jupiter for these purposes) and the personal points in the chart (the Angles, the Moon's Nodes, the Part of Fortune) are where we see interactions and connections on a personality level. All things being equal, it's nice to have a balance between flowing aspects (conjunctions, trines and sextiles) and hard aspects (squares, semi-squares, sesquiquadrates and oppositions). The flowing aspects are where we simply enjoy spending time with our partners and operate naturally; the hard aspects are where the friction and stimulation occurs.

In Natal charts, the Angles, Nodes and Part of Fortune *receive* aspects but do not *make* aspects. What this means is that if Mars trines the Ascendant, it will color the expression of the Ascendant, but it won't affect Mars at all. This is somewhat less the case in synastry. If one person's Mars trines the other person's Ascendant, the Ascendant person will certainly receive a boost from the Mars aspect—they may find that when with their partner, they tend to be more aggressive and direct, more active in their approach to the world. But the Mars person will also experience this connection, albeit in a far more subtle manner.

Karmic Connections (Outer to Personal)

Stephen Arroyo calls aspects between one person's personal points and planets and the other person's outer planets (Saturn, Chiron, Uranus, Neptune and Pluto) "karmic" aspects. These aspects flow one way only: from the outer planet to the inner planet. The outer planet person is often completely oblivious to the effect that they're having on the inner planet person, as well they should be, because what is happening is that they are simply reflecting the inner planet person's projections back to them. The difference between experiencing these connections through relationships and experiencing them through transits is that we have more control over the experience in relationships.

The Universe is far too efficient for relationships to flow only one way, and usually both partners are pretty well matched in the "karmic" aspects department. They're not always working on the same lessons, of course. Person A may experience Person B's Neptune squaring their Moon, and will discover a host of emotional boundary and safety issues that they weren't previously aware of. At the same time, Person B may experience Person A's Pluto conjunct their natal Mercury, and as a result of this, their entire perceptions of the world and communication style will be completely transformed through the relationship.

Generational Connections (Outer to Outer)

Aspects between one person's outer planets (Saturn, Chiron, Uranus, Neptune and Pluto) to another person's outer planets are generational aspects. They represent the background noise of cultural conditioning that define our generations. These aspects have almost no significance whatsoever, except when they reinforce natal aspects.

Reinforced Aspects

Since relationships are primarily ways for us to discover and work out our own, personal issues, it's very important to notice if any of these issues in particular are likely to be emphasized in a given relationship. What we're looking for here are any planetary connections through synastry that reinforce issues with the same planets in the natal chart. For example, if an individual has Venus square Jupiter in her chart, if her partner's Jupiter happens to trine her Venus, this connection will both trigger and reinforce the Venus-Jupiter aspect in her natal chart. As such, it's pretty darned important to understand how this aspect tends to play out for her under normal circumstances, because it will be particularly active in the relationship. In this example, one of the patterns associated with Venus square Jupiter is a tendency towards extravagance and a very bad habit of overspending and living beyond one's means. Having her partner's Jupiter trine her Venus—while it certainly is a pleasurable aspect on a personal level—is also likely to have the effect of encouraging her to spend even more, which is not necessarily a good thing.

Likewise, a person who has the Moon opposite Saturn in his natal chart will have his issues about emotional availability triggered if he creates a relationship with a partner who's natal Saturn quincunxes his Moon.

Double Aspects

Double aspects occur when both individuals share the same synastry connections, such as when person A's Mars squares person B's Sun, and person B's Mars squares person A's Sun. Even when these aspects don't trigger any natal aspects for the individuals, they're important to consider, since both individuals are having the same effect on each other. Obviously, the type of aspect and the planets involved will make a very big difference here. If we're talking about a double aspect of the Moon trine Venus, we're probably looking at some very nice, mutual emotional connections. A double aspect of Uranus quincunx the Moon, on the other hand would tend to bring up serious safety and trust issues for both individuals and would probably be much less fun to experience.

Aspects in Synastry

Now let's take a brief look at how we tend to experience the different aspects in synastry.

Conjunctions

Conjunctions in synastry show a unity of purpose—these are the points where the two individuals align with each other with the greatest precision. The planets involved have to be taken into consideration of course, to look at exactly how this energy is likely to manifest.

Oppositions

Oppositions in synastry indicate the strongest type of attraction between the two individuals. As with all oppositions, these aspects require balance between the two planets. Oppositions between personal planets are some of the best indicators of physical attraction—and when Mars is involved there is often an element of sexual tension thrown into the mix as well.

Trines

Trines in synastry are the areas where the couple can just coast—these are the resting points, the energizing and flowing connections. Trines are very much like the feeling that you can finish each other's sentences. While trines are very comfortable and enjoyable, they can also become routine and somewhat boring—it's important to relate the number of trines back to the individual natal charts and see if this is the type of relationship that these individuals actually want.

Squares

Squares are where the tension and friction come into play. Squares are exciting and stimulating—they encourage the individuals to go out and do something constructive with the built-up energy, and to create something from it. Squares can translate to passion, but they can also translate to restraining orders. Again, it's important to consider the natal charts.

Sextiles

Sextiles are comfortable aspects—they're not as easy or as noticeable as the trines, and they do generally need to be acted on in order to experience them. Sextiles indicate areas where cooperation is very likely.

Quincunxes

Quincunxes are perhaps the most difficult aspects to deal with because it's exceedingly difficult for the two planets involved to ever see eye-to-eye. With quincunxes you either have one person required to compromise and adjust uncomfortably, or perhaps if you're lucky you end up simply "agreeing to disagree."

Semi-Squares and Sesquiquadrates

The 8th harmonic aspects are worth considering in synastry, particularly when they involve very small orbs. The semi-square can be a surprisingly challenging aspect because elementally, the two signs involved are sextile each other, and so it would seem that the two individuals would have an easy time cooperating with each other. However, because of the 8th harmonic energy here, this cooperation tends to involve a great deal of butting heads. Sesquiquadrates are easier to work with because these aspects have a certain amount of perspective built in. The tension and friction of sesquiquadrates is often vented through teasing and joking, sometimes through good-natured bickering. Humor is always the most effective tool when dealing with these aspects; it just comes easier with the sesquiquadrate than it does with the semi-square.

Planets in Houses in Synastry

Synastry aspects are read just like transits, and they do tend to have a similar effect—an outside influence triggering areas of our natal charts. The difference of course, is that while transits come and go, synastry aspects are in effect as long as we interact with the other individual. And just as with transits, in synastry we can consider both the aspects and the house placements.

Looking at the interaction between one person's planets in the other person's houses is one of the last things that I do, since the most that it can tell is *where* some of the synastry aspects are likely to play out in the relationship. I rarely spend much time on this.

COMPATIBILITY PART 4: INTER-PERSONAL CONNECTIONS

The first and most important area of the synastry grid is the inter-personal connections: the aspects between each person's Sun through Jupiter to the other person's Sun through Jupiter. For most people, a balanced mix of easy and stressful aspects is a formula for mutual interest and compatibility. Of course, everything must be evaluated in the context of each individual's natal chart.

Conjunctions, trines and sextiles represent the areas where the energy flows with the greatest ease. This is where the individuals will have the easiest and most comfortable time together. Squares, semi-squares, sesquiquadrates and, to a lesser degree, oppositions, are where the excitement and tension come into play. These, in short, are the sparks in the relationship.

Sexual attraction can be seen in several ways, but the most reliable is aspects between Venus and Mars in the two charts. These can be Venus-Venus, Mars-Mars or Mars-Venus aspects, and while any aspect indicates a potential attraction, the harder the aspect, the more sexual heat in the relationship.

The only aspect to watch out for is the quincunx. Too many quincunxes can create significant challenges in a relationship. Squares and the 8th harmonic aspects create friction, and it's true that over time, these can become frustrating, but in moderate doses, these aspects represent a definite connection between the two individuals. Squares are action aspects, and generally, when two individuals have personal planets squaring each other, the individuals work together, taking action to resolve the tension. Quincunxes, on the other hand, represent outright conflict and a fundamental lack of common ground. They are always stressful—and not in a good way— and always represent a drain on the energy in the relationship.

Compatibility Part 5: Karmic Aspects

The so-called "Karmic Aspects" are aspects between one person's outer planets (Saturn, Chiron, Uranus, Neptune and Pluto) to another person's personal planets. These are the heavier energies in relationship, and they are where we experience our deeper lessons. When our partner's outer planets aspect our personal planets, our partners take on the role of that planet in our lives, allowing us to learn to experience and integrate the energy of that planet more fully.

When we experience karmic aspects in our relationships, it's a very similar energy to experiencing a transit of that particular planet. The difference is that the transits will eventually pass, but the energy of the karmic aspect will always be present as long as we remain in relationship with our partner.

While it's easy to classify the karmic aspects as heavy and generally unpleasant, they're a fact of most relationships. Our relationships are designed to help us learn our spiritual lessons in the fastest and most efficient way possible. In a sense, the entire point of our relationships is found in the karmic aspects. Almost every significant, long-term relationship in our lives will involve at least one major karmic aspect, and most involve several. In fact, even though astrology cannot predict how long a relationship will last, it's worth noting that relationships that don't have any karmic aspects—and specifically, relationships that don't have aspects from Saturn to the personal planets—don't seem to last very long.

Of critical importance are aspects between one person's outer planets and the other person's Moon and/or Venus because these connections will have a direct and significant impact on how well the individuals are able to meet each other's Safety and Validation Needs. In particular, it's essential to note any karmic aspects that reinforce natal aspects and patterns that interfere with feeling safe or validated.

For example, if one individual has Moon square Uranus in his or her chart, *any* aspect from their partner's Uranus to their Moon will reinforce this aspect. The Moon individual will project their own Uranus issues with rejection and abandonment on this Uranus partner and this relationship will present an opportunity for the Moon person to heal some of their core issues with rejection and abandonment. The challenge, of course, is that the opportunity to heal these core issues arises because they will inevitably *experience* these patterns in the relationship. Healing is not possible until these individuals realize that the issues they are experiencing in the relationship are nothing more than projections of their own fears and false beliefs that they are experiencing reflected in the mirror of their partner in relationship.

We might assume that the best way to avoid triggering our core safety and validation patterns in relationship is to avoid partners whose outer planets reinforce our natal aspects. Unfortunately, this advice is almost impossible to follow. The entire point of relationships is that we use them to heal our own false beliefs and reconnect with the truth of who we are. We do this by attracting the perfect partners into our lives, and inevitably, what makes our partners perfect is the fact that they will confront us with the parts of ourselves that we most need to integrate (and that we least want to experience).

Remember that we can always heal our false beliefs and our negative patterns. No matter how many difficult aspects we may have to our Moon or Venus, we are perfectly capable of learning how to work with those energies in a conscious and skillful manner that allows us to feel safe and validated, both on our own and in relationship.

COMPATIBILITY PART 6: SYNTHESIZING SYNASTRY

After pulling things apart, it's very important to put them back together again. Step back and remind yourself of what each person's key relationship needs, desires, and patterns are. Look at the connections between the two charts and try to see where they are strongest—what is it that is drawing these two people together? Reinforced aspects? Double aspects? An elemental connection? Do their charts fill in the blanks for each other, completing aspect patterns or providing "missing" energy? Are the two charts very similar to each other or very different?

Just as when considering transits to the natal chart or themes in the natal chart, the more times a given issue comes up in the relationship charts, the more important and central to the relationship it will be.

When counseling on relationship issues, the most important thing to clarify is what's on each individual's Safety and Validation Checklists. What are their needs and how do they know if they're being met? The vast majority of relationship problems arise because the two partners do not realize that they speak different languages for safety and validation. Once they learn how to speak each other's language, they are able to effectively meet each other's Safety and Validation Needs.

12
Composite Charts

There is one last astrological technique that can be used when considering relationships: the composite chart. Composite charts are basically midpoint charts—that is, two charts are taken together, and a third chart is created from the midpoints of the planetary pairs of the two charts. In general, the near midpoint is used; however, this can occasionally result in an impossible chart (i.e., Mercury or Venus being too far from the Sun), so the opposite midpoint is sometimes used for Mercury and Venus.

Composite charts are a relatively new convention. They do seem to "work" in many circumstances, but frankly, the jury is still out as to exactly how valid they are in the first place, and how to work with them. Composite charts are used almost exclusively when analyzing relationships, and the composite chart is thought to be the chart of the relationship itself. In other words, the composite chart reflects the fundamental nature of the relationship as a separate entity from the two individuals that make up the relationship.

Midpoint composite charts aren't the only type of composite chart. While the midpoint chart averages the longitudinal positions of the planets, the Davidson Relationship Chart averages the charts in time, producing an actual chart for an actual date and time (the average of the birth dates) and an actual location (the average of the birth locations). Granted, the location may well be somewhere in the middle of an ocean somewhere, but nevertheless, it's a "true" chart, and a technique that many astrologers swear by.

I, however, am not one of them.

While midpoint composite charts arguably have some value, I can't find any value or foundation for the Davidson Relationship charts. They have no connection to either of the individuals in the relationship, or to the relationship itself. Personally, I don't find composite charts to be particularly useful—however, I'm willing to make a case for the theoretical value of the midpoint composite chart, with a few considerations.

The first consideration is that composite charts only apply to well-established relationships. The composite chart is, at least in theory, the chart of the relationship itself. A relationship has to grow and mature over time before it takes on its own dynamic. I would consider a composite chart for a couple that had been together for five years, but not for one that had been together for five months. The individuals have to be committed to the relationship, and more importantly, they have to have moved well beyond the courtship phase where they're trying to impress each other.

The next consideration is that because the composite chart is a midpoint chart, it's not possible to be positive of the sign placement of any of the planets. The most that you can do is to be sure of the sign axis. In general, when working with midpoints, the sign and house position is not taken into consideration. Most midpoint work is done using the 90° dial, which ignores the individual signs and houses entirely and operates entirely based on hard aspects. Each point on the 90° dial is actually four points on the 360° wheel, so when working with midpoints, both the direct and the opposite midpoint are combined, along with the two points that square the midpoint axis. Midpoints between two planets can be "triggered" at any of the four points: the direct (or near) midpoint, the opposite (far) midpoint, and also at the two points squaring the midpoints.

On its own then, the composite chart in a traditional 360° wheel has questionable value. We can't be sure of the signs or houses, so interpreting them is pointless. The only information of any direct relevance is the aspects between the composite planets. One could make a case for the fact that aspects in the composite chart would represent core themes or experiences of the relationship. For example, a composite chart with the Moon trine Venus might indicate a nurturing and supportive energy; one with Mars square Saturn could indicate aggression and conflict.

If we consider the composite chart as a collection of sensitive points, however, we're on firmer ground. Any transits to the composite chart would theoretically trigger the charts of both of the individuals, but the energy would play out specifically in the relationship. It might be possible to look at transits to the composite chart to identify some of the core challenges the individuals may experience in the relationship.

For me, the bottom line is that the composite chart doesn't provide me with any practical information that helps me help my clients. In a very real sense, it violates the cardinal rule of relationship counseling: Because it is a chart of the relationship, it does not focus on the individual.

☆13☆
Putting It Together Part 3: Comparing Charts

Now let's take a look at how our first two couples interact—and then we'll take a complete look at our third, and final couple.

Elizabeth Taylor and Richard Burton

Elizabeth Taylor and Richard Burton's synastry grid is shown in Figure 14.

Part 1: Elemental Compatibility

Elizabeth Taylor		Richard Burton	
☉	♓	☉	♏
☽	♏	☽	♍
As	♐	As	♋
Vx	♋	Vx	♐
♀	♈	♀	♑
☿	♓	☿	♐

Elementally, Taylor and Burton have some very nice connections, because of all of the Water and Earth involved. Taylor's Sun in Pisces recharges Burton's Sun in Scorpio and his Cancer Ascendant. Taylor's Moon in Scorpio makes a connection to Burton's Sun in Scorpio (and more than just a connection—they're conjunct each other), and makes a sextile to his Moon in Virgo. All in all, Taylor and Burton will tend to recharge each other energetically.

Across
SYNASTRY GRID
Down

Elizabeth Taylor
February 27, 1932, 2:00 A.M.
Golders Green, England
51°N34 000°W12′

Richard Burton
November 10, 1925, 7:58 P.M.
Pontrhydfendigaid, Wales
52°N17′ 003°W51′

	☽	☉	☿	♀	♂	♃	♄	♅	♆	♇	⚷	☊	☋	As	Mc	Vx	⊗
☽	✷ 3A27	☌ 4S43	☌ 4S33						☌ 5S23		△ 7A07			□ 4S32			
☉	☌ 2S28		⊼ 0S46		□ 2S44		⊼ 0S51		△ 2A18	☍ 1A12						△ 4A10	
☿		□ 0A09	□ 0A19					□ 0S32						☌ 0A20	✷ 1S07	⚻ 0S02	
♀		✷ 2A59	✷ 3A09					△ 2A19		⚻ 0S11				□ 1A43			
♂				△ 3A23	□ 2A08											⊼ 1A06	
♃	✷ 2S57		□ 1S15			□ 1S20		☍ 1A49	△ 0A43					☍ 3A42			
♄	☌ 1S40		⊼ 0A01		□ 1S56		⊼ 0S04		△ 3A05	☍ 1A59				△ 4A58			
♅	△ 6A17							△ 1A31	✷ 2A37	☌ 4S33	☌ 4S33			△ 0S21			
♆			☍ 6A51						⊼ 1A34								
♇	△ 0S50	△ 7A20	□ 2S32			□ 2S27		☌ 5S36									
⚷		∠ 2A47	☌ 7A55			☌ 8A00		□ 4A51				⊼ 1S14		□ 2A58			
☊			☍ 1S51					☌ 8A15		△ 2A11	✷ 2A11			☌ 6A23	△ 0S49		
☋			☌ 1S51							✷ 2A11	△ 2A11			☍ 6A23	✷ 0S49		
As	△ 0S39		□ 1A03	⚻ 0A28		□ 0A58		☌ 4A07	✷ 3A01					☌ 6A00			
Mc	△ 1A37	☌ 6S34	☌ 6S24		⊼ 1A21	∠ 1A28		△ 6A23									
Vx	□ 6A38		⚻ 1A30	□ 0A55		✷ 0A20	⚻ 1A25	□ 5A57		△ 4A21		☌ 6A48			△ 1A22		
⊗								✷ 1A48	△ 2A54	☍ 4A16	☌ 4A16			✷ 0A04	☍ 7A16		

Figure 14: Elizabeth Taylor and Richard Burton Synastry Grid

Part 2: Safety and Validation Needs

In this relationship, Burton's Safety and Validation Needs are likely to be met, and Taylor's Safety Needs are likely to be met. Taylor's Validation Needs, however, will be an issue.

Burton's Moon in Virgo receives a sextile from Taylor's Moon in Scorpio, and opposes Taylor's Sun and Mercury in Pisces. His Safety Needs are getting a lot of energy in the relationship. Likewise, Burton's Venus in Capricorn benefits from sextiles from Taylor's Sun and Mercury in Pisces and (by sign) from her Moon in Scorpio. Although there's less of a direct connection here, Burton's Validation Needs are apt to be supported, at least indirectly.

Taylor's Moon in Scorpio benefits from a conjunction to Burton's Sun in Scorpio, and a sextile from his Moon in Virgo. His Cancer ascendant also contributes to this mix. The result is that Taylor's need for emotional connections is likely to be well supported in this relationship. Her Venus in Aries, however, gets left out in the cold. Remember, Taylor has a core relationship pattern wherein she may feel that she has to choose either safety or validation in her relationships, but finds it exceedingly difficult to meet both sets of needs at the same time. Just as Burton's Sun in Scorpio supports Taylor's Safety Needs by conjuncting her Moon in Scorpio, it *also* triggers her Validation Needs by quincunxing her Venus in Aries, activating and enforcing the Moon-Venus quincunx in Taylor's natal chart.

The fact that Taylor and Burton speak fundamentally different and conflicting Validation Languages adds to the challenge of feeling loved and validated in this relationship. Both Taylor and Burton have Venus in Cardinal signs—they're both fundamentally concerned with being loved and validated for who they are as individuals—but they each have a very different way of expressing their individuality and different ways in which they want to be recognized. Because there is no aspect between Venus in Taylor's chart and Venus in Burton's chart, this represents a somewhat minor challenge in the relationship. It will, however contribute to Taylor's feeling that her Validation Needs are not being met in the relationship.

Part 3: Communication Styles

Taylor's Mercury in Pisces is in a partile square to Burton's Mercury in Sagittarius. This connection is both one of the sources of attraction between Taylor and Burton, and one of the most challenging obstacles for them in the relationship. When Taylor and Burton communicate, they will push each other's buttons. In the short run, this can be stimulating and exciting. Squares are active, 4th harmonic aspects. The 4th harmonic is about building and creating structure. As long as Burton and Taylor have an outlet for their communication energy—somewhere they can direct their joint expression and ideas—they will enjoy this connection. When they're not making a conscious effort to create and collaborate, however, they're likely to get on each other's nerves very quickly. It's interesting, isn't it, that Burton and Taylor enjoyed the happiest stretches of their two marriages to each other when they were working together, which gave them an ideal outlet for their mutual Mercury square.

Without that shared, external objective to channel this square, all communication will require Burton and Taylor to make a conscious effort to translate each other's language. This can become very draining over time; however, without the translation, miscommunication and arguments are inevitable, and these, of course are also very draining.

Part 4: Inter-Personal Connections

Burton and Taylor have one conjunction, two oppositions, one trine, three squares, three sextiles and one quincunx between their personal planets (Sun through Jupiter). The conjunction and the oppositions indicate attraction; the squares show where the passion and excitement is; and the trines and sextiles show where the flowing connections are. All in all, this is a very nice mix of aspects. On a personal level, Burton and Taylor seem very compatible with each other.

Looking at the romantic connections (Venus and Mars aspects), Taylor and Burton have Mars trine Mars, but no other connections. This would seem to indicate sexual compatibility, but not necessarily a tremendous amount of passion in the bedroom.

Part 5: Karmic Aspects
Richard Burton's Planets Aspecting Elizabeth Taylor's Planets

Richard Burton's Saturn is conjunct Elizabeth Taylor's Moon; his Uranus is trine her Moon, and his Pluto is trine her Moon. Once more, we see Taylor's Safety Needs being supported in this relationship. In particular, Burton's Saturn conjunct Taylor's Moon may be the most significant connection for Taylor. Taylor's Moon in Scorpio needs structure and trust before it can feel safe enough to explore the deep, transformational emotional connections it needs. Burton's Saturn conjunct her Moon makes Burton seem to be reliable, responsible, dependable and trustworthy. His Pluto trine her Moon tells her that he's capable of truly intense and powerful emotional connections—something that both appeals to and threatens her Moon in Scorpio. Finally, his Uranus trine her Moon picks up her Moon-Uranus quincunx. He has an element of unreliability that, while certainly not safe, is at least familiar to her (which in many ways, is more important); however, because it's a flowing energy, Taylor is likely to find this comforting rather than threatening.

At the same time, of course, Burton's Saturn quincunxes Taylor's Venus, and his Pluto squares her Venus. He makes her feel safe at the expense of her ability to feel loved and validated as an individual. Taylor is likely to experience Burton as being controlling and manipulative. Remember, this has nothing at all to do with Burton—it's all how Taylor experiences him. Until her Validation Needs reach the critical level, she's more likely to experience him as being supportive and protective, because Saturn and Pluto are meeting her Safety Needs. He will only seem to become controlling and manipulative when she can no longer ignore her Validation Needs in the relationship.

Elizabeth Taylor's Planets Aspecting Richard Burton's Planets

Elizabeth Taylor's Neptune is conjunct Richard Burton's Moon, square his Mercury and trine his Venus. Burton is apt to be dazzled by Taylor's glamour and romance; he will maintain an idealized picture of her. While these connections are wonderful for romance and mystery, they also indicate that he's likely to hold onto the fantasy image of Taylor for as long as he possibly can, and avoid addressing the reality. In particular, her Neptune trine his Venus could make Taylor seem to be the love of his life, his ideal woman in every aspect.

Taylor's Pluto trines Burton's Sun—when he's with her, he will feel powerful. When this is combined with the Neptune trine Venus, however, it could feed into his need to protect and support her, or even to rescue and save her. Her Pluto opposes his Jupiter, emphasizing his natal Jupiter-Pluto opposition on his Ascendant/Descendant axis, and adding to the powerful (and potentially explosive) energy of this relationship.

Taylor's Saturn squares Burton's Mars, indicating that he will feel that she prevents him from doing the things that he wants to do. Her Uranus quincunxes his Sun and squares his Jupiter. What starts out as fun and exciting for Burton may quickly become draining. And, especially with the Uranus quincunx Sun, Taylor's unpredictability and tumultuous nature may prove to be too much for Burton to handle. Staying in the relationship may force Burton to deny his own individual needs and sense of self because Taylor's Uranus energy consistently disrupts Burton's Sun. These challenging and draining energies may also tend to sneak up on Burton, because so long as he's under the romantic thrall of Taylor's Neptune contacting his Moon and Venus, he won't realize that he's not meeting his own fundamental survival needs in the relationship.

Part 6: Synthesizing Synastry

Taylor and Burton's relationship is all about safety and emotional connections. Their mutual attraction is powerful, and Neptune's influence was evidently strong enough to make them forget why they broke up in the first place, and resulted in their second marriage (and their second divorce). When

Taylor and Burton were together, they met each other's Safety Needs with a ferocious intensity. Essential as Safety is, however, once our Safety Needs are met, our Validation Needs become the focus of our attention, and that is where Taylor and Burton encountered their problems.

Jennifer Aniston and Brad Pitt

Jennifer Aniston and Brad Pitt's synastry grid is shown in Figure 15.

Part 1: Elemental Compatibility

Jennifer Aniston		Brad Pitt	
☉	♒	☉	♐
☽	♐	☽	♑
As	♎	As	♐
Vx	♊	Vx	♋
♀	♈	♀	♑
☿	♒	☿	♑

Elementally, Aniston and Pitt have some nice, flowing connections. Pitt's Sagittarius Sun and Ascendant sextile Aniston's Sun by sign (and Aniston's and Pitt's Suns are actually sextile each other as well). Pitt's Sagittarius Sun and Ascendant also connect with Aniston's Libra ascendant as well. And Aniston's Moon in Sagittarius shares the same energy as Pitt's Sun and Ascendant, although this connection is neutral because planets in the same sign do not recharge each other. The connections by sextile are pleasant and moderately recharging, indicating a reasonably high level of elemental compatibility.

We also must consider the larger picture, however, and note that while Jennifer Aniston has no Earth in her chart, Brad Pitt has four personal planets in Earth. And while Pitt has only one personal planet in Air, Aniston has three. This kind of "filling in" of each other's charts is quite common, and is a very strong indication of a mutual attraction between two individuals.

It's also worth noting that Pitt's Ascendant and Sun are both in Sagittarius, an energy that values personal freedom above all else, and one that gives him the appearance of being a rebel. Aniston's Saturn in Aries conjunct her Descendant loves this image. The fact that underneath this "bad boy" image, Pitt is actually very conservative (he's ruled by Saturn and has a very strong Capricorn energy in his chart) could create some challenges in their relationship because Aniston may expect Pitt to be far more adventurous than he actually is.

SYNASTRY GRID

Across: Jennifer Aniston
February 11, 1969, 10:22 p.m.
Sherman Oaks, California
34°N09′04″ 118°W26′54″

Down: Brad Pitt
December 18, 1963, 6:31 a.m.
Shawnee, Oklahoma
35°N19′38″ 096°W55′30″

	☽	☉	☿	♀	♂	♃	♄	♅	♆	♇	⚷	☊	☋	As	Mc	Vx	⊗
☽		☌ 7A37		✶ 1A00		□ 1S42			△ 1A43					□ 1A39	☍ 4A18	⚌ 1S35	
☉	☌ 2S36	✶ 2S30			△ 4S44			□ 1S19	□ 4A44	□ 5A02	□ 5A02			✶ 1S23	⚺ 1A16		☌ 1S17
☿					□ 5A01												
♀		☌ 6A59		✶ 0A22		□ 2S21			△ 1A05					□ 1A00	☍ 3A39		
♂	∠ 1S39		□ 0S48	∠ 1S11	□ 4S47												
♃	∠ 1S28		☌ 0S37	⚌ 1S00	☍ 4S35												
♄		☌ 4A14		□ 4A42	⚌ 1A06	✶ 1A59	⚌ 0S41							△ 5A20			
♅				⚺ 0A51										∠ 0A35		□ 3A49	
♆	□ 6A34				☌ 7A02			∠ 1A40		⚌ 1S12	⚌ 0S54	∠ 0S54					
♇		⚌ 1S13												∠ 2A06			
⚷														⚌ 1S06	⚌ 1A33	□ 4S20	
☊				□ 1S56					⚌ 2A28								
☋				□ 1S56					∠ 2A28								
As				△ 2S41										⚌ 0A13	☍ 5S40		
Mc	□ 3S43	△ 3A28			☌ 8A16		☌ 6A29	✶ 1A39	☌ 2S26	☍ 3A37	☍ 3A55	☌ 3A55		✶ 0A09		□ 2S24	
Vx		☍ 3A05		△ 3A32			△ 1A16	✶ 2A49	△ 3A14	△ 3A32				□ 2A53	☌ 0A14		
⊗				☌ 8A54					⚌ 0A39	⚌ 0A57	∠ 0A57						

Figure 15: Jennifer Aniston and Brad Pitt Synastry Grid

Part 2: Safety and Validation Needs

Aniston's Moon is in Sagittarius and her Venus is in Aries. She has a Fire Safety Checklist and a Fire Validation Checklist. It's relatively easy for her Safety and Validation Needs to be met: All she needs is to be able to take action and do something. Because of her Moon square Pluto, she may be very sensitive to feeling controlled or manipulated by other people. Autonomy and the freedom to act impulsively are key to her ability to feel safe and validated.

Pitt's Moon and Venus are conjunct in Capricorn, and he too has an easy time feeling safe and validated. What he needs is structure, responsibility, and boundaries, and as long as these are present for him, he will be perfectly happy in his relationships. He will tend to feel threatened by things that are abstract, impractical, or irresponsible.

In short, the things that make Jennifer Aniston feel safe and validated are likely to be threatening to Brad Pitt, and the things that make Brad Pitt feel safe and validated will definitely be threatening to Jennifer Aniston. Meeting each other's Safety and Validation Needs will be a challenge, because each one will need to learn to speak the other's language. The irony, of course, is that the things that Pitt and Aniston find the most attractive about each other are the things that will create the most challenges in terms of their being able to meet each other's needs. Aniston is attracted to the Earth in Pitt's chart, and because of his Sagittarius Sun and Ascendant, she believes he embodies the Saturn in Aries rebel archetype she finds so appealing; however, she will quickly find Pitt's need for structure and responsible action to be stifling, and may also interpret it as attempts to control her or otherwise limit her freedom, which are significant issues for her. Pitt is attracted to Aniston's ability to be abstract and social, but ultimately, he needs stability and boundaries in his relationships, and he may come to view Aniston as impulsive and irresponsible, which will significantly interfere with his ability to feel safe and validated in the relationship.

Simply taking Pitt and Aniston's Moon and Venus into account, then, it's unlikely that they will do a very good job of meeting each other's needs in the relationship. Exploring any aspects to Pitt and Aniston's Moon and Venus can show if there are other, more indirect ways that they may meet each other's needs.

The most obvious aspect is Pitt's Jupiter in a partile (same whole degree) conjunction with Aniston's Venus (37 minute orb). This more or less takes care of Aniston's Validation Needs in the relationship. When she's with Pitt, she will feel validated, respected and appreciated for who she is as an individual. It is worth noting, however, that Pitt's Uranus is quincunx Aniston's Venus, and Aniston does have a wide Venus-Uranus opposition in her natal chart. As well as Pitt may meet Aniston's Validation Needs, he may also bring out her core issues with rejection and abandonment.

Aniston's Mars is sextile Pitt's Moon and Venus, which indicates that she has the opportunity to meet Pitt's Safety and Validation Needs when she goes after the things that she wants. Of course, Mars is the sole dispositor of Aniston's chart—in a very real sense, she is ruled by her Mars in Scorpio. This energy may go a long way towards meeting Pitt's needs.

It's also worth noting that Aniston's Saturn is square Pitt's Moon and Venus. Normally, we would consider this aspect to present some challenges in meeting Pitt's Safety and Validation Needs. In this case, however, this connection may not be all bad. Remember that Saturn is Pitt's ruling planet and the sole dispositor of his chart. Moreover, Pitt's Saturn in Aquarius rules both his Moon and Venus in Capricorn. Pitt is apt to be very familiar, comfortable, and above all, safe with Saturn energy, even when it comes in the form of a Square.

These secondary aspects to the Moon and Venus will make some modest deposits in Pitt and Aniston's Need Accounts. However, these deposits are not significant enough to make up for the fundamental differences in their Safety and Validation Languages. They certainly provide some breathing room, but Pitt and Aniston will definitely have to learn how to speak each other's languages in order to meet each other's needs on an ongoing basis. Without that conscious effort, the balance in their Safety and Validation Accounts will steadily decrease over time.

Part 3: Communication Styles

Pitt's Mercury is in Capricorn (part of a Stellium with his Moon and Venus). Aniston's Mercury is in Aquarius. Capricorn and Aquarius have nothing in common by sign, element or modality, and normally this would indicate some fundamental challenges in communication. However, both Capricorn and Aquarius share the same ruler: Saturn. Moreover, Pitt's Mercury in Capricorn is ruled by his Saturn in Aquarius, so Pitt is very comfortable with Aquarian energy. In short, Pitt and Aniston should find it very easy to communicate with each other.

Part 4: Inter-Personal Connections

Pitt and Aniston have four conjunctions, three sextiles, one trine, one opposition, three semi-squares, three squares, and two sesquiquadrates between their personal planets (Sun through Jupiter). This is a very nice mix of energies. The conjunctions show a unity of purpose and shared point of view on many issues, while the sextiles and the trine provide comfortable, flowing connections where they can simply enjoy spending time together. The 4th and 8th harmonic aspects (semi-square, square and sesquiquadrate) provide the excitement and friction in the relationship. All in all, both the number of aspects and the mixture of the aspects indicate a high degree of compatibility between Pitt and Aniston.

Sexually, Pitt and Aniston have some serious heat going on. Pitt's Mars is square Aniston's Venus (partile), which is one of the surest indications of sexual attraction, and Aniston's Venus is sextile Pitt's Mars. That their Mars and Venus mutually aspect each other is an excellent sign of mutual attraction. Finally, Pitt's Mars is semi-square Aniston's Mars, which only contributes to the level of passion in the relationship.

Part 5: Karmic Aspects
Jennifer Aniston's Planets Aspecting Brad Pitt's Planets

Aniston's Saturn is square Pitt's Moon and Venus, and trine his Sun. As already mentioned, this may or may not present a challenge for Pitt because Saturn is such a familiar energy for him. Aniston's Saturn trine Pitt's Sun is a particularly nice energy, supporting as it does, Pitt's ability to express his true and authentic self. It is important to note, however, that the Saturn-Moon/Venus aspect does reinforce a similar energy in Pitt's chart, and that any difficulties Pitt may have in meeting his Safety and Validation Needs because of "Checklists from Hell" may be magnified and brought into the forefront of his relationship with Aniston. Pitt is already predisposed to work hard in order to accomplish his goals and meet his needs—hard work and personal responsibility are coded into his DNA because of his exceptionally strong Saturn. The challenges presented by these aspects may take time to become evident. Eventually, Pitt will discover how different Aniston's Saturn in Aries is from his own Saturn in Aquarius. Saturn in Aries tends to be autocratic, impulsive, and irrational, and Pitt may find that Aniston's Saturn in Aries refuses to give him the rewards he feels he's earned in terms of Safety and Validation.

Aniston's Neptune is semi-square Pitt's Mercury. Although minor, this aspect has the potential to create communication challenges due to misunderstandings and misinterpretations. In essence, Pitt may find that at times he is communicating with the fantasy and not with the reality.

Aniston's Chiron is technically square Pitt's Sun; however, the aspect is separating, and out of sign, as Aniston's Chiron has already moved into Aries. This aspect is not likely to have any significant impact on the relationship.

Finally, Aniston's Pluto is trine Pitt's Moon and Venus and Square his Sun. The Pluto square Sun aspect means that Pitt will be fundamentally changed by this relationship. This is not necessarily a challenging energy, as Pitt does not have any natal issues with Pluto. However, Aniston's Pluto trine Pitt's Moon and Venus is significant because it has a direct impact on Pitt's ability to feel safe and validated in his relationship with Aniston. At first, this energy may be exciting, promising the ability to have his needs met in a powerful and transformational way. However, when combined with the Saturn square Moon/Venus energy, this aspect takes on a less supportive role. The message soon becomes that in order to have his needs met in this relationship, he will have to give up control and accept that his needs will only be met on her terms, and not on his.

Brad Pitt's Planets Aspecting Jennifer Aniston's Planets

Pitt's Uranus is quincunx Aniston's Venus, and his Pluto is sesquiquadrate her Mercury. These are the only two karmic aspects from Pitt's chart to Aniston's chart. They are significant, however, because they play into the two key relationship issues in Aniston's chart: rejection and control.

As we've already mentioned, Aniston has a Venus-Uranus opposition in her natal chart, which indicates that she may find it difficult to feel validated in her relationships. Specifically, it indicates a potential issue or pattern with rejection and abandonment. That Pitt's Uranus is quincunx Aniston's Venus reinforces this energy; however, the quincunx aspect means that Aniston is unlikely to expect to encounter these issues in her relationship with Pitt, and when she does, they will come as a complete surprise to her. Because quincunxes often manifest as circumstances that appear to be beyond our personal sphere of control or influence, it's entirely possible that when Aniston experiences the interruption in her Validation Needs being met, that she may believe that Pitt is not directly responsible for it.

This is, of course, pure speculation and is written with the benefit of a certain amount of hindsight. However, one could assume from the tabloid scandal that Aniston certainly experienced rejection and abandonment when Pitt began his affair with Angelina Jolie. One could also guess that the affair was unexpected, and that Aniston is likely to blame Jolie much more than she blames Pitt. This scenario would, of course, fit perfectly with the interpretation of Pitt's Uranus quincunx Aniston's Venus.

Of lesser importance is Pitt's Pluto sesquiquadrate Aniston's Mercury. This aspect is often experienced as a mild degree of control over the Mercury person's ability and style of communication. The tension of sesquiquadrates often resolve through humor, and this could play out with verbal sparring that Aniston experiences as having perhaps more of an edge than Pitt intends. Since Aniston has a natal Moon square Pluto, she has a natural sensitivity to power, control, manipulation and abuse, and over time this aspect could begin to interfere with Aniston's ability to feel safe in the relationship.

Part 6: Synthesizing Synastry

While the mutual attraction between Brad Pitt and Jennifer Aniston is obvious, both from an elemental standpoint and from a synastry perspective, it was apparently not enough to keep the relationship going. On a fundamental level, Pitt and Aniston simply do not meet each other's Safety and Validation Needs without conscious effort and translation. They share some very nice connections, of course, and many of these connections make small deposits in their respective Need Accounts. However, when left to their natural, comfortable styles of behavior, they will eventually drain each other's Safety and Validation Accounts. As already noted, part of Aniston's attraction to Pitt is likely her belief that he is the rebel/adventurer/bad boy that he appears to be with his Sun and Ascendant in Sagittarius. However, the reality is that Pitt is far more responsible and conservative with his Capricorn Stellium, and this disconnect may have been one of the core reasons for Pitt and Aniston's divorce.

Couple Number 3: Paul Newman and Joanne Woodward

Finally, let's take a look at our final celebrity couple, Paul Newman and Joanne Woodward. We'll begin by looking at each chart individually, and then look at the charts together.

Paul Newman

Paul Newman's natal chart is shown in Figure 16.

Paul Newman
January 26, 1925, 6:30 A.M.
Cleveland, Ohio
41°N29'58" 081°W41'44"

Figure 16: Paul Newman's Natal Chart

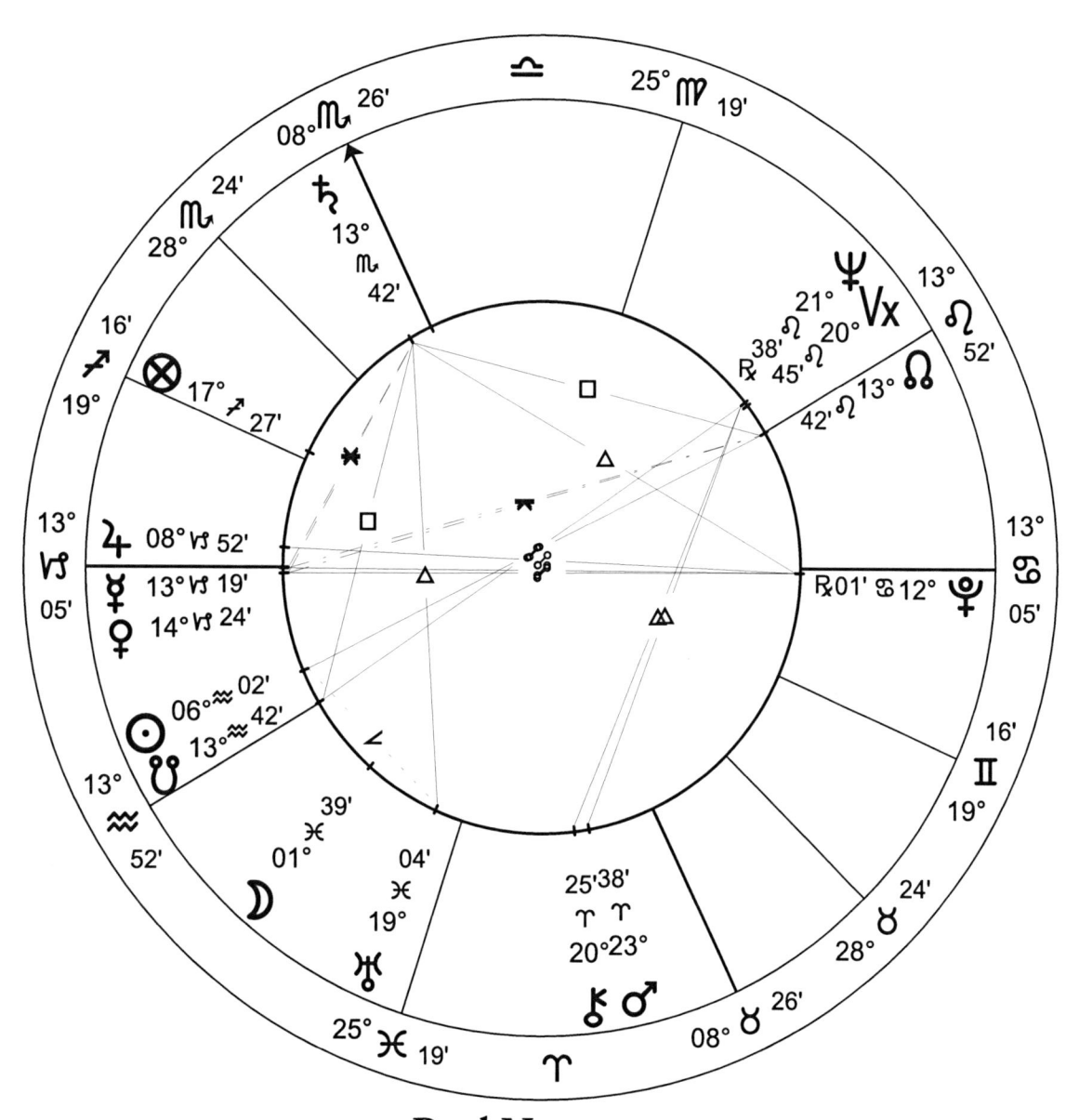

Part 1: Elements and Modalities

Element/Modality	Personal Planets	Personal Points	Outer Planets
Fire	♂	⊗ ☊ Vx	♇ ♆
Earth	☿ ♀ ♃	As	
Air	☉	☋	
Water	☽ ♄	Mc	♅ ♆
Cardinal	☿ ♀ ♂ ♃	As	♇ ♆
Fixed	☉ ♄	Mc ☊ ☋ Vx	♆
Mutable	☽	⊗	♅

Part 2: Temperament

Hemisphere	Planets	Quadrant	Planets
Northern (House 1–6)	☉ ☽ ☿ ♀ ♂ ♇ ♅ ♆	I (House 1–3)	☉ ☽ ☿ ♀ ♂ ♇ ♅
Southern (House 7–12)	♃ ♄ ♆	II (House 4–6)	♆
Eastern (House 10–12, 1–3)	☉ ☽ ☿ ♀ ♂ ♃ ♄ ♇ ♅	III (House 7–9)	♆
Western (House 4–9)	♆ ♇	IV (House 10–12)	♃ ♄

Paul Newman has a moderate emphasis in Earth and Water; he has only one planet each in Fire (Mars in Aries) and Air (Sun in Aquarius). He has an emphasis on Cardinal energy, with four planets in Cardinal signs, which means that he will be very initiating and fundamentally concerned with expressing and defining his identity. Although he has the ability to take action (Mars in Aries), he will tend to be more comfortable expressing himself through his emotions (Water) and the physical realm (Earth).

Temperamentally, Newman is apt to be very self-contained and self-reliant thanks to having six planets in his 1st quadrant, and a total of eight planets in the Eastern hemisphere.

Part 3: Essential Dignities

Pt	Ruler	Exalt	Trip	Term	Face	Detri	Fall	Score
☽	♃	♀	♂	♀	♄	☿	☿	−5 p
☉	♄	--	☿	☿	♀	☉ −	--	−10 p
☿	♄	♂	☽	♃ m	♂	☽	♃	−5 p
♀	♄	♂	☽	♃	♂ m	☽	♃	−5 p
♂	♂ +	☉	♃	♂ +	♀ m	♀	♄	+7
♃	♄	♂	☽	☿ m	♃ +	☽	♃ −	−3
♄	♂	--	♂	♃	☉	♀	☽	−5 p
♅	♃	♀	♂	☿	♃	☿	☿	--
♆	☉	--	♃	♃	♂	♄	--	--
♇	☽	♃	♂	♃	☿	♄	♂	--
⚷	♂	☉	♃	☿	♀	♀	♄	--
☊	☉	--	♃	♀	♃	♄	--	--
☋	♄	--	☿	♀	☿	☉	--	--
As	♄	♂	☽	♃	♂	☽	♃	--
Mc	♂	--	♂	♃	♂	♀	☽	--
Vx	☉	--	♃	♃	♂	♄	--	--
⊗	♃	☋	♃	☿	☽	☿	☊	--

Part 4: Dispositor Tree Diagram

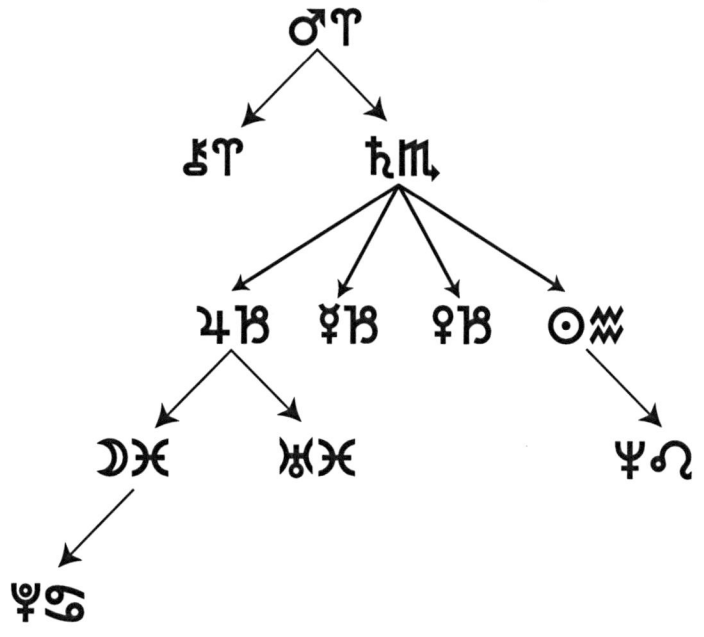

♂♈
├── ⚷♈
└── ♄♏
    ├── ♃♑
    ├── ☿♑
    ├── ♀♑
    └── ☉♒

♃♑
├── ☽♓
└── ♅♓
    └── ♇♋

☉♒
└── ♆♌

Mars in Aries is the sole dispositor of Paul Newman's chart, which would seem to indicate that he is driven by his need to express himself and to take impulsive action. However, this is not nearly as straightforward as it might seem. Even though Mars in Aries is the final dispositor, the only planets in the chart that get to "talk" to Mars directly are Chiron and Saturn. Every other planet in the chart has to go through Saturn before it gets to Mars. Saturn acts as Mars' lieutenant. Mars in Aries may be calling all of the shots, but it is basing its decisions on what Saturn in Scorpio is telling it. Saturn's influence may well be Newman's saving grace because with every planet reporting to Saturn before Mars chooses a course of action, Newman is far less likely to act impulsively, instinctively, or just irresponsibly.

Even so, Mars is the only planet in Newman's chart with any Essential Dignity. Every other planet is Peregrine, and the Sun in Aquarius is both Peregrine and in Detriment. From this we might conclude that Newman may take an unusual and somewhat wandering approach to gathering information; however, once he makes a decision and chooses a course of action, he is more than capable of accomplishing his goals.

Part 5: Relationship Needs

Newman's Moon is in Pisces, and his Venus is in Capricorn. He has a Water Safety Checklist and an Earth Validation Checklist.

Safety Needs

Newman's Moon in Pisces is of particular importance, since this is frequently an indication of poor energetic boundaries. Individuals with the Moon in Pisces are often especially sensitive to other people's emotions, and are virtual magnets for every bit of pain, misery and negative energy that they encounter. The natural function of the Moon in Pisces is to absorb and transmute other people's negative energy; however, individuals with the Moon in Pisces are not always consciously aware that this is going on, and they frequently suffer because of the amount of emotional garbage they attract to their energy fields. It's essential that Pisces Moon individuals take time every day for solitude of some kind; it's also essential that they learn how to clear their energy field of the accumulated emotions they pick up each day. The most effective way of doing this is by spending time every day in, near, and around water. This can be as simple as taking a long shower each day—that alone is sufficient to clear other people's emotions from their personal energy field and help restore the balance in their Safety Accounts.

Validation Needs

Newman's Venus in Capricorn indicates that he values hard work and responsibility in his relationships. In particular, he may value and appreciate people who know how to respect his boundaries—something that he may not experience too often because of his Pisces Moon. Boundaries are apt to be particularly important to Newman, because his Saturn in Scorpio is sextile his Venus. Newman certainly takes his relationships very seriously; he is also apt to consider communication an essential part of healthy relationships because his Mercury is conjunct his Venus in Capricorn. Venus in Capricorn tends to express and interpret appreciation and affection through physical representations (such as gifts) or through physical contact.

Part 6: Can Needs Be Met?
Feeling Safe and Feeling Validated (Moon and Venus Connection)

Although there are no aspects between Newman's Moon and Venus, Capricorn and Pisces are very compatible signs, and it's likely that he will have no difficulty feeling safe and validated at the same time. As already noted, the boundaries that are such a fundamental part of Capricorn energy (and his Validation Needs) may actually help him to feel truly safe, because the Moon in Pisces has inherently poor boundaries.

Pluto Aspects: Power Control, Manipulation and Abuse

Newman's Venus is opposite his Pluto, and since Pluto is on his Descendant, this energy will be prominent in all of his one-to-one relationships. To understand this dynamic, we also have to factor in the fact that Newman's Ascendant/Descendant axis is Capricorn/Cancer. With Pluto in Cancer on the Descendant, he is likely to perceive his partners in relationship as being powerfully—and often destructively—needy. There is a part of him that find this intense emotional need extremely attractive, because it allows him to ride in on a white horse, embodying the Capricorn energy of protector and provider, which is such a powerful part of who he is and how he experiences relationships. The challenge of course, is that this may make it difficult for him to feel truly validated. He may worry that people only love him because of what he does for them, and that if he stopped providing for them or taking care of them, they wouldn't love him anymore.

Part 7: Relationship Wants
Conscious Desires: Descendant in Cancer

As we've already noted, Newman's Descendant in Cancer (and Pluto in Cancer on the Descendant) means that he is powerfully attracted to individuals who are very much in touch with their emotional needs and not afraid to ask for help (putting it mildly!). While his Pisces Moon is thrilled with these partners, the dynamic of need and power could repeat old patterns he might have of enabling others and not knowing when to say no, rather than actually helping them in the most responsible and compassionate manner.

Unconscious Desires: Vertex in Leo

On an unconscious level, Newman is attracted to partners who embody not only the Leo energy of his Vertex, but also the Neptune in Leo energy, since his Neptune is conjunct his Vertex. Neptune in Leo is very much the movie star; these partners are glamorous, beautiful, temperamental, self-centered, and very likely appear to be different than they truly are. Leo energy can be needy just as Cancer energy is; however, the quality of need is very different with Leo, and neither his Pisces Moon nor his Capricorn Venus are likely to have their needs met with Vertex in Leo partners.

Part 8: Parents & Marriage Blueprint

Newman's Father is symbolized by Venus, the ruler of the 4th house, and his mother is symbolized by Mars, the ruler of the 10th house. Mars and Venus do not aspect each other, but they are square by sign: Mars is in Aries, and Venus is in Capricorn. It's not likely that Newman perceived his parents to have a great romance; rather, the foundation of his Marriage Blueprint is probably the belief that relationships take work, something he was already predisposed to believe because of the Capricorn energy in his chart.

Newman was certainly strongly influenced by his father in relationships, and he likely adapted much of his father's relationship styles and beliefs. We can see this because Venus, the planet that rules the 4th house, is in Newman's 1st house, on the Ascendant.

Newman's mother, on the other hand, is also very influential in his life. Although Newman's father was Jewish, his mother was Catholic. In Newman's chart, his mother, the ruler of the 10th house, is Mars in Aries, which is sole dispositor of Newman's chart. Mars is in Newman's 3rd house of early education, siblings, and personal spiritual connections. It's likely that Newman's mother had a profound influence on Newman's spirituality. His mother is certainly the one who encouraged Newman to pursue theatre.

One has to wonder, however, about Newman's mother, and Newman's relationship with her. Mars is conjunct Chiron in Aries, and trine both Neptune in Leo and Newman's Vertex in Leo. The trine from Neptune indicates that Newman may have idolized his mother, and perhaps not been fully aware of the nature of her wound—although with Chiron conjunct Mars, Newman certainly experienced his mother as wounded in some way.

Because Mars, the ruler of the 10th house is trine the Vertex, we could speculate that the qualities Newman is unconsciously attracted to are the qualities he most remembered about his mother.

Part 9: Friends, Lovers or Spouses?

Newman's 5th house of love affairs is ruled by Venus in Capricorn in the 1st house; his 7th house of marriage is ruled by the Moon in Pisces in the 2nd house; and his 11th house of friendship is ruled by Mars in Aries in the 3rd house. Other than the fact that the Moon and Venus are sextile by sign, there are no direct connections between these houses, and it's unlikely that Newman would be able to move his relationships from one house to the next. In particular, he may find it difficult to move from the 5th house to the 11th house or vice versa, because Mars and Venus are square by sign, if not by aspect.

JOANNE WOODWARD

Joanne Woodward's natal chart is shown in Figure 17.

Joanne Woodward
February 27, 1930, 4:00 A.M.
Thomasville, Georgia
30°N50′11″ 083°W58′44″

Figure 17: Joanne Woodward's Natal Chart

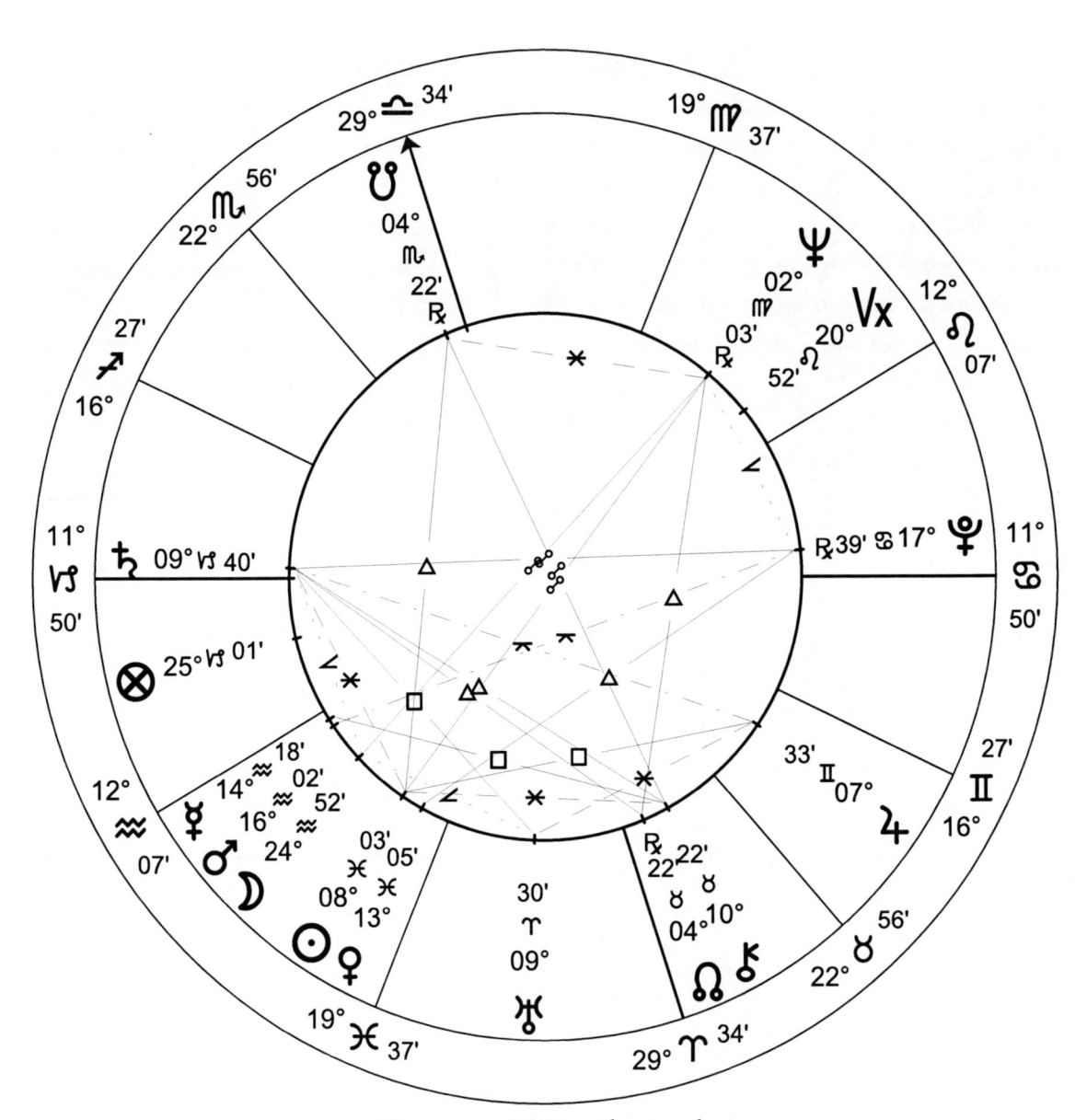

Part 1: Elements and Modalities

Element/Modality	Personal Planets	Personal Points	Outer Planets
Fire		Vx	♅
Earth	♄	As ☊ ⊗	⚷ ♆
Air	☽ ☿ ♂ ♃	Mc	
Water	☉ ♀	☋	♇
Cardinal	♄	As Mc ⊗	♅ ♇
Fixed	☽ ☿ ♂	☊ ☋ Vx	⚷
Mutable	☉ ♀ ♃		♆

Part 2: Temperament

Hemisphere	Planets	Quadrant	Planets
Northern (House 1–6)	☉ ☽ ☿ ♀ ♂ ♃ ⚷ ♅	I (House 1–3)	☉ ☽ ☿ ♀ ♂ ♅
Southern (House 7–12)	♄ ♆ ♇	II (House 4–6)	♃ ⚷
Eastern (House 10–12, 1–3)	☉ ☽ ☿ ♀ ♂ ♄ ♅	III (House 7–9)	♆ ♇
Western (House 4–9)	♃ ⚷ ♆ ♇	IV (House 10–12)	♄

The first thing we notice about Joanne Woodward is that she has a significant emphasis in Air, with four planets (Moon, Mercury, Mars and Jupiter) in Air signs, three of which make up a Stellium in Aquarius. Communication, social interaction, and intellectual stimulation will be essential to her overall health and happiness. Although she only has two planets in Water, these planets are the Sun and Venus in Pisces, so emotional connections are also very important to her. The combination of Aquarius and Pisces energy indicates a great deal of compassion for humanity, and because of the Pisces influence, she is able to experience and express this energy on a personal level rather than on an exclusively abstract and intellectual level, as is usually the case with Aquarius energy. Woodward has only one planet in Earth; however, this planet is Saturn in Capricorn, so she is apt to have no difficulty with being grounded and practical when she needs to be.

The lack of Fire in her chart indicates that she will need to supplement this energy by engaging in some kind of physical activity every day. It's rare that individuals with no Fire in their charts overcompensate by being too driven, and especially considering that the only Cardinal planet Woodward has is Saturn in Capricorn, she's more likely to require a conscious effort to overcome her inertia and get moving. Once she does get moving, however, with three Fixed planets and three Mutable planets, she is apt to keep going. The three Fixed planets are the three planets in Aquarius, so she's likely to be especially attached to her point of view and her ideals. She may also base her sense of self-worth on how other people respond to her in a social and intellectual setting. She is also skilled at adapting and changing, because of the three Mutable Planets (Sun, Venus and Jupiter).

Part 3: Essential Dignities

Pt	Ruler	Exalt	Trip	Term	Face	Detri	Fall	Score
☽	♄	--	☿	♃	☽ +	☉	--	+1
☉	♃	♀	♂	♃	♄	☿	☿	−5 p
☿	♄	--	☿ +	♀	☿ +	☉	--	+4
♀	♃	♀ +	♂	♃	♃	☿	☿	+4
♂	♄	--	☿	♀	☿	☉	--	−5 p
♃	☿	☊	☿	♃ +	♃ +	♃ −	☋	−2
♄	♄ +	♂	☽	☿	♃	☽	♃	+5
♅	♂	☉	♃	♀	♂	♀	♄	--
♆	☿	☿	☽	☿	☉	♃	♀	--
♇	☽	♃	♂	☿	☿	♄	♂	--
⚷	♀	☽	☽	☿	☽	♂	--	--
☊	♀	☽	☽	♀	☿	♂	--	--
☋	♂	--	♂	♂	♂	♀	☽	--
As	♄	♂	☽	☿	♂	☽	♃	--
Mc	♀	♄	☿	♂	♃	♂	☉	--
Vx	☉	--	♃	♃	♂	♄	--	--
⊗	♄	♂	☽	♄	☉	☽	♃	--

Part 4: Dispositor Tree Diagram

$$\saturn \capricorn$$
↓ ↓ ↓
$$\mercury \aquarius \quad \mars \aquarius \quad \moon \aquarius$$
↓ ↓ ↓ ↓
$$\jupiter \gemini \quad \neptune \virgo \quad \uranus \aries \quad \pluto \cancer$$
↓ ↓
$$\sun \pisces \quad \venus \pisces$$
↓
$$\chiron \taurus$$

If we had any doubts about Woodward's ability to express and experience the element of Earth, they're certainly laid to rest now. With Saturn in Capricorn ruling her entire chart as the sole dispositor (not to mention that it is the ruler of the Ascendant, conjunct the Ascendant, and the rising planet in the chart), Woodward is all about the grounded, practical, and above all responsible energy of Earth in general, and Saturn in Capricorn in particular. That Saturn's lieutenants are all planets in Aquarius—her Moon, Mercury and Mars, to be specific—does set up an interesting dynamic. Capricorn energy respects the rules and traditions and never questions them because they are the rules and traditions. Aquarius energy, on the other hand, always questions and tests the rules, making sure that the rules still work, and still support the greatest amount of personal freedom for the individuals in the group. Everything about the ways that Woodward expresses emotions and experiences Safety (Moon), communicates and experiences reality (Mercury) and goes after the things that she wants in the world (Mars) is about questioning and testing the accepted rules, and yet her fundamental programming is to respect the rules without questioning them. The result may be a tendency to live on the edge—pushing the envelope as far as it can go without ever once actually crossing the line.

The most "masculine" planets in Woodward's chart, the Sun and Mars fare the worst, as both are Peregrine. Neither Mars in Aquarius nor the Sun in Pisces is able to take the kind of direct, focused action that these planets need. They are forced to learn how to accomplish their goals in other ways. Woodward's Jupiter in Gemini is also notable, because even though it is in the sign of its Detriment, it receives dignity by both Term and Face. This is a Jupiter that, even though it worries (Detriment) about overlooking the little details, has learned how to keep an eye on the big picture while addressing the smaller components. This is important to consider, because Woodward's Sun and Venus in Pisces both report to this Jupiter.

Part 5: Relationship Needs

Woodward's Moon is in Aquarius, and her Venus is in Pisces.

Safety Needs

Woodward's Moon is in Aquarius, so she has an Air Safety Checklist. Her Moon has dignity only by Face, and Face means fear. The Moon in Air signs is extremely uncomfortable because Air signs do not like to express deep emotions; Air signs prefer to operate in the mental, social, and intellectual realms, making connections along the surface, but rarely exploring what lies beneath. Aquarius is entirely a group oriented energy, and individuals with the Moon in Aquarius need to believe that they are in relationship with people who share the same group affiliation in order to feel safe. With Aquarius, the group can be defined by one single idea or value, but that idea or value can never be questioned. It's likely that Woodward has a core fear that she is not, in fact, a rightful member of the group, because her Aquarius Moon has dignity only by Face. If her Moon were Peregrine as opposed to having dignity by Face, she would be far less aware that she might not be in the group she thinks she's in. Her ignorance might actually help her to feel more safe.

Validation Needs

Woodward's Venus is in Pisces, so she has a Water Validation Checklist. Individuals with Venus in Pisces value the emotional and spiritual connections in relationships above all else. She will feel loved and appreciated when she is able to merge energetically with her partners.

Part 6: Can Needs Be Met?
Feeling Safe and Feeling Validated (Moon and Venus Connection)

Woodward may have some fundamental challenges in feeling both safe and validated at the same time, because she has an Air Safety Checklist and a Water Validation Checklist, and Air and Water have the most difficult time working together. The one saving grace is that her Moon and Venus are only one sign apart, and even though Aquarius and Pisces have nothing in common in terms of modality, polarity or element, they do share a fundamental connection because one sign naturally evolves into the other. Since her Venus in Pisces (Exaltation) is so much stronger than her Moon in Aquarius (Face), it's likely that her Validation Needs will take precedence. Once she experiences the spiritual and emotional connections, she can then tell herself that she is only able to experience these connections because she and her partner share the same ideals and values, which is what her Moon in Aquarius needs in order to feel safe.

Saturn Aspects: Checklists from Hell
Uranus Aspects: Rejection, Abandonment and Unreliability

Woodward has a partile square in her chart between Saturn (at 9 Capricorn) and Uranus (at 9 Aries). Her Moon, at 24 Aquarius is at the exact midpoint of this square, and is semi-square to both her Saturn and her Uranus. While the Saturn-Uranus square is more or less a generational aspect, the fact that Woodward's Moon is tied in with it means that this energy—the tension between Saturn in Capricorn's need to respect the existing rules and social structures, and Uranus in Aries' need to break free of the rules and express a unique, individual identity—is inexorably linked to Woodward's Safety Needs. She experiences this tension on a very personal level, and her ability to feel safe depends entirely on how well she is able to balance these conflicting energies.

This, of course, repeats the theme we first noted when looking at Woodward's dispositor tree: the tension between Aquarius' need to revise rules that no longer support the group and Capricorn's rigid adherence to the rules. Woodward is most likely acutely aware of the rules, expectations, boundaries and limitations of any given situation, because on the one hand, she needs to respect them, and on the other hand, she needs to make sure that she has the greatest amount of personal freedom to express herself within those rules. In order to feel safe, she must always operate on the edge, going as far as she possibly can without crossing over the line. It's also likely that in order to feel safe, she will always need to know where the line is, and in relationship, she may do this by testing the boundaries of her partners.

Pluto Aspects: Power Control, Manipulation and Abuse

Woodward's Venus is trine Pluto, indicating that for her, relationships will always carry a powerful, transformational emotional component. Her Pluto is also in her 7th house, on her Descendant (although it does not aspect her Saturn or Uranus). Relationships will always have an element of power and control in them for Woodward, and because we tend to project planets in the 7th house on our partners, she is apt to see her partners in relationship as the ones with the power. Since her Venus is trine her Pluto, this is most likely something that appeals to her. She may feel that the entire purpose of relationships is to be transformed. The only issues she has with Pluto come from her Mars quincunx Pluto. This aspect would indicate that she does have a very specific limit to how much she is willing to be influenced or transformed by her partners in relationship, and once that limit is reached, she will act out and defend herself.

Even though her Mars and Moon are not conjunct each other, and her Moon is out of aspect and separating from a quincunx to Pluto, when her Mars-Pluto quincunx is triggered, this is likely to have an impact on the balance in her Safety Account. However, it's unlikely that Woodward has a fundamental safety issue with Pluto.

Part 7: Relationship Wants
Conscious Desires: Descendant in Cancer

Woodward's Descendant in Cancer, combined with her Pluto in Cancer on the Descendant means that she will be powerfully attracted to partners who have deep emotional needs, and the ability to experience and initiate powerful emotional connections. These partners will do an excellent job of meeting her Venus in Pisces Validation Needs; however, Woodward's Moon in Aquarius is especially uncomfortable with the emotional energy of Cancer. If these partners get too needy or too emotionally intense, they will trigger Woodward's Safety Needs, and she will have to pull back, retreating to the abstract, theoretical and intellectual realm of Aquarius—something that her Descendant in Cancer partners will not appreciate at all.

Unconscious Desires: Vertex in Leo

On an unconscious level, Woodward is attracted to partners who embody the Leo archetype. These partners are warm, charismatic, generous, loving, dynamic, creative and above all, self-centered and in need of validation and attention. The Vertex in Leo partners will actually do a better job of meeting Woodward's Safety Needs, because Leo is the opposite sign of Aquarius. Not only is Woodward apt to find partners with Leo energy very attractive (remember, she has no Fire in her chart), but they will also help her to balance the Aquarius Stellium in her chart by helping her to learn to feel safe being the center of attention. In the meantime, her Moon in Aquarius will be perfectly happy being an appreciative audience for her Vertex in Leo partners.

Part 8: Parents & Marriage Blueprint

Woodward's Father is represented by Mars in Aquarius, the ruler of her 4th house. Her mother is represented by Venus in Pisces, the ruler of her 10th house. Once again, we encounter the

Pisces/Aquarius connection. Even though there is no aspect between her Venus and Mars and they are in signs with nothing in common by element, modality or polarity, there is still some connection between the two signs. Also, the fact that both Mars and Venus are in Woodward's 2nd house is another indication that her impressions of her parent's marriage are largely favorable.

Part 9: Friends, Lovers or Spouses?

Woodward's 5th house of love affairs is ruled by Venus in Pisces in the 2nd house; her 7th house of marriage is ruled by the Moon in Aquarius in the 2nd house; and her 11th house of friendship is ruled by Mars in Aquarius in her 2nd house. Obviously, the most direct connection is between friends and marriage partners, because the rulers of the 7th and 11th are in the same sign; however, as the rulers of all three houses are in the same house, it's very easy for Woodward to move her relationships from one house to the next. It's also worth noting that because the rulers of the three relationship houses are each in Woodward's 2nd house of resources, that she is apt to consider her relationships to be very important and valuable parts of her life.

PAUL NEWMAN AND JOANNE WOODWARD

Paul Newman and Joanne Woodward's synastry grid is shown in Figure 18.

Part 1: Elemental Compatibility

PAUL NEWMAN		JOANNE WOODWARD	
☉	♒	☉	♓
☽	♓	☽	♒
As	♑	As	♑
Vx	♌	Vx	♌
♀	♑	♀	♓
☿	♑	☿	♒

Newman and Woodward share the same elemental energies in their charts; both have Capricorn on the Ascendant, and while Newman has Sun in Aquarius and Moon in Pisces, Woodward has Sun in Pisces and Moon in Aquarius. While these connections are definitely very strong, they are ultimately neutral in quality. Newman and Woodward will not drain each other's energy; however, the also won't recharge each other.

PUTTING IT TOGETHER PART 3: COMPARING CHARTS

Across

Paul Newman
January 26, 1925, 6:30 A.M.
Cleveland, Ohio
41°N29′58″ 081°W41′44″

SYNASTRY GRID

Down

Joanne Woodward
February 27, 1930, 4:00 A.M.
Thomasville, Georgia
30°N50′11″ 083°W58′44″

	☽	☉	☿	♀	♂	♃	♄	♅	♆	♇	⚷	☊	☋	As	Mc	Vx	⊗
☽	☌ 6A47			✱ 1S14	∠ 1S01				☍ 3S15	⚻ 2A09						☍ 4S07	
☉	☌ 6S24			∠ 0A35	✱ 0A49	△ 5A39			△ 3A58					△ 0A22			
☿						□ 0S36		☍ 7A20			☍ 0S36	☌ 0S36				☍ 6A27	✱ 3A09
♀		✱ 0A14	✱ 1A20			△ 0A37	☌ 5A59		△ 1S03		⚻ 0A38		✱ 0A00	△ 4S39		☍	□ 4A22
♂						□ 2S20		☍ 5A36			☍ 2S19	☌ 2S19				☍ 4A43	✱ 1A25
♃	□ 5S54	△ 1S31			∠ 1A05	⚻ 1A19					△ 6A09			⚻ 0A52			
♄			☌ 3A39	☌ 4A45		☌ 0S48			☍ 2A22					☌ 3A25	✱ 1S14		
♅			□ 3A49	□ 4A55		□ 0S38			□ 2A32		△ 4A13			□ 3A35	⚻ 1S04		
♆	☍ 0A24																
♇	⚻ 1A00		☍ 4A20	☍ 3A14		△ 3A57	△ 1S25		☌ 5A38	□ 2S46		☍ 4A34				⚻ 0A12	
⚷		□ 4S20	△ 2A57	△ 4A03		△ 1S30	☍ 3A20		✱ 1A40		□ 3A21	□ 3A21	△ 2A43	☍ 1S56			
☊	✱ 2A43	□ 1S39				△ 4S30			∠ 0A19					☍ 4S03		⚻ 1A55	
☋	△ 2A43	□ 1S39							⚻ 0A19					☌ 4S03		∠ 1A55	
As			☌ 1A28	☌ 2A34		☌ 2S59	✱ 1A52			☍ 0A11		⚻ 1A52		☌ 1A14			
Mc	△ 2A05	□ 6A28			☍ 5S56										☌ 8A52		
Vx					△ 2A46			⚻ 1A48	☌ 0A46		△ 0A27	☌ 7A09	☍ 7A09			☌ 0A07	△ 3A25
⊗					□ 1A23				□ 4A36								

Figure 18: Paul Newman and Joanne Woodward Synastry Grid

Every partner in every relationship is our mirror. Of course, when two individuals share so many essential energies in common, the fact that they mirror each other becomes even more obvious. Whether or not these individuals get along or are attracted to each other depends entirely on how well each individual loves and accepts him or herself. If either individual is not comfortable and accepting of him or herself, they will see the parts of themselves that they most wish to disown magnified and embodied in the other. On the other hand, the more they love and accept themselves, the more they will love and accept their partner.

Part 2: Safety and Validation Needs

The most obvious connection in terms of Newman and Woodward's relationship needs is between Newman's Moon in Pisces and Woodward's Venus in Pisces. That Newman and Woodward have this language in common means that Newman's Safety Needs and Woodward's Validation Needs will easily be met in the relationship. Newman and Woodward's Validation Needs are also taken care of because of the very harmonious relationship between Newman's Venus in Capricorn and Woodward's Venus in Pisces. Not only are the two signs compatible, but the two planets are actually sextile each other indicating a very strong connection between Newman's and Woodward's Validation Accounts.

While Newman's Safety and Validation Needs are easily met, and Woodward's Validation Needs are also easily met, Woodward's Safety Needs may present some minor challenges in the relationship. Woodward's Moon in Aquarius is largely uncomfortable with deep emotional connections. Where Newman needs emotional connections to feel safe, Woodward needs distance and objectivity. The saving grace is that Woodward is extremely familiar with the Aquarius-Pisces dynamic, since this dynamic is one of the dominant themes of her chart. Newman's strong Capricorn influence—and particularly his Venus in Capricorn—indicates that he values boundaries, so it's likely that he will be able to give Woodward the space she needs when she needs it, helping her to meet her Safety Needs. All in all, it's likely that Newman and Woodward do an excellent job of meeting each other's Safety and Validation Needs.

Part 3: Communication Styles

Newman and Woodward have very different communication styles, and yet once again, they share connections and common themes in their charts that most likely overcome any potential challenges. Newman's Mercury is in Capricorn, and Woodward's Mercury is in Aquarius. Capricorn and Aquarius have nothing in common by element, modality or polarity, but they do share two connections. First, one sign evolves into the other, which always indicates a certain level of connection. Second, and most importantly, both Capricorn and Aquarius are ruled by Saturn. Because of this, we can look at the relationship between Newman's Saturn and Woodward's Saturn for more information. Woodward's Saturn in Capricorn is the sole dispositor of her chart; Newman's Saturn in Scorpio is also exceptionally important, as every planet in his chart reports to it, and then Saturn reports to Mars, the sole dispositor of his chart. Both Newman and Woodward are very powerfully influenced by Saturn, and Newman's Saturn in Scorpio is sextile Woodward's Saturn in Capricorn. In short, while they may have differing communication styles, they have a tremendous amount of common ground, and communication is apt to be very easy for them.

Part 4: Inter-Personal Connections

Newman and Woodward have two conjunctions (although one is out of sign), four sextiles, one trine, three semi-squares, one square and one quincunx between their personal planets, (Sun through Jupiter). Overall, this emphasizes the more flowing, easy connections. There may not be a tremendous level of excitement in their relationship, but there is probably a great deal of comfort and support.

Sexually, the only connection between Mars and Venus in their charts is the sextile between Venus in Newman and Woodward's chart. This certainly indicates a strong attraction, although again, it's apt to be more comfortable than torrid.

Part 5: Karmic Aspects
Paul Newman's Planets Aspecting Joanne Woodward's Planets

Newman's Saturn is in a partile trine to Woodward's Venus, and a wide trine to her Pisces Sun. As Woodward's Sun and Venus are both sextile her Saturn, this energy is very familiar and very supportive to her. Newman's Saturn also squares Woodward's Mars/Mercury conjunction. Taken together, Newman provides structure and support to Woodward, while at the same time, he will tend to challenge her ideas and desires (Saturn square Mercury/Mars). Considering how familiar Woodward is with Saturn energy, and the fact that Newman's Saturn is sextile her Saturn, these connections are likely to be familiar and quite supportive. Newman's Saturn may challenge Woodward to refine and define the ways that she communicates and goes after the things that she wants.

Newman's Uranus is widely conjunct Woodward's Venus. Since Woodward does not have any major patterns with rejection or abandonment, Woodward probably experiences this aspect as exciting. More importantly, in the absence of any Venus-Mars aspects between their charts, this aspect could be responsible for turning up the heat in the bedroom.

Newman's Neptune in Leo opposes Woodward's Moon, Mercury and Mars in Aquarius, and conjoins her Vertex in Leo. Woodward is likely to project her ideal romantic fantasy on Newman. She may also tend to let her energetic and emotional boundaries down around him, which allows for deeper connections. Since her Moon in Aquarius does not especially appreciate deeper emotional connections, this could potentially create Safety issues for Woodward. However, since Woodward does not have any core issues with Neptune in her natal chart, this Neptune-Moon opposition (which, by the way, is another generational aspect that Woodward would experience with any partner born in the same year as Newman), could help Woodward to become comfortable with experiencing and expressing her feelings on a deeper level.

Finally, Newman's Pluto trines Woodward's Sun and Venus. This does repeat Woodward's natal Venus trine Pluto aspect, and even though it is an aspect that Woodward would share with everyone born within a few years of Newman, it indicates that Newman has the power, depth and deep emotional reserves that Woodward needs in relationship.

Joanne Woodward's Planets Aspecting Paul Newman's Planets

The most significant connections for Newman come from Woodward's Saturn, which is conjunct Newman's Mercury, Venus, Jupiter and Ascendant. These connections are very supportive, and quite familiar to Newman. Each of these points is ruled by Newman's Saturn in Scorpio, and all three planets, plus his Ascendant are sextile his Saturn. While some people might experience this kind of aspect from Saturn to be limiting and restrictive, Newman almost certainly experiences it as easy, comfortable, and supportive in every way.

Of course, the fact that Woodward's Saturn is conjunct Newman's Mercury, Venus, Jupiter and Ascendant also means that her Uranus is square these points. Since Newman does not have any particular issues with Uranus in his chart, and indeed, since his Uranus is trine his Saturn, he is likely to have a very healthy relationship with Uranus, Newman is likely to experience these squares as energizing and exciting. Too much Saturn energy can become oppressive. The squares from Woodward's Uranus are just the thing to keep him challenged, interested, and energized.

Woodward's Neptune opposes Newman's Moon. This is an aspect that Newman and Woodward share—each one's Neptune opposes the other one's Moon. Again, this aspect is an indication of a definite romantic attraction, and a tendency to idealize their partners. Newman's Moon in Pisces is far more comfortable with this energy, because his Moon in Pisces enjoys the experience of merging with another person on an emotional and spiritual level. The one challenge with this aspect is that it will tend to magnify the Moon in Pisces's core boundary issues. Considering how much Saturn energy Newman has in his chart, however, it's unlikely that poor boundaries will be a factor in his relationships.

Woodward's Pluto is sesquiquadrate to Newman's Moon, and opposes his Venus and Mars. This is largely a repeat of the aspects in Newman's natal chart: his natal Pluto opposes the Capricorn Stellium of Jupiter, Mercury and Venus. For the most part, this energy will be very familiar to Newman and does not present any challenges. The one component that is not present in Newman's chart, however, is any aspect between his natal Moon and natal Pluto. Even though Newman expects his relationships to be powerful and transformational because of his Pluto on the Descendant, this particular relationship is apt to challenge him to transform on levels that may occasionally trigger his safety alarms. Once again, however, since Newman does not have any Moon-Pluto aspects in his natal chart, this aspect does not necessarily present any challenges.

Finally, Woodward's Chiron squares Newman's Sun, and Trines his Mercury, Venus and Jupiter. Chiron aspects in synastry indicate opportunities to heal our core wounds. Although Newman does not have any Chiron patterns in his chart that specifically relate to his relationships, it's worth noting that he does have Chiron conjunct his Mars in Aries, which is the sole dispositor of his chart. Newman has a fundamental wound with his identity, and the way that he goes after the things that he wants. His relationship with Woodward may present an opportunity for him to address and explore this wound in a supportive, non-threatening, and above all, indirect way. The planets being aspected by Woodward's Chiron are all in Capricorn, so they share the core issue of identity; however, none of these planets are connected to Newman's Chiron natally. It's an interesting connection to consider, but once again, not an aspect that presents any challenges in the relationship.

Part 6: Synthesized Synastry

The reasons for the success of Newman and Woodward's marriage are obvious. First and foremost, they individually have few inherent difficulties in feeling safe and validated, and they have so much in common that they naturally and easily meet each other's Safety and Validation Needs. The glue that holds their relationship together comes from the many Saturn aspects between their charts, and the fact that Saturn is such an important planet for each of them. They each have an inherent understanding that relationships take work, and require dedication, responsibility and person accountability.

As indicated earlier, the deciding factor in this relationship is how well Newman and Woodward love and appreciate themselves. Because they share so many common energies in their charts, they will be especially powerful and, more to the point, obvious mirrors for each other. The success of their relationship with each other is largely a product of the success of each of their relationships with themselves.

☖14☗
Relationship Counseling

With the wealth of information and insight that astrology can provide about human relationships, astrology can be a particularly effective tool in relationship counseling. Each counselor develops his or her own approach to working with clients, whether they use astrology as a tool or not. All that I can share in this chapter are some insights to how I, personally, use astrology as a tool for relationship counseling.

For me, the first and most important rule of any kind of counseling is the **Universal Law of Relationships.** Our partners in relationships are our mirrors. They reflect our own issues back to us. It is *never* about the other person. I believe that this is the most important rule to embrace and understand when undertaking any kind of counseling because when we sit down to counsel a client, *we are in relationship with that client, and therefore we are subject to the Universal Law of Relationships.*

It's *never* about the other person. Ever. Even when the other person is a client who has come to us for advice and guidance. On a very fundamental level, *every bit of advice we ever give to a client has nothing to do with them and everything to do with us.*

The person who most needs to follow the advice given during a counseling session is the person who is giving the advice in the first place.

Even though every bit of advice and guidance we give to our clients really applies to us, this is not to say that the advice does not have merit or use for our clients as well. Being aware of this truth, however, is one of the most effective ways to keep our own egos in check—not to mention a powerful way to advance rapidly along our own spiritual path.

The biggest problem that I personally have with the more mainstream types of therapy and counseling is my perception that the therapists are trained to be objective to the point of denying their own issues, lessons and biases. While most therapists participate in some kind of peer counseling (most therapists are, themselves, also in therapy), my perception is that the culture of modern psychology and psychiatry forces most therapists—at least during the time spent with their clients—to pretend that they, themselves are entirely free from the neuroses and relationship challenges that plague their clients.

Again, I want to emphasize that these are my own, personal perceptions and may not in fact have any objective truth. However, I personally believe that most therapists would be far more effective if they were willing to acknowledge, at least to themselves, that they pursued a career in therapy in order to attempt to heal their own wounds, and that they inevitably attract clients who share the same issues as they do themselves.

I always endeavor to be very open about this for myself. I have become an expert on relationships not because I am inherently skilled at human relationships, but rather because I spent most of my life in relationships that did not support me. I teach relationship skills because I am continuously in the process of learning how to apply and master these skills myself, integrating them into my own life. Just because I've been very successful at "walking my talk" and using my understanding of Safety and Validation Needs to improve the relationships in my life doesn't mean that it's *easy* for me—nor does it mean that my relationships, or my behavior in relationships, is always exemplary. All it means is that I am continuously surrounded with opportunities to improve my interpersonal relationship skills, and I have arranged my life so that I am always reminded of these skills and how to apply them.

This also brings up an important point: We ourselves do not have to have healed all of our own issues in order to be able to help others to heal their issues—even when we're helping others to heal issues in themselves that we have yet to heal in ourselves. In fact, we will tend to attract clients who reflect our own unhealed issues back to us so that through helping and supporting our clients to heal these issues, we can become aware of how to heal these issues ourselves.

It is not possible to attract the "wrong" client. Every client who comes into our lives is there for a reason, and presents an opportunity for mutual healing. They have come into our lives because in this time and place, we are the most appropriate person to reflect their issues back to them. When we are no longer the appropriate person, they will move on.

Even though it's important to become aware of our own personal biases and judgments, it's also important to recognize that our clients have come to us *because of* our biases and judgments.

In my practice, I have two fundamental rules that I follow. These rules fall under the heading of what I consider to be ethics, but perhaps it's more accurate to say that they come out of my own, personal code of integrity. Violating these guidelines would be wrong for me, personally, but I don't necessarily consider violations of these guidelines to be fundamentally wrong.

The first rule is that I do not make choices for my clients. I do not tell them what to do, I do not tell them what they *should* do, and I do not tell them what I would do if I were in their shoes. I help my clients to understand their options, and I endeavor to provide them with questions that will help them to find the answer and make the choices that are right for them. However, I make every possible effort to remain completely neutral and to avoid influencing their decision in any way. I also endeavor to refrain from any judgments about choices my clients have made, and it is always my intention to support my clients to the best of my ability.

The second rule is that I will not discuss another person's chart with a client except in the most general terms. I will talk about another person's Moon and Venus sign in order to help my client to understand how better to meet this person's Safety and Validation Needs. I will not, however, discuss any specifics of the chart, nor will I speculate on any relationship patterns or issues this person may or may not have. I only discuss a person's chart when that person is present. When I have a client who insists on knowing what's going on in another person's chart, or even how compatible they might be, I gently but firmly remind my client that it's never about the other person, and return to looking at their own relationship beliefs, patterns, and needs.

This may seem curious to many of you, particularly since when most people come to an astrologer for relationship counseling, what they really want is an analysis of how compatible their chart is with their intended romantic partner's. When my clients insist on knowing this, I sell them one of my $30 computer reports. I rarely do chart comparison with actual clients because there is rarely a need to. I've yet to have a client come to me who wanted a compatibility analysis done, who was actually *in* relationship with the person they were interested in.

It may also seem curious that even though most of my practice focuses on relationships, that I have only worked with a handful of couples. While I do believe that couples counseling has some inherent value, I also believe that most couples counseling is a complete waste of time.

My perception is that the vast majority of the time, when two people begin couples counseling, Person A has dragged Person B to the counseling session, usually under extreme duress. Person B doesn't want to be there, and Person A expects that the therapist will prove that Person A is right and Person B is wrong. I personally think this is a waste of both time and money.

While I'm perfectly happy to work with couples, in order for me to work with a couple, I first have to have a one-on-one session with each individual. Only then will I meet with the two as a couple. Needless to say, this happens quite rarely. Most of the time, I simply work with Person A, and when Person A learns how to understand and take responsibility for meeting his or her own Safety and Validation Needs, there's no longer a need to work with Person B because the relationship has improved dramatically.

When I do work with couples, it's generally to help them to create a new and more supportive blueprint for their relationship. The challenges they experience have less to do with meeting each other's Safety and Validation Needs and more to do with moving beyond their limiting and often disastrous Marriage Blueprints. These individuals are looking for guidance so that they can consciously choose to avoid the pitfalls and traps that they have experienced in their previous relationships. I usually help guide the couple through a Relationship Definition Talk (see Chapter 9 of *The Relationship Handbook*), and help them to create a vocabulary that they can build on so that they can facilitate future Relationship Definition Talks on their own.

The Six Steps to Improve Every Relationship in Your Life

Essentially, my approach to relationship counseling is to help my clients to move through the Six Steps to Improve Every Relationship In Your Life. These steps are covered in great detail in Chapter 17 of *The Relationship Handbook*. Here, I will share how I walk my clients through these steps.

Step 1: Identify What Needs Aren't Being Met in the Relationship

The first things I cover with my clients, once we've moved into talking about relationships, are their Safety and Validation Needs. Whether my client is looking for help with a specific relationship or not, it's essential that they know about Safety and Validation Needs and understand the specific languages they speak to meet these needs.

Usually, we spend about 30 to 45 minutes exploring their Safety and Validation Needs. During this time, I also explore any patterns they may have that make it difficult for them to feel safe or validated, and offer strategies and suggestions so that they can begin to alter these patterns and maintain the minimum required balances in these accounts on their own.

Once they have a context for the discussion, we can then look at the specific relationship or relationships that they want to improve. Every problem we have in a relationship comes from either a lack of safety, a lack of validation, or both. So the first question to answer is which need is not being met in the specific relationship: safety or validation.

Usually, we will explore this by looking at the specific wants that aren't being fulfilled, and then identifying the specific Need Account that would receive a deposit from that want being fulfilled.

Step 2: Identify How We Would Like Those Needs to Be Met

Once we've identified whether the issue is a lack of safety or a lack of validation, the next step is to identify what their partner would have to do in order to meet that need. This process is about uncovering the client's expectations in the relationship, and it's important to help the client move beyond the original *want* that caused the problem in the first place.

What are other things their partner could do to meet their Safety Needs? How else could their partner meet their Validation Needs?

I always encourage the client to be absolutely honest and forthright. If the client is holding back or seems to be censoring him or herself, I help them to become a little more emotionally invested in the situation so that they can uncover and express their *real* wants and expectations, no matter how extreme they may be.

Step 3: Reality Check—Are Our Expectations Reasonable?

Once the client has uncovered his or her wants—his or her expectations in the relationship, it's time to explore how reasonable those expectations are. Before doing this, it's important to help the client return to a safe, objective space. If the client became emotional or otherwise invested during Step 2, a few cleansing breaths, or even a brief "Present Moment Safety Exercise" (on page 48 of *The Relationship Handbook*) may be appropriate. It's essential that the client be able to look at their list objectively in order to proceed.

Consider each expectation in the context of the relationship and ask if that expectation is, in fact, reasonable. Often, the client will realize that his or her expectations are unreasonable, given the nature and context of the relationship. When this is the case, I help the client to adjust their expectations for the relationship. Often, this is all that is required to vastly improve a relationship.

When our expectations for a specific relationship are unreasonable, however, it's often a sign that we're working on the wrong relationship. Our needs are not being met in one relationship, and we turn to another relationship where our needs *are* being met, and expect that relationship to make up the deficit. The most common scenario for this is when we expect our romantic partners to make up for the fact that our Safety and Validation Needs are not being met in our professional relationships.

When a client discovers that their expectations are unreasonable, I will usually explore his or her other relationships to see if we can identify the real source of the problem and address how to improve that relationship.

If the client's expectations are, in fact, reasonable, we move onto the next step.

Step 4: Determine What Needs We Aren't Meeting

Relationship problems always work both ways—if one person isn't happy in the relationship, then the other person is probably not happy in the relationship either. This also means that if our needs aren't being met in the relationship then we're not meeting our partner's needs in the relationship. We must find out what needs we are not meeting.

Since our partners are our mirrors, it's usually safe to assume that if we're not feeling validated than neither are our partners. Likewise, if we're not feeling safe, then our partners are probably feeling unsafe as well.

Often, the problem here is a language barrier. We're speaking in one language and our partners are listening in another. I always take a few moments to help the client understand that what means "safe" to us, may not mean "safe" to our partners. I usually remind the client of the languages they speak for safety and validation and then explore which languages their partners may speak. If I have the birth data for their partner, I will look at the Moon and Venus in the partner's chart and help the client to understand the specific languages that their partner speaks.

Step 5: Meet Our Partner's Needs First

This is the single most important step in the process. If we want to improve our relationships, we must do everything we can do to meet our partner's Safety and Validation Needs.

There are two reasons for this: one is spiritual/metaphysical, and the other is pragmatic.

The spiritual/metaphysical reason why we must first meet our partner's needs in relationship if we want our own needs to be met, is that since our partners are our mirrors, when we meet their Safety and Validation Needs, we're actually meeting our own Safety and Validation Needs. In fact, most people discover that all they need to do to improve their relationships is meet their partner's needs.

The pragmatic reason to meet our partner's needs first is that we want our partners to go out of their way to meet our Safety and Validation Needs. Ask yourself when our partners are the most likely to want to do this for us: when they're feeling unsafe and unloved, or when they're feeling safe, secure, nurtured, content, and appreciated? It's always better to ask someone for a favor when they're in a *good* mood.

When I teach these steps in the Relationship Workshops, I always stop here and remind everyone that we must meet our partner's *needs*; we are under no obligation to meet our partner's *wants*. We have to find ways to make our partner's feel safe and validated. We don't necessarily have to do this the ways that our partner's expect us to, however.

Usually, this step is about learning how to speak our partner's Safety and Validation Languages. It's not that we're not trying to meet our partner's needs, it's just that we're speaking our languages and our partners are listening in theirs. In order to meet our partner's needs, we must speak *their* language, and do things that make deposits in *their* Safety and Validation Accounts, even if these things have little or no value to us, personally.

Often my clients reveal that their partners are adamant about one particular issue, and the main cause of the conflict is their partner's refusal to negotiate about this particular point. This means that their partners are *attached* to that specific want, and whatever need getting that want may fulfill, the bigger issue is that anytime we are attached to something, it has become a Safety Need for us. The first priority for my client, then is to find ways that they can make regular deposits in their partner's Safety Account. Once their partner is feeling safe, they will release their attachment to that specific want, and it will be possible to explore it without getting into a fight.

Step 6: Ask to Have Our Needs Met

As already indicated, most people find that when they succeed at Step 5 and meet their partner's needs, that their own needs are also being met perfectly well. If, however, after completing Step 5, our needs are not being met to our satisfaction, it's time to ask our partners to meet our needs.

As long as we have mastered Step 5, the only issue left is a language barrier. Our partners are certainly trying to meet our Safety and Validation Needs; however, they are speaking their languages and we are listening in ours. Step 6 is about helping our partners to understand the specific things that meet our needs.

It's essential that we avoid triggering our partner's egos by making them feel that they're doing something wrong. Avoid pointing out that they have failed to meet our needs in the past. Instead, let them know the kinds of things that we really appreciate. If we have truly mastered Step 5 and are meeting our partner's Safety and Validation Needs, they will go out of their way to do the same for us.

Remember, however, that getting what we *need* does not always mean getting what we *want*. We have to be certain that our requests and expectations are reasonable, and we also have to be responsible for maintaining the minimum balance of safety and validation in our accounts on our own.

⁎Appendix⁎
Relationship Astrology Worksheets

This appendix contains the worksheets used throughout this handbook to find the core relationship themes in a natal chart and to compare the natal charts of two individuals to evaluate compatibility.

You can download Adobe PDF copies of these worksheets (that you may view and print using Adobe Acrobat Reader from http://www.TheRealAstrology.com/relationship/.

These worksheets include a blank Essential Dignity table. You can use this table, along with the reference table on page 31 to fill in the Essential Dignities by hand. Alternatively, you can simply print out a copy of the correct Essential Dignities using Solar Fire™ software by Astrolabe, Inc. (http://www.alabe.com). I highly recommend the latter option. Solar Fire is only available for Windows; however, if you're a Macintosh user like me, simply purchase a copy of Mircosoft Virtual PC and you can run Solar Fire in on your Mac using the virtual machine.

Natal Chart Relationship Interpretation Worksheet

Part 1: Elements and Modalities

Element/Modality	Personal Planets	Personal Points	Outer Planets
Fire			
Earth			
Air			
Water			
Cardinal			
Fixed			
Mutable			

Part 2: Temperament

Hemisphere	Planets	Quadrant	Planets
Northern (House 1–6)		I (House 1–3)	
Southern (House 7–12)		II (House 4–6)	
Eastern (House 10–12, 1–3)		III (House 7–9)	
Western (House 4–9)		IV (House 10–12)	

[Comments]

Astrological Relationship Handbook

Part 3: Essential Dignities

Planet	Ruler +5	Exalt. +4	Trip. +3	Term. +2	Face +1	Detr. −5	Fall −4	Score
☽								
☉								
☿								
♀								
♂								
♃								
♄								
♅								
♆								
♇								
⚷								
☊								
☋								
As								
Mc								
Vx								
⊗								

Peregrine planets receive an *additional* score of −5.

A-3

Part 4: Dispositor Tree Diagram

[Draw Dispositor Tree Diagram]

[Comment on Essential Dignities and Dispositor Tree]

Part 5: Relationship Needs

Safety Needs [Moon Sign]

Validation Needs [Venus Sign]

Part 6: Can Needs Be Met?
Feeling Safe and Feeling Validated (Moon and Venus Connection)

Saturn Aspects: Checklists From Hell

Uranus Aspects: Rejection, Abandonment and Unreliability

Pluto Aspects: Power, Control, Manipulation and Abuse

Chiron Aspects: Core Wounds
[Note any Chiron Aspects and observe.]

Part 7: Relationship Wants
Conscious Desires: Descendant

Unconscious Desires: Vertex

Planets in the 7th and 8th Houses

Part 8: Parents & Marriage Blueprint
[Observe relationship between ruler of the 4th (father) and ruler of the 10th (mother).]

Part 9: Friends, Lovers or Spouses
[Observe and evaluate relationship between rulers of the 5th (lovers), 7th (spouses) and 11th (friends) houses.]

Relationship Compatibility and Synastry Worksheet

Part 1: Elemental Compatibility

A:		B:	
☉		☉	
☽		☽	
As		As	
Vx		Vx	
♀		♀	
☿		☿	

[Comment]

Part 2: Safety and Validation Needs

[Comment on connections between A's Moon and Venus and B's Moon and Venus. Evaluate how easily A and B are apt to meet each other's Safety and Validation Needs.]

Part 3: Communication Styles
[Comment on A's Mercury in relationship with B's Mercury.]

Part 4: Inter-Personal Connections
[Evaluate number and kinds of aspects between Sun through Jupiter between both charts.]

Part 5: Karmic Aspects
Person A's Planets Aspecting Person B's Planets
[Evaluate Person A's Saturn through Pluto aspecting Person B's Sun through Jupiter.]

Person B's Planets Aspecting Person A's Planets
[Evaluate Person B's Saturn through Pluto aspecting Person A's Sun through Jupiter.]

Part 6: Synthesized Synastry

Bibliography

Arroyo, Stephen. *Astrology, Psychology and the Four Elements.* Sebastopol, California: CRCS Publications, 1975.

Arroyo, Stephen. *Chart Interpretation Handbook.* Sebastopol, California: CRCS Publications, 1989.

Burk, Kevin. *Astrology: Understanding the Birth Chart.* St. Paul, Minnesota: Llewellyn Publications, 2001.

Burk, Kevin. *The Relationship Handbook: How to Understand and Improve Every Relationship in Your Life.* San Diego, California: Serendipity Press, 2004.

Gunther, Bernard. *Energy Ecstasy and Your Seven Vital Chakras.* North Hollywood: Newcastle Publishing Company, Inc., 1983.

Lehman, J. Lee. Essential Dignities. West Chester, Pennsylvania: Whitford Press, 1989.

Maslow, Abraham. *Motivation and Personality.* New York: Harper & Brothers, 1954.

Wakefield, June. *Cosmic Astrology: The Religion of the Stars.* Tempe, Arizona: American Federation of Astrologers, 1982.

therealastrology.com
with Kevin B. Burk
Relationship Astrology
Correspondence Course

Yes! You can learn how to use Classical Astrology to reveal key relationship patterns in the natal chart and to understand and improve every relationship in your life!

Study astrology with internationally-acclaimed author and astrologer, Kevin B. Burk!

When most people begin to study astrology, the first thing they want to know is what their birth chart has to say about them. The second thing they want to know is what their birth chart has to say about their relationships.

Now, you can learn the secrets of relationship astrology—including the *only* accurate way to evaluate compatibility—and discover how to use astrology for relationship coaching and counseling!

✓ Listen to live recordings of an actual 12-week class in your web browser.

✓ Download PDF files of all handouts, charts, and assignments—and receive feedback on your homework assignments.

✓ Study at your own pace, in your own time.

Plus, when you register for the course, you will receive...

✓ Access to exclusive video clips and animations that further illustrate key techniques and concepts.

✓ Unlimited eMail support on class topics and assignments.

✓ A total of one hour of one-on-one telephone tutoring with Kevin B. Burk.

✓ A Certificate of Mastery upon successful completion of the final project.

All reading assignments will be from the *Astrological Relationship Handbook* and *The Relationship Handbook* by Kevin B. Burk.

therealastrology.com/classes

by Kevin B. Burk

The first truly comprehensive guide to human relationships has finally arrived! *The Relationship Handbook* is guaranteed to help you to improve *every single relationship* in your life! Inside, you will learn the secrets to improving your romantic relationships, your family relationships, your professional relationships, and even your friendships!

Filled with practical, compassionate, often humorous but always useful advice, *The Relationship Handbook* guides you through the ins and outs of all human relationships.

The Relationship Handbook changes people's lives. In the words of one of the many participants in Kevin B. Burk's Relationship Workshops, "This information makes my world a better place to live!"

In The Relationship Handbook you will discover…

- The **two most important needs** in every relationship—*and why we're almost never aware of one of them!*
- The three elements that define *every* romantic relationship.
- The **Relationship Blueprints** that determine how you **create every single one of your relationships**.
- How to **overcome your negative thinking** and **create the loving, supportive relationships** that you deserve.
- The *real* differences between men and women (and it's got nothing to do with being from different planets)!
- The **Relationship Definition Talk**—the key to successful romantic relationships.
- **Six steps** that are guaranteed to **improve** *every* **relationship in your life.**
- …and much more!

THE RELATIONSHIP HANDBOOK *by* KEVIN B. BURK
SERENDIPITY PRESS, OCTOBER 2004
HARDBACK/ISBN 0-9759682-1-1/$29.95 U.S.
619.807.2473 • 6161 EL CAJON BLVD #306, SAN DIEGO CA • www.EveryRelationship.com
CONTACT: KEVIN B. BURK, 619.807.2473 • KEVIN@EveryRelationship.com

by Kevin B. Burk

Learn All of the Astrology math You Will Ever Need—The Easy Way!

Don't Panic! Math is your *friend*. Granted, it's the kind of friend that wakes you up in the middle of the night, raids your refrigerator, and then passes out on your living room floor, but it's still your friend. And if you're serious about learning astrology, especially if you plan to take any of the certification exams through NCGR or AFA, you do have to be able to do the math—or at the very least understand how the math is done.

This workbook is designed to help you to overcome your fears about astrology math. if you didn't have at least some fears about learning how to calculate charts by hand, you wouldn't be reading this book. This is nothing to be ashamed of. Unless you have kids in high school, the last time you were presented with an algebra problem was when *you* were in high school.

And face it: you probably hated it then, too.

I promise you that this will be much easier for you than it was in high school. For one thing, you're allowed (and even expected) to use a calculator here. The Valium, which you're also allowed, is optional.

Astrology Math Made Easy starts at the beginning and teaches you the basic elements of astrology math: time conversions and latitude and longitude conversions. You then learn how to interpolate the planets, find the Sidereal time of birth, and interpolate the house cusps. Each time you learn a new skill, you have ample opportunity to master it with exercises and examples—and the answers are all provided for you in the back, so you can check your work!

ASTROLOGY MATH MADE EASY *by* KEVIN B. BURK

SERENDIPITY PRESS, JANUARY 2005

TRADE PAPERBACK/ISBN 0-9759682-4-6/$16.95 U.S.

619.807.2473 • 6161 EL CAJON BLVD #306, SAN DIEGO CA • TheRealAstrology.com/MathBook

CONTACT: KEVIN B. BURK, 619.807.2473 • Kevin@TheRealAstrology.com

therealastrology.com
with **Kevin B. Burk**

Natal Chart Interpretation
Correspondence Course

Yes! You can learn how to use Classical Astrology to unlock the secrets of any birth chart—and create your own, synthesized interpretations, even if you've never studied astrology before!

Study astrology with internationally-acclaimed author and astrologer, Kevin B. Burk!

Whether you have studied astrology in the past or you are new to astrology, when you complete this comprehensive course, you will be able to come up with your own, in-depth, synthesized interpretation of any birth chart using Classical Astrology!

From the building blocks of the planets, signs and houses, you will learn how to use Essential Dignities to become fluent in the language of Astrology.

✔ Listen to live recordings of an actual 14-week class in your web browser.

✔ Download PDF files of all handouts, charts, and assignments—and receive feedback on your homework assignments.

✔ Study at your own pace, in your own time.

Plus, when you register for the course, you will receive...

✔ Access to exclusive video clips and animations that further illustrate key techniques and concepts.

✔ Unlimited eMail support on class topics and assignments.

✔ A total of one hour of one-on-one telephone tutoring with Kevin B. Burk.

✔ A Certificate of Mastery upon successful completion of the final project.

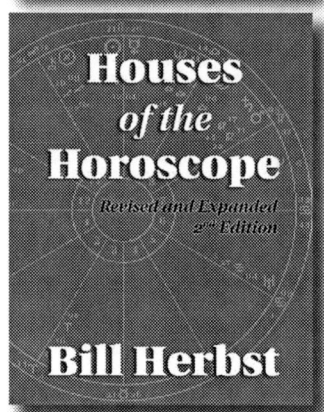

All reading assignments will be from *Astrology: Understanding the Birth Chart* by Kevin B. Burk and *Houses of the Horoscope* by Bill Herbst.

therealastrology.com/classes

by Bill Herbst

The Definitive Book on the Houses is Back In Print in a Revised and Expanded 2nd Edition!

"*Houses of the Horoscope* is my favorite astrology book of all time."

—Tem Tarriktar, creator and publisher of *The Mountain Astrologer*

"An astrological tour de force! Rich and deep insights uncover hidden vistas in your understanding of the astrological houses. This book deserves recognition as one of the most important guides to houses ever to see print."

—Richard Nolle, review in *Horoscope*

"Herbst's explanations of the meaning of the houses and the significance of planets contained in certain houses are without parallel in contemporary astrological research and approach. Herbst offers interpretations that are insightful, incisive and often humorous. One of the best things is that he leaves the thinking to you, the reader. He gets us into the houses in a deeper way than has been previously explored, and lets us rearrange the furniture. This is definitely a book which should occupy a prominent place in the library of any student or professional involved with astrology."

—Timothy Minger, review in *The Mountain Astrologer*

"*Houses of the Horoscope* is a clear, comprehensive and wonderfully illuminating text. The book is destined to become a classic reference work on the houses. Perhaps we might subtitle it as 'Everything You Ever Wanted to Know About Houses.' The house meanings are covered in an impeccable manner, and every planetary placement by house is analyzed with extraordinary insight. I loved it! With this goldmine and Dane Rudyhar's *The Astrological Houses*, you will be able to understand this essential field of astrological knowledge as an expert."

—Mark Lerner, review in *Welcome to Planet Earth*

HOUSES OF THE HOROSCOPE *by* BILL HERBST
SERENDIPITY PRESS, FEBRUARY 2006
TRADE PAPERBACK/ISBN 0-9759682-6-2/$24.95 U.S.
619.807.2473 • 6161 EL CAJON BLVD #306, SAN DIEGO CA • www.EveryRelationship.com
CONTACT: KEVIN B. BURK, 619.807.2473 • Kevin@EveryRelationship.com